Deregulation and Competition

Deregulation
and
Competition

Lessons from the Airline Industry

Jagdish N. Sheth • Fred C. Allvine
• Can Uslay • Ashutosh Dixit

⑤SAGE | Response Business Books

Los Angeles | London | New Delhi
Singapore | Washington DC | Melbourne

First published in 2007 by

SAGE Publications India Pvt Ltd
B1/I-1 Mohan Cooperative Industrial Area
Mathura Road, New Delhi 110 044, India
www.sagepub.in

SAGE Publications Inc
2455 Teller Road
Thousand Oaks, California 91320, USA

SAGE Publications Ltd
1 Oliver's Yard, 55 City Road
London EC1Y 1SP, United Kingdom

SAGE Publications Asia-Pacific Pte Ltd
3 Church Street
#10-04 Samsung Hub
Singapore 049483

Published by Vivek Mehra for SAGE Publications India Pvt Ltd, typeset in 10/13 Bookman old style at InoSoft Systems, Noida.

Library of Congress Cataloging-in-Publication Data
Sheth, Jagdish N.
  Deregulation and competition: lessons from the airline industry/
Jagdish N. Sheth, Fred C. Allvine, and Can Uslay.
    p. cm.
  Includes bibliographical references and index.
    1. Airlines. 2. Airlines—United States. I. Allvine, Fred C. II. Uslay,
Can, 1973– III. Title.

HE9774.S44   387.7—dc22   2007   2007033633

ISBN: 978-07-619-3596-4 (HB)

SAGE Team: Sugata Ghosh, Koel Mishra

Contents

List of Tables

List of Figures

Acknowledgements

WE WOULD like to express our gratitude and thanks to Navijit Gill, who rewrote parts of the book and to Mark Hutcheson who provided end-to-end editorial and administrative support. Mark Hutcheson also coordinated day-to-day communication and routine operational decisions with the publisher. Finally, we want to thank Dr Sugata Ghosh, Vice President, Commissioning, for his confidence in the book and for making it available to the professional market.

Prologue: The Battle for Open Skies

CONCEPT ARBITRAGE has allowed enterprising industrial moguls in emerging economies to build companies in industries as diverse as retail and telecom. The story of deregulation and privatization in the most advanced capitalist nation provides fertile ground for predicting the evolution of industries. It's not a perfect science, but the business models that emerge are examples of what is possible.

The story of airline deregulation and privatization is being played out in many emerging economies, including India and Malaysia, as discount carriers take on erstwhile protected carriers. The similarities and differences with the US experience give a clue as to how successful they will be. To that effect, this book looks at the history of deregulation in the US—the players, the strategies and the continuing battle for the open skies.

The US airline industry was deregulated in 1978, based on the expectation that a large number of new discount airlines would enter the field and provide the public considerably lower airfares. In fact, over the first few years following deregulation, a number of new discount airlines did come into existence and provided the public considerably lower airfares. However, the major airlines developed a strategy to eliminate the discount airlines. Ten years after deregulation, all but one of the new airlines were shut down, and the one remaining airline was in bankruptcy.

The major airlines—Delta, American, United, Northwest, Continental, and US Airways—took a number of steps to dominate the industry during the 1980s and early 1990s. One of the weapons they deployed was to control most of the gates at airports in large cities. The major airlines obtained exclusive leases for use of many of these gates for 20 years or longer. This was in spite of the fact that the Federal government originally provided the money to build major airports and their runways. To develop customer loyalty, the major carriers introduced costly frequent-flyer programs that provided an incentive for passengers to fly a particular airline. They also built luxury lounges where frequent business travelers could relax and have a drink. In addition, the major airlines paid premium fees to travel agents to book flights on their airlines. In summary, the major airlines created an expensive hub-and-spoke system and provided many costly amenities.

Despite these steps, they still experienced a problem when start-up discount airlines started to fly routes to the major hub airports. Given that the discounters had much lower operating costs, they were able to charge considerably lower fares than the established airlines. In many retail fields there are high-cost operators as well as low-cost firms, and they tend to co-exist by meeting the needs of two different market segments. However, the major airlines developed a strategy to keep the discount airlines from successfully competing in their high-cost hub markets.

The strategy was to respond aggressively when discount airlines started flying on some of the major airlines' high-price routes. The major airlines would temporarily lower their prices and meet the low fares of the discount airline. In the process, the major airlines were selling tickets far below their operating costs. When the small discount airlines were unable to gain enough volume to sustain their operation, they would withdraw from these routes. The major airlines would then increase ticket prices back to the original level or in many cases to a higher level than before. The major airlines were able to subsidize temporary losses on select routes with the profits from the vast majority of their routes, where they experienced no competition from discount airlines.

The outlook for the discount airlines sharply improved from 1993 to 2000 (during the Clinton administration). A number of studies were conducted and hearings held regarding major airline dominance of large airports and the monopoly fares they charged. In 1998, the Department of Transportation (DOT) tried to introduce guidelines to stop predatory pricing, but this effort failed. The US Justice Department attempted to bring a predatory-pricing case against American Airlines, but the judge refused to hear the case. Nonetheless, the DOT was able to remove many of the barriers to entry faced by discount airlines in the large markets of the major airlines. As time wore on, the resourceful discount airlines began competing on three-fourths of the 1,000 busiest routes in the country. Many airline analysts believe that the discount carriers that offer good service and some amenities will continue to expand their market share. This is the reason the outlook for the six major airlines remains bleak and action needs to be taken to reduce the number and costs of the major airlines.

Southwest Airlines is the oldest, biggest, and most profitable discount airline. Following airline deregulation in 1978, it systematically expanded its operation across much of the country by offering lower fares. It is also the largest airline in the United States in terms of domestic passengers boarded, and has been consistently profitable for more than 30 years. Southwest has held its costs down by offering basic airline service with few frills. There are additional savings due to its low cost, point-to-point method of operating that avoids the costs and delays of flying to many of the major airports.

AirTran Airways (originally called ValuJet) came into existence in 1994 when it took over the gates of Eastern Airlines after Eastern withdrew from Atlanta airport. The small discounter began flying two airplanes to a few cities in Florida, and has steadily expanded its fleet of airplanes and service routes, mainly in the southeastern part of the United States, to become the second-largest discount airline. Recently, it started flying long-distance routes to the western part of the country.

JetBlue Airways began operating in 1999 by providing low-cost transcontinental service from the under-used John F. Kennedy (JFK) Airport located outside of New York City. It was the first discount airline to compete on long-distance domestic flights, which had been a highly profitable part of the major airlines' business. JetBlue has ordered 200 feeder airlines to fly passengers from small cities in the northeast to its major airport in New York City. JetBlue intends to fly these passengers and others originating in New York City on its profitable long-distance flights across the country.

The discount airline movement spread to Europe in the 1990s, and discount airlines have sharply cut into the market share of the high-cost national airlines. The largest discounter in Europe is Ryanair. It is modeled after Southwest with an even more bare-bones approach to services.

There is some concern that discount airlines are now expanding too rapidly and that they could be setting themselves up for a shakeout along with the major airlines. The major airlines and their affiliates have witnessed the growth and profitability of the discount airlines, and some have decided to reorganize as discount airlines. In 2002, Arizona-based America West sharply lowered its cost and converted from a full-service airline to a discount airline.

In 2004, Atlantic Coast Airline, which was a feeder to two major airlines, changed its name to Independence Air and became a discount airline flying to 35 cities from Dulles International Airport in Washington, D.C. In early 2005, American West acknowledged that it was holding discussions with US Airways about forming a new discount airline that would be even larger than Southwest.

In chapter one, we will look at how the stage was set for deregulation in the US. In the second chapter we visit two start-up airlines that tried to capitalize on the opportunity presented by deregulation—and failed. The next couple of chapters discuss the cut-throat response by the major airlines and the tactics they adopted to combat competition.

Most of the subsequent chapters are devoted to the new airlines that came in with a low-cost model and how some of them managed to break the cozy oligopoly of the majors. International events in Europe and Asia and the relevance of the US experience is also discussed.

The book concludes by addressing the big question: what will be the fate of the majors airlines? With four airlines in bankruptcy in 2006, the US airline industry is experiencing a significant crisis. The major airlines incurred an incredible loss of more than $20 billion from 2001 to 2004. These losses are expected to pile up throughout 2006 and could continue even longer. Furthermore, the Federal government loaned the troubled airlines $15 billion in 2002 based on the argument that the "September 11, 2001 crisis" was a primary reason for the plight of the major airlines. There is no doubt that their losses were in part due to the aftermath of a troubled economy and reduced demand for air travel. But a significant and ongoing factor in the huge losses of the principal airlines is that too many of them have high cost structures. Their expensive hub-and-spoke systems are broken, and need extensive repair. Permitting the major airlines to consolidate and downsize could help reduce their financial problems, but even this move will not totally resolve these issues.

The remainder of the decade is going to be very challenging for the US airline industry. As it braces for the inevitable rationalization, there will be new lessons for the global airline industry. In the meantime, it is possible to predict how the battle for the skies is likely to turn out in fast-liberalizing economies by comparing and contrasting deregulation in the US.

Chapter One

Flight Plan for Deregulation

IN THIS chapter, we will briefly review the history of airline regulation from 1938 to 1978. This provides the context for the push towards deregulation—and its initial failure to achieve the desired results. Airline deregulation was expected to create more airlines, greater choice of airline services, and lower prices. Initially, the promise of more competition and lower fares turned out much as expected. However, 10 years after deregulation, there were fewer airlines in existence than before deregulation. There was only one new airline in existence at that time, and it was in bankruptcy. Furthermore, several of the original legacy airlines had gone out of business and industry concentration was increasing. The heightened competition that had been expected following deregulation was stillborn.

But now, more than 25 years after the deregulation (in 1978), it appears that the policy is finally paying off for airline consumers. There are both stable, profitable low-cost carriers and new, fast-growing discount airlines that are providing the public with lower fares. In contrast, the legacy carriers lost billions of dollars from 2001 to 2004, and Delta and Northwest executives have speculated that by 2010 as few as two of the six legacy carriers operating in 2004 (American, United, Delta, Northwest, US Airways and Continental) will still be in existence.

A SHORT HISTORY OF REGULATION

First we will consider legislative history leading up to the passage of the Civil Aeronautics Act of 1938, which regulated the development of the emerging commercial airline industry. Coming out of the Great Depression of the late 1920s and 1930s, the Federal government recognized that the airline industry was in its infancy and that it was vulnerable. There was concern that in the absence of regulation, the competitive environment would impede the industry's ability to stabilize and grow. The existing airmail legislation was believed to contain features that would weaken the development of the commercial airline industry. Congress also wanted to create legislation that would avoid the economic chaos experienced in the railroad and motor-carrier industries. The goal was to establish legislation that would nurture the development of a field perceived as a public utility type of industry. While the airline industry was in its infancy, there was the belief that it was a field with vast potential and of great significance to the economic development of USA.[1]

The goal of Congress was to pass legislation that would promote orderly development of a competitive airline-transportation industry. It wanted to avoid a period of destructive competition resulting from bad competitive practices and uneconomical capital structure. Some members of Congress expressed concern that the emerging air-transportation industry might experience destructive price wars and wasteful practices. They advocated legislation that would preserve competition and prohibit industry monopolization. In the actual drafting of the legislation, Congress explicitly stated that the purpose of the legislation was to create a competitive airline industry.[2]

CREATION OF THE CIVIL AERONAUTICS BOARD

President Roosevelt signed into law the Federal Aviation Act that established the Civil Aeronautics Board (CAB) in 1938. It was an independent regulatory agency whose purpose was to provide regulation to help guide sound growth in the emerging air-transportation industry. The responsibility of the CAB was divided into three major categories as described below:

1. Entry: prescribe which routes will be flown, the cities to be served, and the airlines to provide the service.
2. Rates: determine whether fares are "just and reasonable" and authorize the airfares to be charged on different routes.
3. Antitrust: the authority to approve or disapprove a number of airline agreements, some of which violated major antitrust laws.[3]

Entry

Immediately following the passage of the Act, the CAB was primarily concerned with issuing certificates to those airlines that had provided service to cities during the "Grandfather" period (May 14, 1938 to August 22, 1938). The applicants were air carriers that had provided continuous service over the Grandfather period. After certifying service to the Grandfather carriers, the CAB started certifying new routes for airlines to serve. Some of the criteria used included: (a) route integration, (b) frequency of service, (c) equipment to be used, (d) fares to be charged, (e) effort to promote route, (f) need of applicant to strengthen routes, (g) profitability of route for applicant and existing carriers, and (h) level of diversion of traffic from existing carrier(s).[4]

The CAB tended to favor issuing new routes to smaller carriers who were at a competitive disadvantage due to the limited routes they served. Favoring new route requests of smaller carriers was also done to reduce industry concentration. Permitting smaller carriers to fly on lucrative routes was viewed as an important way of improving route structure for the nation. In addition, by strengthening the smaller carriers, the CAB was often able to reduce the Federal subsidy it was paying. The CAB also tended to favor route requests of some large carriers who were experiencing financial difficulty.[5]

It was Congress's intention in passing the 1938 Act that the CAB would implement a cautious but moderately liberal approach to entry of new airlines as the market expanded. From 1950 to 1974, the CAB received 79 applications from firms seeking authority to provide scheduled airline service. However, no new airlines were allowed to enter the industry. Furthermore, between 1969 and 1974, the CAB refused to accept any applications to serve new routes. Of the 16 trunk-line carriers that were "Grandfathered" in 1938, there were only 10 in existence four decades later in 1978 when the airline industry was deregulated. In spite of rapid growth of the airline industry, the CAB did not see it fit to allow new firms to enter the field. The "big-four" airlines in 1938 (United, American, Eastern, and TWA) were the same four airlines in the mid 1970s.[6]

Airfares

From 1938 to 1974, the CAB set airline fares using a methodology that determined rates for regulated monopolies such as public utilities. The CAB examined the costs and revenue figures for the entire airline industry. It then adjusted these figures to determine what cost and revenue would have been, had the entire airline industry operated with a load factor of 55 percent (it assumed that planes should fly at this level of capacity). A 12 percent return on investment was added to determine the total cost that had to be covered by revenue. Finally, fares were set to generate revenue to cover costs, with adjustments made for the distance of different routes.[7]

Congress determined that while this system was administratively efficient, it tended to keep airfares at unreasonably high levels. The load factor of 55 percent was considered to be too low in comparison to intra-state airlines in Texas and California that were achieving load factors of 60 to 70 percent. One reason for the legacy carriers not achieving higher load factors was that the board prohibited selective price cuts and required the airlines to charge the same fares for equal-distance flights. More efficient carriers were prohibited from lowering their price to take business away from less efficient carriers. The prohibition on competing on price led some airlines to add services to attract customers, which in turn, drove up their costs. Some airlines offered lavish services and had large advertising budgets which contributed to driving up customer costs. As cost spiraled and profits diminished, the airlines sought fare increases.[8]

There was a fundamental drawback to rate-making by the board. The focus was on "cost-based pricing" and not "demand-oriented pricing". The general public that might take a vacation or visit friends if the price was lower was largely ignored by the pricing regulations of the CAB.

Antitrust

Firms in unregulated industries are not allowed to collude in any way, such as in the setting of prices, reduction in capacity, and the use of promotion. Officials of the Justice Department and Federal Trade Commission carefully monitor the behavior of unregulated firms. However, the CAB was responsible for monitoring the competitive behavior of the airline industry. In the late 1960s, excessive optimism led the airline industry to overinvest in large-capacity jet aircraft and during the recession of the early

1970s, demand for air travel fell. The CAB allowed several major carriers (e.g., United, TWA, and American) to agree collectively to reduce flights on a number of major domestic routes from 1971 through 1975. There was also some evidence of other collective agreements made by airlines without permission of the CAB, but no action was taken against the airlines.[9]

MAJOR CRITICISMS OF AIRLINE REGULATION

One problem with airline regulation that was often cited was "inefficient pricing". In free markets, prices are normally determined by the interplay between "supply" and "demand". The interplay of market forces tends to produce a level of price and supply of service that consumers demand. However, rate setting by the CAB interfered with the normal workings of the market and created a suboptimal fare structure. The competition that did exist was trying to create better services that resulted in higher costs and, in turn, higher prices. There was a strong sentiment that prices tend to be higher than an unregulated market would have set. The decline in prices in the early years following deregulation in 1978 was used to support the conclusion that regulations contributed to higher prices.[10]

A second problem related to airline regulation was "inefficient routing decisions". The CAB had the authority to require airlines to show public need when requesting authority to fly different routes. The burden was on a new entrant to prove that public need existed before new routes would be approved. It was common for the incumbent carrier(s) to challenge applicants of other carriers wishing to fly on their existing routes. By making it difficult for new airlines to enter existing routes, the CAB prevented more efficient carriers from challenging less efficient airlines, causing fares to fall.[11]

A third problem associated with airline regulation was that it "impeded new airlines from entering the industry". A new firm was confronted with substantial hurdles in obtaining certification to enter the commercial-airline industry. Existing airlines were permitted to present evidence in opposition to application for certification of a new carrier. This process worked very well for the "Grand-fathered" carriers and allowed them to prohibit any new airline from entering the industry during airline regulation.[12]

A fourth problem of airline regulation was that it contributed to inefficiencies due to sanctioned actions and other illegal conduct. The Federal Aviation Act of 1958 gave the CAB authority to agree to anticompetitive and harmful practices that otherwise would have been deemed illegal by the antitrust laws. For example, the CAB sanctioned agreements among competing airlines to decrease their service on given routes in order to increase their load factor and improve profitability.[13] In addition, there was evidence of persistent unsanctioned collusive behavior while the CAB regulated the airline. For example, the airlines allegedly used the Air Transport Association to coordinate price increases.[14]

ADVOCATES OF DEREGULATION

There was a growing body of academic literature by economists during the 1960s and early 1970s that was critical of airline regulation. Economists specializing in the airline industry were frequently asked to testify before congressional hearings regarding the shortcomings of airline regulation. Many economists claimed that the airline industry was close to being "perfectly competitive", and that deregulation would remove the harmful consequences of regulation by the CAB. The view was often expressed that airline deregulation would contribute to greater efficiency, a different level of airline services, lower prices, and more competition.[15]

William A. Jordan conducted a study that was important in two respects. His research supported the conclusion that regulation often protects "producers" and not "consumers". He also noted the much greater efficiency of intrastate airlines that are free of CAB regulation.[16]

George W. Douglas and James C. Miller researched the regulated airline industry and stated that:

> ... we concede that the airline industry, if deregulated, would probably contain certain market imperfections.... However, the preconditions for pure competition appear to be present.

Later in a congressional hearing Miller stated:

> A regulator is inherently less capable of administering resources "correctly" than is an individual competitive entrepreneur.[17]

Michael E. Levine, writing in a law journal, avoided much economic rhetoric and stated:

> Such regulation ... cannot add economic benefits to those already provided by free-market competition.... Regulatory experience ... suggests that the ultimate result will be government protectionism, the proliferation of inefficient practices, and oligopolistic market behavior.[18]

Alfred E. Kahn wrote two books on economic theory and became chairman of the CAB as deregulation was being implemented. His second book contained a large section on the airline industry where he stated:

> The airline industry is structurally suited for effective competition. Economies of scale are evidently quite limited, and barriers to entry—except for the Federal Aviation Act and the CAB itself—are relatively low.

Kahn expressed his strong conviction in favor of airline deregulation to Congress and said the following:

> It is time to replace a protectionist stature with one that will genuinely encourage competition. It is time to return this industry to the free enterprise system .... Everything about the air transportation industry persuades me that competition is feasible ....The CAB is simply not capable of making business decisions as good as the ones that business itself will make in a competitive environment. It is that simple and that fundamental.[19]

A number of government agencies were also influential supporters of deregulation and they employed an increasing number of economists. These agencies included the Federal Trade Commission, the Antitrust Division of the Department of Justice, the Department of Transportation, and the Council on Wage and Price Stability. The mission of these agencies was predicted on the assumed benefits of competition. In addition, economists on the Council of Economic Advisors, the Office of Management and Budget, and the CAB joined in support of airline deregulation.[20]

One of the top priorities of both the Ford and Carter Administrations was regulatory reform. During the Ford Administration, the Domestic Council Review Group for Regulatory Reform was created. It helped to organize reform groups and assisted in drafting reform proposals. President Carter supported key legislative leaders such as Senators Edward Kennedy and Howard Cannon, who worked on legislation to deregulate the airline industry. Carter also assisted in the development of ad-hoc groups in favor of deregulation. These included organizations such as the National Federation of Independent Business, the American Farm Bureau Federation, Nader's Aviation Consumer Action Project, and the National Association of Manufacturers. Several businesses with large airline shipping costs joined in support of deregulation. Many consumers also supported the principle of airline deregulation believing they would experience better service and lower fares.[21]

In summary, during the 1970s, many economists and industry analysts developed a consensus that airline regulation was contrary to the public interest. These problems were associated with setting of airfares, restriction on competition on different routes, entry of new airlines, and the sanctioning of inefficient and collusive behavior.

GOVERNMENT POLICY TURNS IN FAVOR OF DEREGULATION

Upon taking office in 1974, President Ford targeted double-digit inflation as the centerpiece for his administration's new domestic program. A number of conferences were held in September 1974 to solicit views from academics, government officials, Congressmen, and interest groups regarding ways to curb inflation in the country. The administration and academic economists were united in their view that much economic regulation was costly and anticompetitive. Deregulation was extremely compatible with the Administration's position of reducing costs and curbing inflationary pressures.[22]

President Nixon sent a message to Congress on October 8, 1974 where he reinforced an earlier Nixon linkage between inflation and excessive regulation. He stated that "the Federal government imposes too many hidden and too many inflationary costs on our economy." He recommended that Congress establish a National Commission on Regulatory Reform that would "identify and eliminate existing Federal rules and regulations that increase costs to the consumer and return to vigorous antitrust enforcement."[23]

There were a large number of Congressional hearings regarding the pros and cons of airline deregulation. The sentiment was growing that something had to be done about airline regulation, with an increased belief that it was a large contributing factor to the country's inflationary problem. Senator Kennedy's oversight committee held one of the hearings in early 1975. In his opening remarks, Senator Kennedy set the stage for the hearings by noting that "regulations all too often encourage or approve unreasonably high prices, regulation is also passed on the consumer, and that cost is astronomical."[24]

The Ford administration then stated its position on aviation reform. The Secretary of Transportation explained that the administration was preparing a legislative proposal that represented "a major departure from the regulatory regime we have relied upon in the past [and] will fundamentally redirect our air transportation regulation policy." The secretary went on to endorse the position of economists that the current regulatory system

> misplaces incentive and disincentive, distorts competitive advantage, protects inefficient carriers from effective competition, over-restricts market entry, artificially inflates rates, and misallocates our nation's resources.[25]

Over the next eight days of hearings, widespread dissatisfaction of CAB control of the airline industry was expressed, even by some of the regulated airlines. But there was disagreement on the type of reform necessary to improve the situation. Economists and officials from the Department of Justice and the Council of Economic Advisors joined together in favor of "total deregulation" of the airline industry over time. Existing carriers were in favor of "incremental change" in the CAB authority, but opposed total deregulation. One airline executive said, "the types of changes we feel are worthy of consideration are those that would tend to improve the present system, and not destroy it."[26] Existing carriers were strongly opposed to elimination of the CAB's certificate of routes airlines could fly. However, they were in favor of increased carrier pricing freedom.

AIRLINE DEREGULATION

Kahn was appointed chairman of the CAB in June 1977. He was the first economist to serve on the CAB and he endorsed reduction of airline competition restrictions. One month later, a second economist, Elizabeth Bailey, was appointed to be a member of the CAB and was also an advocate of airline deregulation. One of Kahn's first decisions was to wrest control of rate and route responsibility from staff members who were known to support regulation.[27]

Kahn encouraged his staff to explore ways to reduce CAB interference in airline rate and route decisions. Actions taken by his staff violated regulatory precedent and raised questions of legality. Fortunately, deregulation legislation was passed before Kahn's liberal policies could be challenged in the courts. With his encouragement, more price restrictions were lifted and price competition was encouraged. The CAB promoted low-cost air service and price competition between scheduled airlines and charter carriers. Discount pricing regulations were relaxed, which contributed to the introduction of lower fares for schedule carriers. Two policy changes were made to encourage carriers to adopt more competitive pricing strategies. First, preferential treatment in route cases would be given to carriers who planned to use low fares on a route. Second, the CAB introduced a zone of downward pricing flexibility and carriers were permitted to reduce prices by as much as 50 percent below the standard industry fare.[28]

Route awards became one of the most controversial policy changes made by the CAB. Steps were taken to speed the route-award process and to bypass the long evidentiary process. The CAB adopted procedures to reduce the obstacles to route expansion by existing carriers. New applicants were no longer required to prove that their services would be profitable. Furthermore, a carrier impacted by a new entrant was no longer able to block it on the grounds that it would divert traffic from existing operations. The CAB also implemented a multiple permissive policy on new routes. Rather than selecting a single carrier to serve a new route, all applicants were granted permission to fly a new route as long as they were "fit, willing, and able" to serve the route. The adoption of the permissive entry route policy came close to being de facto deregulation.[29]

In March 1978, Chairman Kahn stated in a Congressional hearing that the issue of airline deregulation had been studied to the point of absurdity. He said that:

> Since November of 1974, there have been eight sets of hearings by five separate congressional committees over a period of 60 days .... There have been dozens of studies and reports by the CAB, the Department of Transportation, the General Accounting Office (GAO), and several congressional committees—an accumulation of evidence totaling nearly 20,000 pages ....There is certainly no point in still further study.[30]

Kahn observed that more studies represented a delaying action, and that there was clear evidence supporting the benefits of airline deregulation.

By the end of the summer of 1978, the CAB had on its own initiative implemented most of the provisions of the pending deregulation bill. The adverse consequences that opponents of the deregulation had predicted did not initially occur. Instead, airline profits significantly increased during 1977 and 1978, diminishing opposition by the major legacy airlines.[31]

President Carter signed the Airline Deregulation Act on October 24, 1978. It was designed to relax and then terminate direct government control over the airline industry. CAB's authority over routes that an airline could serve was to terminate by December 31, 1981, and regulation of fares that airlines could charge was to cease by January 1, 1983. New airlines were permitted to enter routes served by scheduled airlines, and certified carriers found it much easier to enter new routes. Existing intrastate airlines were permitted to enter one new route during the calendar years of 1979, 1980, and 1981. In addition, existing carriers were precluded from abruptly terminating service to small communities. Service was to be maintained for 10 years and supported by a new subsidy program. Price freedom was also increased. Carriers were permitted to increase fares by as much as 5 percent above the Standard Industry Fare Level (SIFL) or to reduce them by 50 percent below the SIFL.[32]

SUCCESS OF LOW-COST INTRA-STATE AIRLINES

One of the frequently heard arguments in favor of airline deregulation was the success of services provided by Pacific Southwest Airline (PSA) in California, and Southwest (SW) in Texas. Congressional hearings often note that their fares were 50–60 percent below those of the regulated airlines, particularly in comparison with the northeastern part of the country. It was believed that if deregulation occurred, low-cost fare competition would spread across the country, meeting the needs of the general public who could not afford to pay the high fares of the regulated airlines.

Realizing that the general population could typically not afford to pay the fares of the major intra-state airlines, PSA and SW decided to provide rock-bottom prices. In the 1960s, PSA provided air service between San Francisco and Los Angeles for a mere $12. Similarly, SW only charged $10 to $13 per ticket for its flights between Houston and Dallas.[33,34] Its very low prices were a key factor in the success of both of these intrastate airlines. The rock-bottom prices not only attracted the price-sensitive general public, but were also well received by business travelers.

Both PSA and SW benchmarked their fares against the cost of one-way bus and train ticket prices. They felt that unless their fares were competitive, passengers would simply continue to travel by bus or train.[35] Their low fares accomplished just what they were supposed to do and attracted larger and larger numbers of passengers from buses, trains, and from long car trips to distant destinations.

The low-fare intrastate airlines took a number of steps that contributed to holding down their costs. They flew smaller aircraft that were better suited for frequent flights on short distances (a few hundred miles) between intrastate cities and achieved good fuel efficiency. Furthermore, SW decided to use only one airplane model, the Boeing 737. This decision reduced its capital cost and airplane maintenance expense.[36] The decision to fly only Boeing 737 meant less pilots and ground-crew training. The familiarity of all employees with one aircraft helped to produce faster turn-around times and permitted planes to be flown more hours per day. SW was able to achieve a remarkable turn-around time of only 10 minutes.[37,38]

Fast turnarounds allow individual aircraft to make more flights per day. SW seized this opportunity from the very beginning, as the Dallas to Houston route scheduled 12 roundtrip flights each day.[39] If, for some reason, a flight was cancelled, or passengers missed their flight, they knew that an hour later there would be another flight to take them to their destination. With short runs and quick turnarounds, both PSA and SW built a reputation of being highly reliable airlines.

A final element of the low-cost model derives more from customer-centricity. The attitude toward passengers at most of the big carriers, prior to deregulation, was that of herding cattle. The employees were indifferent as to how these customers felt about the flying experience. However, at PSA and SW, customers always came first and everything from boarding the plane to making safety announcements was approached from the aspect of having fun. To help create a friendly and fun atmosphere, these airlines shunned the typical stuffy business attire. In the 1960s, PSA had stewardesses wearing form-fitting mini skirts. When SW came onto the scene, their flight attendants were the first to have brightly colored hot pants as the uniform of the day.[40,41] Although these smaller airlines did not provide the usual frills seen at most of the larger carriers, passengers increasingly grew loyal to them because everything they did revolved around making the customer happy and providing a superior flying experience.

In summary, the new model adopted originally by PSA in California and later imitated by Texas-based SW, was driven by three main factors: (a) low cost, (b) reliable flight schedules, and (c) a superior flying experience.

Before deregulation, the major intra-state airlines operated primarily under a monopolistic or duopolistic structure. These airlines were heavily entrenched in their respective markets and acted much like a government-controlled utility provider. With these conditions, the question remains, "How were PSA and SW able to carve out their niche markets without being squashed by the big boys?" From a federal standpoint, the CAB regulated all interstate routes, but neither PSA nor SW flew interstate routes in the 1960s and 1970s. Instead, both these airlines began as intra-state carriers—PSA concentrating on serving San Diego, Los Angeles, and San Francisco in California, and up until deregulation, SW only providing service between Houston, Dallas, and San Antonio in Texas. Due to being intra-state airlines, PSA was regulated by the California Public Utilities Commission (PUC) and SW fell under the authority of the Texas Aeronautics Commission (TAC).[42] These individual state-controlled regulatory boards provided the necessary approval for both PSA and SW to operate when the CAB, prompted by the larger carriers of the time, wanted to deny them any such access.

The major airlines that existed at the time wanted to protect their market share and certainly put up a fight when this new competition showed up. The legal battles for SW were something fierce as the two major carriers in Texas, Braniff and Texas International, filed for multiple injunctions along the way. SW spent its first four years and more than $500,000 in legal fees fighting case after case, some of which went all the way to the US Supreme Court, and all of this before SW got its first plane off the ground.[43] These initial struggles could have been the very seed that created such an entrepreneurial attitude and culture among all of SW's employees for years to come. One thing is for sure: without the perseverance of SW's founders, the company could never have survived the intimidating climate of the time.

PSA and SW both had to find their fair share of differentiators that allowed the smaller companies to compete successfully with the larger airlines. Without the oversight of the CAB, PSA was not "saddled with costly monthly reporting requirements and protracted legal proceedings on routes and fares. (PUC requirements [were] considerably easier to meet.)"[44] Also, since PSA did not join the Air Transport Association, it was able to attract more passengers by paying travel agents a commission of 8 percent instead of the usual 5 percent offered by Western and United.[45] SW found that by serving smaller, out-of-the-way airports, they were able to reduce airport user fees sharply and, in turn, provide lower fares and attract an abundance of customers. After testing service to Houston Hobby Airport, SW found that the average passenger loads doubled, so they abandoned service to Houston's larger and better-known airport, Intercontinental, in favor of the almost desolate Hobby airport.[46] Once again, this was a case of SW recognizing an underserved need and responding with exactly what the flying public wanted.

Overcoming the regulatory barriers and staring down the so-called "800-pound gorillas" of the monopolistic carriers was a monumental undertaking at the time. PSA and SW had to find innovative ways of circumventing the existing laws simply to get started, and then to continue to stay in business. Time has shown that these airlines' low-cost model is tremendously viable, as SW continues to grow and is the most consistently profitable airline in existence. The idea works today just as it worked then: provide reliable and affordable flights while taking care of customers, and people will come back to fly with you again and again.

The subsequent chapters will demonstrate just how robust the low-cost model is—and its vulnerability to predatory pricing since deregulation. Attempts to stop predatory pricing have been made, but unfortunately certain major airlines still use this practice to defend their monopoly markets at the expense of the public. The next chapter uses the example of two discount airlines, Skytrain and People Express, that were formed in the early years of deregulation, and how they were driven out of business by predatory practices.

Chapter Two

Lost Opportunities

AS WE are about to discuss in this chapter, one of the major reasons for airline deregulation was the expectation of economists and politicians (including Presidents Nixon and Carter) that a large number of new airlines would emerge and make the industry more efficient. In particular, they expected that several new low-cost and low-price airlines would be created similar to the intrastate airlines, Southwest (SW) and Pacific Southwest Airline (PSA). These airlines often sold tickets for 50–60 percent less than the fares of the major full-service airlines. Economists strongly argued that there were no barriers to entry in the industry and that new airlines could fly routes where no discount service was offered.

This chapter describes the rise and fall of two discount airlines that emerged with the beginning of airline deregulation in 1978. Kahn, the new chairman of the CAB, and a leading advocate of airline deregulation, was glad to see these new discount airlines come into existence, but he was disappointed by the failure of most of them. The first discount airline to be discussed involves international air travel, and explains how the colorful Freddie Laker started his airline, Skytrain, which flew from London to New York and a few other US cities before it collapsed. The second case describes the rise and fall of People

Express, the largest of the new discount airlines started in the United States.

A major problem contributing to the failure of these two start-up airlines, as well as several others, was that the major established airlines (American, United, Delta, and Northwest) used "predatory pricing" to drive the new low-price discount airlines out of business. The major airlines would temporarily lower their fares on select routes where they competed with new discount airlines. In the process, they siphoned off their competitors' customers and eventually drove them into bankruptcy.

The possibility of "predatory pricing" was raised during the debate on airline deregulation, but the issue was dismissed on the basis that it was a violation of the antitrust laws. The expectation was that the Justice Department would take action to stop this illegal practice should it occur. However, President Reagan did not have the same view regarding the benefits of airline deregulation as President Carter, and did not urge the Justice Department to act. He believed in big business, which played a major role in his election, and he was not going to "bite the hands that fed him."

The Justice Department literally did nothing to stop the large, established airlines from stomping all over the new discount airlines. This policy decision left the many small and struggling new carriers vulnerable to deadly attack by the large established airlines. The major airlines often reduced their prices on just a small portion of their routes (e.g. 10–20 percent) when waging a war of destruction against a small discounter. Their size made a big difference in the battle with new start-up discount airlines. Once the new discounters were eliminated, the major airlines simply raised their fares back to, or above, their prior level.

While much of the history of airline deregulation is gloomy, there may yet be a happy ending to the story. Airline deregulation may at long last be working—with the public able to choose between one of the more costly legacy airlines (United, American, Delta, Northwest, Continental, and US Airways) or a low-fare discount airline (SW, AirTran, JetBlue, and Frontier). During the Clinton Administration (1993–2000), the Federal government became concerned about the growing dominance of the major airlines and the premium fares they were charging in many large cities. In recent years, the CAB has taken a number of steps to open up routes to the discount airlines that had been controlled by the high-cost legacy carriers. Public response to the discount airlines has grown rapidly in recent years. The share of passengers flown by the low-cost carriers increased from 10 percent in 1990 to close to 30 percent in 2004.[47] Officers of Delta and Northwest have publicly stated that the six major airlines of 2004 could be reduced to two or three over the remainder of the decade if the lower-cost, discount airlines continue to expand.

There is no question that the high-cost legacy carriers are being threatened by the expanding low-cost discount airlines. Legacy carriers lost more than $9 billion from 2001–04, while the low-cost discount airlines recorded profits and expanded their market share. However, the legacy carriers have a great deal of political clout in Washington and may yet figure out a way for the Federal government to bail them out of their critical financial situation so they can battle the low-cost discount airlines.

Freddie Laker's Skytrain

Freddie Laker was a very successful airline entrepreneur in England. He became a self-made millionaire by developing a charter airline business that flew troops, cargo, and vacationers throughout Europe and also internationally. One day, Laker hit on the idea that he would create a discount airline to fly vacationers and family travelers on a regularly scheduled basis at low fares. This was a unique concept at the time since the major international airlines largely ignored this segment of the market. Laker did not, however, plan to compete with the major trans-Atlantic airlines, whose primary customers were business travelers wanting more services for which they paid high prices.[48]

Laker petitioned the British government in 1970 for a certificate to start a discount airline to fly from London to New York City—the busiest international route in the world. He argued that his economy-oriented airline would have a minimal impact on British Airways, Pan Am, and TWA, which were serving the more affluent airline customers flying across the Atlantic to New York City. He was going to provide limited service to economy-minded air travelers who would purchase tickets a few hours before the flight time. He modeled his airline after the railroad business, where people would go to a train station, buy a ticket, and then be transported to another city; hence, he named his airline Skytrain.[49]

Laker envisioned that his Skytrain service would not appeal to business travelers who had to make plans in advance to fly across the Atlantic. He claimed there would only be a minimal diversion of business travelers to his economy airline, since business travelers would not be willing to stand in line for hours to purchase last-minute tickets. Business travelers were also looking for a higher level of service than what his bare-bones airline would provide. Laker's was an airline targeted at younger people and families who could not afford to pay the high fares of the established carriers from London to the United States. He believed that most of Skytrain's passengers would carry their luggage aboard his airplanes, and that they would pay for food and drinks consumed while flying.[50]

Laker's first obstacle was to gain clearance from the British authority to initiate his Skytrain service. However, British Airways strongly objected to Laker's discount airline obtaining a charter to fly from London to New York.

Issues were raised concerning the diversion of passengers from the established full-service airlines, and whether Laker had the financial backing to launch and support a new airline. He faced one obstacle after another in order to obtain permission to launch his discount airline. However, Laker won support from Queen Elizabeth for Skytrain to obtain a license to start flying across the Atlantic. Laker actually came from a humble background, and thought there was a need for the economical air service he proposed. Finally, Laker obtained a license to fly from Heathrow Airport in London to Newark Airport in New York City beginning January 1, 1973.[51] Laker purchased several new DC-10 aircraft that would hold 345 passengers each. He felt the high capacity of the DC-10 would give him an advantage over his competition, which flew planes with half the capacity.

Laker's next challenge was to obtain certification from the United States to fly his discount airline back from New York to London. He thought this process would be relatively simple since the United States had two airlines flying between New York and London (Pan Am and TWA), while England only had one airline (British Airways) providing this service. The major international airlines were permitted to make agreements on who would be permitted to fly internationally and the fare that would be charged. The Consortium of International Airlines discussed Laker's request to start service from London to the United States but denied it. Laker sued the consortium for not permitting him to start his discount airline service. The suit was dropped when the international airlines agreed not to contest his certification to fly from New York to London.[52]

Laker was finally certified to start flying between London and New York City. His first flight was on September 26, 1978, seven years after he had started the process of trying to launch his discount airline. Over the years, Laker gained a great deal of free publicity through his fight to start a low-cost airline to meet the needs of the common person. On his first flight to the United States, he had many European journalists and television people anxious to cover the historic event, despite the fact that they had to pay their own round-trip fares to fly the inaugural London–New York route. Similarly, there were many US reporters who boarded the plane in New York to provide their readers and viewers information about the first discount airline to fly the busiest international route in the world. Skytrain's free publicity helped the discount airline to attract many customers with minimal advertising.[53]

There were definite obstacles placed in the way of Skytrain's success. While hard to imagine today, passengers flying from London to New York could not purchase their tickets before 4 a.m. on the day of the flight. They could either purchase their tickets at the Gatwick Airport in London, or at a converted tobacco shop at London's Victoria Station, which provided service to the airport. The shop had been empty for some time, and Laker stripped everything out except the shelves along the wall, where passengers could complete ticket information. In the back of the shop, he installed a partition with several sales windows.[54] The New York Port authority did not want long lines of people waiting to buy tickets at Kennedy Airport, and required tickets to be purchased off the airport property. Laker found a new building with an empty first floor close to the Van Wyck Expressway leading to the airport that was also near a subway station with service to the airport.[55]

The process of purchasing a Skytrain ticket was kept simple. Customers either paid cash or used a VISA credit card to make the purchase. At that time, VISA was only charging a 2.5 percent fee. Laker created the least expensive ticketing and sales promotion effort in the industry. While Laker's cost of ticketing came to 4.7 percent of its operating expenses, the cost of ticketing by British Airways was 19 percent and was about 15 percent for a consortium of international airlines.[56]

Skytrain was a success from the start. All seats on its first Sunday flight were sold, and it was highly profitable in its first year of operation. In less than four years, Laker's Skytrain became the fifth largest airline flying North Atlantic routes. During 1980, Skytrain flew 177,600 passengers and made a profit of $3.6 million. Laker claimed that his success was due to the major airlines failing to provide air service for the ordinary person who could not afford to pay the high fares of the major full-service carriers.[57]

Shortly before the first year anniversary of Skytrain, Laker dropped a bombshell on a dumb-founded aviation industry. The early success he experienced seemed to have gone to his head. He announced plans to buy 15 new wide-bodied airplanes. Newspaper articles questioned, "Where will Freddie get the cash"? Laker announced that he planned to use some of the airplanes to start an around-the-world Skytrain to be called GLOBETRAIN. However, he was unable to get permission to fly from London to Hong Kong, and from there to Los Angeles.[58] He used some of the new airplanes to provide charter service, the area where he got his start and had acquired much of his experience. He also secured permission to fly from London to three cities in Florida (Miami, Fort Lauderdale, and Orlando).

Laker's dream of further expanding his discount airline continued. In February 1981, he signed an agreement to purchase three Airbus airplanes for $131 million. His plan was to provide low-cost airline service from London to 37 cities in nine European countries. The law was clearly on his side, but governments of the European Economic Community were concerned since most of the countries had their own national airlines and did not like the idea of competing with Laker's low-price airline. Laker also planned to connect the 37 cities into a network of some 630 routes, but this was unacceptable under the laws of the European countries that banned a third country from providing scheduled service between two other nations.

As it turned out, Laker did not receive authority to fly to a single city in Europe.[59]

As Laker planned his airline, he expected that major US airline competitors would create their own discount airlines to combat his Skytrain. However, that was not the strategy of his major competitors. Instead, each of the major airlines offered a number of discount tickets that would collectively equal the number of seats Laker planned to fly. Until this time, the major airlines had primarily offered just one fare and class of service. Witnessing Laker's success, Pan Am lowered the price of more of its tickets to undercut Laker's Skytrain. Pan Am reduced its prices in spite of the fact that it was already losing millions of dollars flying between New York and London. Freddie complained that Pan Am was selling below cost and was using predatory pricing to try and destroy his airline. The major airlines' sharp fare reductions, and particularly those by Pan Am, caused Skytrain traffic to decrease significantly, resulting in large losses for the discounter. In addition, Laker had taken on a huge debt to purchase more aircraft that were not being used in the face of the competitive pressures; he simply could not stimulate enough demand to make use of the new aircraft. He tapped every source of capital he knew of to obtain additional funding, but failed to do so. Laker finally shut down Skytrain at 8 a.m. on February 5, 1982.[60]

Laker's creditors brought a $350 million anti-trust case against British Airways and nine other airlines as also aircraft manufacturer McDonnell Douglas for conspiring to drive Skytrain out of business. The case charged that the major airlines agreed through the International Air Transport Association to use predatory pricing to drive his discount airline out of business. McDonnell Douglas was included in the suit since it allegedly agreed (under pressure from Skytrain competitors) to stop offering favorable terms to Laker for purchases of its aircraft. After Laker went out of business, fares on its former routes, now only serviced by the major airlines, increased by 50–60 percent. This move supported Laker's contention that Skytrain was a victim of predatory pricing. An article in *Barron's National Business and Financial Weekly* stated: "I think there can be no doubt that during the days of Laker Airways there was obvious predatory pricing."[61]

The settlement of the anti-trust case was divided into three parts. The payment of $48 million went to Laker's creditors, which included 16,000 small firms, 14,000 ticket holders, and 2,300 employees. Also, larger creditors received a portion of the money they were owed. Laker personally accepted a settlement of $8 million, and the lawyers in the case received $12 million from the defendants.[62]

PEOPLE EXPRESS

One of the most compelling arguments for airline deregulation starting in 1978 was that supposedly a large number of new discount airlines similar to SW in Texas and PSA in California would emerge. These two airlines charged intrastate fares that were often 50–60 percent less than fares of the major airlines.

In fact, several new discount airlines were created soon after deregulation in 1978 to the delight of the flying public and the dismay of the established airlines. Some of the first discount airlines to start flying were People Express, Midway, and New York Air. These new discount airlines offered large savings, which was expected for two primary reasons: First, they had lower labor cost since they paid lower wages and provided fewer costly services. Second, they initially bought used aircraft at a fraction of the cost of airplanes flown by the major airlines.[63]

People Express began providing discount air service in April 1981 from Newark International Airport, just outside New York City. The airport was relatively deserted, with the major airlines choosing to fly from the more convenient LaGuardia and JFK airports located in New York City. During its first four months of operation, People Express hired 600 employees, flew to eight eastern cities, and carried 400,000 passengers charging fares as low as $23. There were some similarities between the original design of Laker's Skytrain and Donald Burr's People Express. Burr eliminated as many costly services as possible to allow his airline to sell tickets with large discounts. Customers either purchased their tickets from travel agents or paid for their tickets after boarding the airplane. Baggage handling was a "do-it-yourself" process with an alternative option to pay $3 per bag checked. And there was no complimentary food service.

Given the initial strong response to its low-price discount service, Burr went on a buying spree. In just under three years, People Express had purchased 20 737s and 18 727s (twice the capacity of the 737s) that it used to provide service on 21 East Coast routes. In addition, Burr established a two-year lease on one of the high-capacity Boeing 747s with 490 seats. The Boeing 747 was used to fly from Newark to London five days a week. People Express became popular and successful with considerable customer savings and an initial sale of 85 percent of its seats. People Express planned to lease three more 747s to provide cross-country service in the United States and to fly more international routes.[64]

Burr's early success with People Express was phenomenal. In just three years he had 150 flights per day from Newark, the largest number of flights of any airline in the New York area. Burr vowed to keep growing. His goal was to have an operation as large as Delta in Atlanta with 334 departures a day. The early success he experienced led him to purchase 35 new aircraft in 1984 and 1985. He planned to use the new aircraft to add more flights onto existing routes such as Newark to Boston, Buffalo, Pittsburgh, and Columbus in the northeast, and he looked to add a number of cities in Florida and even a route to

London. He also planned to begin service to New Orleans, St. Louis, Denver, and Minneapolis.[65]

Financial analysts and other airline executives questioned whether People Express was growing too fast and at a pace that could lead to its downfall. Some worried that Burr was placing too much capacity on existing routes that could not be profitably employed. His capacity usage was continuing to slide from the high 70 percent level to the low 70 percent range.

Burr decided to start flying important routes of the long-established airlines to better maximize use of his expanding fleet of airplanes. One airline executive stated, "If they start flying New York-to-Chicago, American or United may pull out a cannon and blast them." Burr disregarded the idea that his airline could be shot out of the skies, since People Express had an extremely low cost structure relative to the major airlines and had withstood fare wars in the past. He added that People Express controlled so much traffic from Newark that it would be impossible for other airlines to add significant capacity. He stated "anybody who attacks us in Newark has to be a slow wit."[66]

People Express had earned $1 million on sales of $138 million in 1982, and its earnings climbed to $10.4 million on sales of $292 million during 1983. But trouble was brewing at corporate headquarters where Gerald Gitner, co-founder and first president of People Express, began to worry that fares were set unnecessarily low. He thought that People Express "was giving away the store." A financial analyst agreed, and stated: "I don't think that the airline is being run for the benefit of stockholders." However, Burr was adamant about keeping fares down. People Express typically entered a market charging about one-third of the existing coach fare. For example, the coach fare on the Newark to Buffalo route had been $99 and when People Express started serving the route it only charged $38 at peak travel times, and $25 for off-peak times. Had Burr taken the advice to reduce slightly the level of discount it offered, People Express might have survived the hard times that were just around the corner.[67]

People Express began experiencing a number of problems in 1984. Competition reacted as Laker added capacity on his airline's existing routes. People Express tripled its capacity on its route from Newark to Pittsburgh from four to 12 flights a day. An executive of USAir stated that the move "caught us by surprise." But once awakened, USAir quickly responded and withdrew its hefty premium, sharply narrowing the gap with the price charged by People Express. People Express flights to West Palm Beach, Florida, began to divert customers from Delta flights to Fort Lauderdale. Therefore, Delta increased its capacity by 66 percent, setting fares only slightly more than People Express. Similarly, major airlines on other People Express routes sharply lowered their prices, attracting a large numbers of travelers who would have otherwise flown on Burr's discount airline.[68]

The competitive response to People Express began to take its toil. The airline was reporting huge gains in revenue per flown-passenger miles, often more than double that of the year before, but the problem was that its load factor (percent of seats sold) had started to plummet. Its load factor declined from 76.3 percent to 69.7 percent for the first three months of 1984, and this was just the beginning. Fewer passengers per plane placed a real cloud on the future of People Express. For the first quarter of 1984, its profit plunged to $18,000 from $2.1 million the year before, the first decline in earnings since it began operating.[69]

With the purchase of large numbers of new aircraft in 1984, People Express was forced to change its strategy from flying more obscure routes and drawing people out of their cars and from buses to "start flying routes of the major airlines." In June 1984, People Express announced a new service from Newark to Los Angeles. Five major airlines flew this major high-volume transcontinental route. People Express's one-way standard fare was $149 and for off-peak seasons $119, while the lowest fare of the major airlines had been $400. United Airlines quickly met People Express's fare, but required a 14-day advance purchase of a round-trip ticket with a seven-day minimum stay. American Airlines took the battle to a new level by announcing that its low fares would apply to 14 daily flights. TWA and Pan Am matched American's fares, but only on a few of their flights, stating that their cross-country flights were nearly full with passengers flying on to overseas locations.[70]

People Express next took on the major airlines by offering a route from Newark to Chicago. It offered 10 flights a day on one of the most heavily traveled routes in the country, causing a major challenge to the two largest US airlines—United and American. People Express, with its frequent service and low fares, was now aiming at business travelers who were the backbone of the major airlines. People Express's one-way fare was $79 for peak times and $59 for the off-peak times, and was considerably less than the coach fare of $258 charged by the major airlines. United, the nation's largest airline, announced a one-way peak fare of $79 and an off-peak fare of $59 in response to People Express's low fare. To qualify for this significantly reduced fare, United required a seven-day advance purchase and a stay over the weekend. In turn, American cut its fare and terms of travel, and met those of United.[71]

In September 1984, People Express announced it would begin flying from Newark to Detroit and Newark to Miami, intensifying its challenge on routes served by the major airlines. It started flying seven nonstop flights a day to Detroit, charging a peak fare of $65 and an off-peak fare of $45. It also began flying four flights to Miami, charging $99 for mid-day flights and $79 for early-morning and late-night flights. People Express already flew to small cities in Florida including Jacksonville, Melbourne, Sarasota, St Petersburg and West Palm Beach—a legacy of the time that it used to stay away from routes served by major airlines.[72]

On September 28, People Express also began flying from Newark to San Francisco, its second coast-to-coast route, continuing its strategy to take on the major airlines on their own turf. Fares were comparable to its peak-time fare, from Newark to Los Angeles, of $149. It started service with one jumbo Boeing 747, making a round-trip flight each day. Burr's discount airline was scheduled to take delivery of three additional 747s in the spring of 1985, which would allow People Express to increase its transcontinental capacity substantially.[73]

People Express continued its strategic offering of discount service on major airline routes to use its growing fleet of aircraft. It began flying from Newark to Cleveland in October 1984,[74] its one-way peak fare being $65, and $45 for off-peak flights. The major airlines' primary unrestricted fare had been $173. Then, in November 1984, People Express started operating three flights a day from Newark to Denver. Its peak-time fare was $99 and off-peak fare was $79.[75] In December, it began two flights a day from Newark to Orlando, charging a peak-time fare of $99 and $79 for off-peak flights.[76] In addition, in December, People Express started flying five daily round-trip flights to North Carolina—Newark to Greensboro, High Point, and Winston-Salem.[77]

Given the new routes added during 1984 and price reductions of several of the major airlines, People Express produced both positive and negative operating results. Its revenue–passenger miles flown more than doubled from 3.67 billion in 1983 to 7.7 billion in 1984, but its load factor decreased from 74.6 percent in 1983 to 69.8 percent in 1984.[78] In addition, People Express reported a loss during the fourth quarter of 1984 after seven consecutive quarterly profits. People Express blamed the loss on its expansion to 10 new cities during the second half of the year as it took possession of a large number of new aircraft.

People Express's profit problem intensified in January 1985, when American slashed fares on routes flown by People Express and other discounters. American cut its coach fares by 70 percent for flights between 7 p.m. and 6 a.m. Its new fare, directed at People Express, was called its "Ultimate Super Saver." The tickets were for round trips and had to be purchased 30 days in advance, with a Saturday-night stay over. Several other major airlines matched American's sharp price cuts.

Some industry observers suggested that American might be waging a war to destroy People Express and other discounters. An official of another airline that competed with American called the move "Armageddon"; he said, "The shakeout has now started. This will flush down the weak ones. They're after People Express and others that have been cutting fares."[79] Several major airlines' sharp price cuts took place on a selective basis, and were targeted at weakening or destroying discount airlines. For example, United stated that its Super-Coach fares were being offered only in "10 percent of its markets where it competed with People Express and other discounters."

Selective price cuts by major carriers to weaken and destroy discount airlines is known as "predatory pricing."[80] There was some concern during the discussions leading up to airline deregulation in 1978 that predatory pricing might be used to drive new discount airlines out of business. Some feared that the major airlines, which often flew more than 1,000 flights every day, could selectively lower their prices on certain routes and temporarily meet those of the discounters. In the process, they would drive the discounters out of business.

Deregulation enthusiasts declared that anti-trust laws prohibited predatory pricing. These enthusiasts anticipated that the US Justice Department would take action to stop this unfair and destructive practice by the large airlines. However, according to some government officials, the Justice Department would not respond to predatory pricing claims since the Reagan Administration considered most types of price cutting by the major airlines to be legal and pro-competitive.[81] The major airlines' selective price cuts against People Express and other discounters did its job, as People Express reported its second consecutive loss for the first quarter of 1985 after seven consecutive quarters of profitability.

People Express's purchase of 36 aircraft during 1984 and 1985 created a fleet of 64 airplanes. Consequently, it could no longer use its airplanes to fly mostly secondary routes that were of limited interest to the major airlines. The movement into routes where it competed directly with the major airlines was now hitting the bottom line.[82] One of the cities where it offered this new service was Newark to Dallas, one of American's primary hubs. People Express also started flying from Newark to Atlanta, Delta's major hub.[83] It also expanded internationally and started flying from Newark to Brussels, Belgium, its second transatlantic route. It had been flying from Newark to London since 1983, and had increased its flights on that busiest of international routes.

People Express experienced difficulty in obtaining gates to new cities it wanted to serve, so Burr decided to change his strategy where he would buy existing airlines with advantageous route structures. The discounter had been operating a few flights to Denver, but could not get a single gate of its own, and had to lease gates from other carriers at considerable cost. Late in 1985, Burr outbid Continental Airlines and paid $300 million for Frontier Airlines based in Denver, Colorado. This represented a bold move by the discounter in two respects. First, it was a huge financial expenditure for People Express, which had already taken on a large amount of debt to expand it fleet from three aircraft in 1981 to 64 in 1985. Second, Frontier had been struggling financially for much of the year in its battle with United, which was striving to grow its position in Denver. Although, this battle was expected to continue, Burr wanted to buy Frontier in order to open up new routes to People Express. The merger would link People Express's 49 cities operating primarily in the eastern half of the country, to Frontier's 52 cities concentrated in the west and southwest.[84] The US government approved the merger on November 25, 1985, and the deal created the ninth largest passenger airline in the United States—quite a feat for an airline that only began flying in 1981.

Before Burr purchased Frontier, the airline had provided a high level of service and operated much like a major airline. It was one of the most heavily unionized airlines, and its cost-per-seat mile was 3.2 cents more than that of People Express. When purchasing Frontier, Burr indicated that he would not change the company's image. However, shortly after taking over management of Frontier, Burr sharply slashed Frontier's fares. The People Express–Frontier combination effectively created a discount airline serving 43 states. But for the year ending December 31, 1985, People Express reported a loss of $27.5 million on sales of $977.9 million. While People Express had made a small profit for the year, the loss was attributed to the expenses incurred due to its purchase of Frontier.[85] The Frontier purchase was followed shortly thereafter with Burr purchasing two smaller airlines, a regional carrier called Britt Airways, and Provincetown-Boston Airlines which operated in Florida and the northeast.

By March 15, 1986, Frontier's operation changed to be similar to People Express. There would be no more free lunches and checked baggage. Prices were cut by as much as 60 percent to more than 100 cities. Larry Martin, Frontier's president, told reporters, "We intend to be the dominant carrier in the Denver market." A new three-tier price structure was also announced with premium, economy, and discount fares. Depending on the flight distance from Denver, the "discount fares" would be $29,

$39, and $49; "economy fares" would be $69, $79, and $89; and "premium fares" would be $99, $109, and $119. The announcement led to the prediction of heightened competition from Denver, since it was a major market for both United and Continental Airlines.[86] People Express, which acquired Frontier late in 1985, reported a record net loss of $58 million for the first quarter of 1986. Part of the loss was attributed to the fierce price war taking place in Denver between Frontier and United.

Burr shocked many people when he announced a "major change in the strategy" for People Express beginning May 1, 1986. The airline had experienced trouble filling enough of its seats on its larger Boeing 727 that it had purchased over the past two years. The discounter was giving up its "Spartan operation" and was going to add a number of services to compete for more business travelers. It added first-class service on its 747 flights and was now going to add a first-class section to its 50 Boeing 727 jets and its 23 Boeing 737 jets. First class would include free food and drinks, which previously its passengers had to purchase. People Express also announced a new Travel-Award Program, permitting business travelers to earn free tickets similar to that of the major airlines. Trying to attract more business travelers, the new strategic plan also included selling its tickets through United's Apollo and American's Sabre computer-reservation services. This plan permitted travel agents to book tickets automatically, no longer having to use their phones to book reservations. Pushing Burr to make these changes was the fact that People Express posted a record net loss of $58 million in the first quarter of 1989. Some financial analysts felt that converting People Express from a discount airline to one with services similar to the major airlines was Burr's last-ditch effort to try and save his airline from bankruptcy— a course the airline was rapidly headed toward.[87]

People Express's meteoric growth contributed to a growing number of service problems. According to the

Department of Transportation, complaints soared to 10.3 per 100,000 customers in the first quarter of 1986. That number was about triple the level of complaints for all other airlines and 17 times worse than Delta, which had one of the best service records. The discounter overbooked its flights during holiday seasons and the summer in order to make sure that its planes were jammed full at peak times—hoping to offset weak demand at other times of the year. People Express also overbooked its flights since it was the only airline not requiring advance payment, which was a benefit to customers but also led to a larger number of "no shows." Furthermore, its reservation system was not sophisticated enough to eliminate reservations for a return trip for a "no show", which further contributed to its overbooking problem. A People Express manager said that on some flights, the airline overbooked in excess of 100 percent. On most flights, there were enough "no shows" that passengers were able to board their scheduled flight. But on other flights at peak times, some ticket holders were left behind. Furthermore, given its low level of staffing, there were times where lost baggage became a real problem.[88]

People Express's financial condition sharply deteriorated during the first half of 1986. It lost $58 million during the first quarter and $74.5 million during the second quarter of the year. As a consequence, Burr made a number of changes during the second half of 1986 to try and save People Express. He had purchased Frontier in December 1985 for $300 million, hoping to open up the western part of the country for People Express, but Frontier entered a costly price war with United and Continental in Denver, Colorado. It was estimated that Frontier was losing around $10 million each month. Burr negotiated with United to buy Frontier. However, when that effort failed, he shut down Frontier in August 1986, and filed for Chapter 11 bankruptcy. In addition, the shut-down of Frontier put 4,700 employees out of work.[89]

Burr tried a number of things to keep his faltering People Express from slipping over the edge. He sold several of his aircraft to raise badly needed cash. He reduced the number of cities served from its Newark base. It even stopped flying to Brussels, Belgium. However, his operating model no longer worked and capacity usage had fallen to 57 percent for all of 1986, while People Express needed to operate in the high 60 percent range to break even. On December 21, 1986, People Express was sold to Texas Air.[90]

SUMMARY

Airline deregulation was expected to lead to the formation of several new airlines similar to the low-cost intrastate airlines SW and PSA. These intra-state airlines fares were 50–60 percent below those of the major airlines. For a period of two–three years, the proponents of deregulation found in People Express everything they expected deregulation to produce.

However, there is no question that People Express grew too fast and should never have purchased Frontier (a full-service money losing airline). But the failure of People Express and a number of other start-up discount airlines was also due to anti-competitive conduct of the major airlines with which they tried to compete. Initially, People Express flew more obscure routes and stayed away from the routes dominated by the major airlines. During its initial years, the discounter grew rapidly and prospered, but in order to continue to grow, People Express started flying routes dominated by the major airlines such as Newark to Chicago, Denver, Los Angeles, San Francisco, Atlanta, and Miami. For a while, People Express was flying more airplanes from the New York area than any of the major airlines.

Trying to compete with the high-cost, full-service airlines on their routes was a major reason for the downfall of People Express and other new low-cost discount airlines. The major airlines would temporarily lower their fares on select routes to meet People Express's low fares as well as those of other discount airlines. In the process, the major airlines would keep the discount airlines from obtaining enough volume to operate profitably. The end result for People Express and other discount airlines' forced withdrawal from major routes and liquidation.

It was common for long-established major airlines to lower their prices temporarily on a small fraction of their routes (10–20 percent), while maintaining high prices on routes where they dominated with little to no competition; hence, they were making large profits on these routes. Furthermore, on many of the major airlines' routes, the discounters could not obtain the gates required to provide service. In a sense, the discounters were trying to compete with one hand tied behind their backs.

During the exhaustive hearings regarding airline deregulation, the subject of predatory pricing usage was discussed. However, concerns about predatory pricing were largely discounted on the basis that the Federal regulatory agencies would take action to stop the practice. Both Presidents Nixon and Carter were strongly in favor of deregulation, believing that discount airlines would come into existence and lower the cost of flying in the United States. But under President Reagan, despite several complaints, the Department of Transportation and the Justice Department took no action to stop predatory pricing. Reagan's plan was unexpected when economists and government officials enthusiastically endorsed deregulation in the mid-1970s.

In summary, over the first five years following deregulation in 1978, several discount airlines emerged. However, by the tenth anniversary of deregulation in 1988, they had all but disappeared. Similarly, while there were 15 major airlines in 1978, the number had declined to 10 a decade later. The Reagan Administration approved 17 out of 18 mergers between 1985 and 1988. The market share of the eight major airlines climbed from 74.1 percent in 1983 to 91.7 percent in 1988. Given the majors' monopoly positions in the big markets, they frequently charge 20–40 percent premiums in comparison to routes served by discount airlines.[91]

Development of Fortress Hubs

ONE OF the primary justifications for airline deregulation in 1978 was that a large number of new low-cost airlines were expected to enter the high-price markets and drive down the price of flying. Anticipating the growth of new low-cost airlines, the legacy airlines that existed before deregulation were permitted to either lower their prices initially by as much as 50 percent, or to increase them by no more than 10 percent.

Airline deregulation was based on the premise that "there were no barriers to entry that would prohibit new low-fare airlines from entering high-price markets." But the reality turned out to be a far cry from that. Entry into markets dominated by the legacy carriers was extremely difficult. Following deregulation, the major airlines developed a set of large markets they dominated; often, one or two airlines had 70 percent or greater market share. With their dominant/monopoly positions, the major airlines were able to charge large fare premiums with little worry about competition from low-cost discount airlines.

One of the most devastating impacts on deregulation was the Reagan Administration's decision to approve 17 out of 18 mergers proposed from 1985 to 1988. While there were 15 major airlines in 1978, there were only eight a decade later in 1988. The market share of the eight surviving airlines climbed from 74.1 percent in 1983 to 91.7 percent in 1988.[92]

The events occurring in the airline industry were concisely summarized in a 1988 *Wall Street Journal* article titled "Ten Years After Deregulation, Carriers Appear To Avoid Competitors' Flight Paths." The article explained how the major airlines had put the toughest dog-fighting behind them with 168 carriers being wiped out over the past 10 years. Now, with only eight airlines dominating the nation's air traffic, "the industry is slipping cozily into the comforts of oligopoly."[93]

During his confirmation hearing in 1989, Samuel K. Skinner, President George Bush's Transportation Secretary stated: "It was not the intent of deregulation to give anyone a monopoly. ... It's time to review the impact of that. We have to find ways to instill competitiveness in the system."[94] Unfortunately, words were louder than action, and little was done to even the playing field and increase competition.

DEVELOPMENT OF THE "HUB-AND-SPOKE" SYSTEMS

When the airline industry was deregulated in 1978, the major legacy carriers fundamentally had a point-to-point system. The point-to-point system essentially involved major airlines flying from one city to another, such as from Denver to Chicago, Chicago to Cincinnati, Cincinnati to Atlanta, and Atlanta to Miami.

Following deregulation, all major airlines developed what has become known as a "hub-and-spoke" system. The major airlines changed their route structure to concentrate flights from small nearby cities to their large hub airports.

This hub-and-spoke system is often compared to the wheel of a bicycle with many small spokes leading to the center (or hub) of the wheel. The major airlines operated a number of hub-and-spoke airports, often located several hundred or thousands of miles from one another. They flew most of their customers from one of their hub-and-spoke cities to another of the hub-and-spoke cities they dominated.

The hub-and-spoke cities the major airlines dominated over several years include:

- American—Dallas (Fort Worth) and Miami
- TWA—St. Louis (bought by American)
- Continental—Houston and Newark
- United—Denver, Chicago (O'Hare), and San Francisco
- Delta—Atlanta, Cincinnati, and Salt Lake City
- US Airways—Charlotte, Philadelphia, and Pittsburgh
- Northwest—Detroit, Minneapolis and Memphis

Shortly after deregulation in 1978, the first major airline to develop a hub-and-spoke system was Delta, headquartered in Atlanta, Georgia. As Atlanta had the only airline hub, a common joke told was that "when someone died he/she had to go through Atlanta before moving on to heaven." Despite the joke, Delta's hub system became a model that all major airlines eventually adopted. The system involved flying customers from several small cities to Atlanta. Passengers originating in Atlanta, and those arriving from many small cities, were then flown on to other large hub-and-spoke cities Delta operated, including Dallas (shared with American), Cincinnati, and Salt Lake City.

Thomas G. Plaskett, the Senior Vice President of Marketing at American, provided insight into the advantages of the hub-and-spoke system. He commented:

> The primary advantage of the hub-and-spoke system is that it gives us more product to sell. The total number of markets in which we are selling air transportation is currently 3,751 as compared to 357 before we began our hub here in Dallas in 1981.

Furthermore, it was commonly the case that more customers originated from smaller cities (the spokes) than from the large hub cities.[95]

United was one of the last of the major airlines to adopt the hub-and-spoke system. Following deregulation, United felt that the biggest profits came from long-haul routes that made more efficient use of its airplanes. However, finding that it was losing customers to its major competitors, United also adopted a hub-and-spoke system in 1983. Three of its major hub cities were Chicago, Denver, and San Francisco. As its major competitors had discovered, United's hub-and-spoke system permitted the airline to provide more frequent service than when it flew a linear point-to-point system, and to control more of the traffic in its large hub markets.

Another advantage of this system was that it permitted the major airlines to move from broad-based fare cuts to narrow price slashing to keep new discount airlines from successfully penetrating their major markets. Richard Farris, United's Chairman and Chief Operations Officer, said that its hub-and-spoke system permitted United to keep new discount airlines from successfully penetrating its markets. He said,

> In some big markets, a price-cutter may affect only 5 percent of our business. So if we have, say, 60 percent of the business, we aren't going to drag down the other 55 percent to meet the five percent.[96]

On the other hand, the hub-and-spoke system has its drawbacks as well. In 1985, only 2 percent of passengers arriving at a hub from smaller spoke cities were able to stay on the same plane. Thus, they had to hurry to another gate to fly on to their final destinations, creating major passenger inconvenience. The major airlines also had to hold their larger hub-city airplanes on the ground for a long time while passengers made their way from short incoming flights. In Delta's case, airplanes carrying customers on to other large destinations were often on the ground for a full hour.[97] This was two-to-three times the turn-around time of airlines flying from point to point. In addition, bad weather conditions often contributed to long flight delays, increasing the chance that many passengers would miss their connections. Furthermore, there was an increase in misplaced luggage due to the transfer of luggage from small incoming flights to the longer flights between the hub airports. Nevertheless, the hub-and-spoke system was the overall winner for the major airlines. It allowed them to expand and dominate most major airports across the country.

Large legacy airlines also dominated the major airports by controlling as many airport gates as possible. The major airlines could often acquire most of the gates at their large hub airports, thus denying the opportunity for small, discount airlines to compete. In 1986, 10 years after airline deregulation, business at 15 of the top national airports was either dominated by one airline with 50 percent or more of the gates, or two airlines controlling 70 percent or more of the gates. Stephen A. George, the director of Pittsburgh Airport where USAir carried about 80 percent of its passengers, stated that the airline industry is "an oligopoly again ... and just a surviving handful" of airlines exist at major airports. The consequence of increasing concentration at major airports was obvious—increased market power and higher fares. For example, after TWA purchased Ozark Airline, its airline ticket price in St Louis increased 33 percent between May 1986 and May 1987.[98]

The major airlines dominating the larger airports used their influence to reduce competition. Local airport authorities do not have much power to make gates available to new discount airlines. Airlines that control most of the leases at the major airports have a great deal to say about construction of new gates and who can use them. For example, in Denver, United agreed to pay $55 million of bonds for the improvement of concourse B. According to Anthony Chaitin, United's Senior Vice President for Customer Services, "I do not intend to let competitors use (the concourse)." Similarly, Pittsburgh wanted to build a new terminal that would cost $503 million to ease congestion at its single-airport terminal, but USAir delayed signing the new lease agreement, given concerns that gates might go to new competitors. At that time, USAir controlled 33 of the 52 gates. According to Associate Professor of Transportation Marketing, Lawrence Cunningham, "Airport construction is a Catch-22 scenario. The airport authority is in the unenviable position of negotiating with the dominant airline to bring in new competition."[99]

THE CONSEQUENCES OF MARKET DOMINANCE

Traditional economics postulates the relationship between market concentration and the prices firms charge for their products or services. As concentration—measured by market share held by the largest competitors—increases, there is an increase in market power that permits dominating companies to increase their prices. A major rationale for airline deregulation was that there were no barriers to entry and that there would be large numbers of new airlines entering high-priced markets to drive down airline fares. However, the large airlines that existed at the time of deregulation developed a game plan to stop competition from entering their dominant markets.

Government policy had much to do with setting the economic tone—either by creating an environment where competition thrives, or by encouraging some businesses to develop high market share, giving them the power to increase their prices. While President Carter was a fervent supporter of airline deregulation with a large number of new airlines, his successor, President Reagan, had a different orientation, favoring big business. President Reagan did not encourage the Justice Department to take vigorous action to stop the predatory pricing that was hurting the smaller major and new discount airlines. Moreover, the Reagan Administration approved 17 of the 18 mergers that took place between 1985 and 1988. Due to the wave of mergers in the airline industry, the number of major airlines declined from 12 in 1978 to eight in 1986.[100] Consequently, the aforementioned result was that the national market share of the eight largest airlines climbed to 91.7 percent in 1988.

Kahn, considered the father of airline deregulation, expressed considerable dismay over the growing monopoly trend in the airline industry. He laid the blame on the Reagan Administration's "abysmal dereliction" in preventing mergers.[101]

When the airline industry was deregulated in 1978, the major airlines could either compete in more markets across the country, or they could concentrate their business in a select set of large markets. They chose the latter case, selecting sets of markets they could dominate and charge premium fares. According to an article in the *Los Angeles Times* in 1989, the effect of this concentration is clear.

> ... in hub airports dominated by one carrier: Consumers there can expect to pay as much as 50 percent more than people flying comparable routes in cities with some competition.[102]

Similarly, a study conducted by the General Accounting Office found fares 60 percent higher at four highly concentrated hub airports in 1988, 10 years after airline deregulation. The study also reported that fares were 27 percent higher at 15 concentrated airports compared to other major airports.[103]

TAKING OVER THE REGIONAL AIRLINES

The first step in the large airline strategy of dominating the major airports was to tie up its gates (as discussed in the previous section). A closely related aspect of this strategy involved the major airlines' relationships with the small regional airlines that provided service between smaller cities and also to large airports. The major airlines determined that if they were going to tightly control the air traffic at major airports, then they needed to purchase or develop contractual agreements with the regional airlines. By 1988, the major airlines had gained control over 48 of the 50 largest regional airlines.[104]

The major airlines effectively took control of the smaller airlines by either purchasing them or by developing contractual agreements. In the mid-1980s, the regional airlines flew over 30 million passengers a year to 800 cities. The regional airlines were permitted to use the name and color of planes of the major airlines and to participate further in their frequent flyer programs. One of the most controversial provisions of the agreement between the regional/commuter carriers and the major airlines was that the smaller carriers were permitted to use the same reservation system as the major airlines. To both passengers and travel agencies, this implied that service of the regional carriers was actually handled by the major airline. This system also gave the small carriers priority-listing in the major airlines' reservation systems.[105]

The arrangement between the major airlines and the commuter airlines was so successful for both parties that there was a stampede to become a regional partner of a major airline. According to King Morse, the president of Command Airways, "We were like lemmings going over the cliff." He stated that in 1984, only 12 regional carriers had agreements with the major airlines, while two years later this number rose to 66. In the process, the regional

carriers were often compelled to restructure their services to feed customers into and out of the major airline
hubs. This restructuring process encouraged regional
carriers to discontinue service between many small cities. Major airlines taking over many of the regional
carriers caused a negative impact on the small remaining
regional carriers. In many cases, their business was
siphoned off by the regional carriers that partnered with
the major airlines. As a result, a large number of small
regional carriers were forced out of business.[106]

Some airlines experts feared that the major airlines'
takeover of the smaller regional airlines further stifled
competition, but federal regulators decided not to inter-
fere, as the airline industry oligopoly tightened. Critics
noted that the regional airlines became the birthplace of
many new airlines. However, as regional carriers were
largely under major airline control, they were unlikely to
emerge as competitors. Some critics further noted that it
is very difficult for a new discount airline to break into
major airports as long as regional airlines were controlled
by major airlines in their large hub networks, nor would
it be able to obtain customers from regional airlines
associated with the major airlines in their large hub
markets.[107]

The significance of the major airlines taking over most
of the regional/commuter airlines is that the latter often
account for over 50 percent of passengers the major
airlines fly between their hub and other large cities. For
this reason, it is easy to understand why they wanted to
control the regional airlines—it simply allowed them to
dominate their hub-and-spoke markets even more strongly.

Michael Boyd, President of Regional Management System, stated: "The Department of Transportation let the
commuter-airline industry get merged into the major-
airline industry." Kahn charged that changes in the regional carrier market jeopardize "a major source of possible
competition" in the airline industry. He went on to state

that he feared "consumers are more likely to be exploited" through higher fares, poor service, or both.[108]

OTHER TACTICS USED BY MAJOR AIRLINES

Up to this point, three factors have been discussed as contributors to the growth of hub airports dominated by a few major airlines:

1. Mergers of major airlines.
2. Control of most of the landing slots at large hub airports.
3. Purchase or development of exclusive contracts with most of the feeder airlines.

However, there are three more factors that made the major airlines literally "fortress hubs," permitting them to dominate large airports and charge premium fares. Some of these additional factors include frequent-flyer programs, premiums paid to travel agents, and computer reservation systems.

Frequent-Flyer Programs

American introduced the first frequent-flyer program in 1981. The idea behind frequent-flyer programs was to encourage passengers—particularly the higher-paying and frequent-flying business travelers—to direct most of their business to a single carrier that flew to and from the major hub airports. The frequent-flyer programs were particularly attractive to business travelers who flew more frequently, collecting points they could eventually use for leisure travel. Furthermore, the business travelers' companies generally paid for their tickets. Thus, business travelers had little incentive to fly discount carriers selling tickets for less, without frequent-flyer programs. Moreover, the dominant major airlines served many more cities, permitting passengers to acquire enough frequent-flyer points and obtain free tickets faster.

The Transportation Research Board is an independent agency consisting of experts studying developments involving several forms of transportation (i.e. automobiles, railroads, and airlines). In 1988, 10 years after airline deregulation, the Transportation Research Board issued a statement regarding the use of frequent-flyer incentive by the major airlines. The Transportation Research Board's reaction to frequent-flyer programs was summarized in an article entitled "Skyway Robbery."[109]

The article stated that the first purpose of frequent-flyer programs was to "build brand loyalty in a business where the products are pretty indistinguishable." The second was that frequent-flyer programs "make straightforward pricing competition pointless." According to the article, frequent-flyer programs are a rip-off in the following four ways:

- They contribute to higher airline prices.
- They encourage travelers to select the airline that distributes frequent-flyer points instead of flying an airline offering the lowest price.
- They encourage flyers to take needless trips to obtain more points.
- They protect established airlines from new competitors offering lower prices.

The article concluded that the best way to protect the success of deregulation was to prick the bubble of frequent-flyer programs through taxation.[110]

Travel Agent Commission Overrides (TACO)

Following airline deregulation, the major airlines used travel agents to book most of their tickets, accounting for 90 percent of airline ticket sales in the early 1990s. The travel agents helped flyers understand the growing array of fares based on how far in advance tickets were purchased, the day of the week, quality of seating, and so on. It might have been expected that the airlines would pay a certain percentage—say 5 percent—for the tickets the agents sold. However, that was not the case. Instead, the major airlines paid special fees to agents who booked flights on the major airlines in their hub markets. These fees were called Travel Agent Commission Overrides.[111]

The Travel Agent Commission Overrides turned out to be another marketing tool, like frequent-flyer programs, that the major airlines used to dominate their respective hub markets. Following deregulation, the major airlines paid a fare premium to agents who booked a large percentage of their flights in their respective hub markets. As can be observed from Table 3.1, the travel agent booked airline flights for a commission of 4.2 percent of the ticket price in 1978, when the industry was deregulated. Shortly thereafter, the travel agent commission rapidly increased from 4.8 percent in 1980 to 7.4 percent in 1985, on to a peak of 10.8 percent in 1993.

The Clinton Administration (1993–2000) undertook a major investigation of a wide variety of marketing practices involving the airline industry, one of which was Travel Agent Commission Overrides. There was concern

Table 3.1: Airline Ticket Information

Year	Total Cost ($ millions)	Cost per Revenue Passenger Mile	Travel Agent Commission (percentage)
1978	893.67	0.377	4.2
1980	1,586.38	0.611	4.8
1985	3,098.50	0.929	7.4
1990	6,387.90	1.396	9.8
1991	6,810.59	1.528	10.8
1992	7,135.97	1.518	10.8
1993	6,649.60	0.586	10.8
1994	5,818.11	1.143	8.7

Source: Air Traffic Authority.

that this practice was harmful to low-price airlines that had not been so successful during the Reagan and Bush Administrations between 1981 and 1992. The expense of airline ticketing was also becoming a concern to the major airlines, which were suffering from a profit squeeze.

Computer Reservation Systems

The third of the closely related marketing-power techniques used by some of the larger legacy airlines was company-owned Computer Reservation Systems (CRS). The CAB found that several of the largest airlines used their CRS to gain advantage over their competition by ensuring their flights were displayed first. The majority of flights are booked from the first page of the computer screen for the cities to which passengers want to fly, but the CAB ruled this discriminatory practice to be anti-competitive in 1984.[112]

The Department of Transportation (DOT), which assumed responsibility for regulating the airlines, ruled that CRS could not be biased. The DOT put in place rules in 1984 and 1990 that prohibited airlines from biasing their CRS. However, Darryl Jenkins, an airline authority, stated in a white paper in 2002 that loopholes in the DOT rules allowed programmers to bias their CRS indirectly. Jenkins further stated:

> Not coincidentally the largest CRS system (American's Sabre) that was at the heart of the bias issue 20 years ago is now—at least since the beginning of this decade—acting in a similar manner with Travelocity, its wholly-owned travel website.[113]

In 1988, the DOT also found that the major airlines who owned the CRS earned an excessive return from it. The booking fees for the two major CRS' were approximately double the cost of providing the service. The revenue transfer from the non-CRS vendor airlines to the CRS-vendor airlines was substantial, resulting in significant income loss for the smaller airlines. Thus, CRS made it more difficult for new airlines to successfully penetrate markets dominated by major airlines.[114]

Most booking agents would use the CRS of the dominant airline serving a market. Thus, other airlines attempting to compete at a major airline hub market found themselves at a competitive disadvantage since their schedules were often presented after the dominant airline. Major airline competitors also experienced higher costs due to the high booking fees they were charged for using a competitor's CRS. Thus, CRS often discouraged major airlines from effectively competing in hub markets of other airlines with strong CRS systems such as those of American and United.[115]

In summary, six factors have been discussed that contributed to competitive concentration in the major airline hub-and-spoke markets. The first three are:

1. Mergers of major airlines.
2. Control of most of the landing slots at large hub airports.
3. Purchase of most of the feeder airlines.

Three additional factors contributing to market dominance of the large-legacy airlines include:

4. Frequent-flyer programs.
5. Travel agency commission overrides (TACO).
6. Computer reservation systems (CRS).

FARE PREMIUMS CHARGED BY MAJOR AIRLINES IN THEIR HUB MARKETS

Airlines that existed at the time of deregulation in 1978 developed an elaborate program (using the six basic steps listed in the previous section) to dominate the largest markets. The large markets they dominated became known as "fortress hubs," since in most cases it was difficult, if not impossible, for the new discount airlines to penetrate these markets.

An internal memo from the Vice President of USAir to its President and CEO, written in July 1987, stressed that it was the goal of the major airlines to establish concentrated hub markets where they could charge higher fares.[116]

> [T]here is still much to do before we can be confident that we have *established a northeast stronghold that is as impervious as possible* (emphasis added). Ideally, we should control a major portion of the traffic at each of the cities in the northeast. The beauty of the niche strategy is not just the marketing identity and control that it gives us. In addition, *it enables us to keep control of prices within our niche territory, thus insulating a significant position of our traffic from the devastating effects of unbridled price competition* (emphasis added).

Hub airports are often defined as those where one airline controls 60 percent or more, or two airlines control 85 percent or more, of flights. Given their market dominance due to barriers to entry, the major legacy airlines have been able to charge significantly higher fares than airlines providing service in more competitive markets.

There were several reports during the 1990s issued by the United States General Accounting Office (GAO) discussing the fare premiums charged by the major airlines in their hub markets. The reports often stated that something needed to be done to correct the situation and reduce airfares. Unfortunately, few, if any, of the recommendations to increase competition were adopted during the 1990s.

Kenneth M. Mead, an administrator of the GAO, made a presentation in 1991 titled *Airline Competition: Industry Competitive and Financial Problems*, in which he stated:

Our analysis of 1988 fares (ten years after deregulation) on routes of 15 concentrated airports found that when one or two airlines dominated an airport, fares were about 20 percent higher than on routes from less concentrated airports.[117]

Mead acknowledged there was widespread belief that steps needed to be taken to increase competition in the hub markets to drive down airfares. He stated,

Competitive access to airport facilities, a level playing field for marketing airline services, and better access to domestic and international capital markets would provide an atmosphere to enhance competition.[118]

The GAO next reported the fare premium for 14 hub markets for the year ending 1992—four years after the previously discussed report; this report was titled *Higher Fares and Less Competition Continue at Concentrated Airports*. The report stated that for the year ending March 31, 1992, "fares at concentrated airports were 22 percent higher than fares at 35 less concentrated airports....[119] In 1988 fares were about 21 percent higher."

Three years later, in 1995, the GAO issued a second report, also called *Higher Fares and Less Competition Continue at Concentrated Airports*. However, this report used a different set of airports. It included five highly concentrated slot-controlled airports where one airline accounted for more than 75 percent of the passengers. These airports included Charlotte, Cincinnati, Pittsburgh, Minneapolis, and Detroit. The other five airports were slot-controlled airports (i.e. the number of landing and take-offs were limited) and they included Washington National, New York LaGuardia, Newark, JFK, and Chicago O'Hare, which had not been included in the earlier report. The fare premium for the 10 airports with operating barriers was 31 percent higher than 33 other large airports.[120]

The report stated that six years ago the GAO had made a number of policy recommendations to the DOT to improve

the competitive situation. However, none of the recommendations had been adopted. Again, the GAO urged the
DOT to take steps to address a number of serious barriers
to entry.[121]

Professor Severin Borenstein delivered a report to the
Transportation Research Bureau in 1999 showing the
changes in hub premiums for 16 major airports from 1984
through 1997. The average hub premium increased over
the 13-year period from 15 percent in 1984 to 27 percent
in 1997. The fare premium would have been still higher
if the study had included slot-controlled airports in Washington, D.C. and New York City.

The fare premium grew for some of the 16 airports over
the 13-year period. The airports with increasing fares
included Charlotte, Cincinnati, Dallas-Fort Worth, Houston, Minneapolis, Pittsburgh, and Washington (IAD). In
many instances, these were hub airports where the dominant airlines had very high market shares and little
competition. By contrast, other hub airports' fare premiums decreased over time. In many cases, the decline in
hub airport premiums was due to the entry of low-cost
discount airlines such as SW and AirTran. Airports experiencing a decreasing premium, particularly in the later
years, included Atlanta, Salt Lake City, and St. Louis.

The GAO reported that 470 million passengers traveled
in the 31 largest US airports in 1999. Their analysis
further indicated that the major airlines dominated 16 of
the large hub airports (i.e. one airline had 50 percent or
greater market share) in which 260 million passengers
traveled. Furthermore, in the most dominated airports,
six major airlines had 80 percent or greater market
share. An additional indication of the dominance of the
major airlines is that at nine of the 16 airports, the
second largest airline carried less than 10 percent of
the passengers. Only in Atlanta, Salt Lake City, and St.
Louis did low-fare airlines account for 10 percent of total
passengers.

Table 3.2: Sixteen Largest Hub Markets Dominated by a Single Airline in 1999

Hub City	Dominant Airline	Market Share (%)
1. Cincinnati	Delta	94
2. Charlotte	US Airways	90
3. Pittsburgh	US Airways	86
4. Houston	Continental	83
5. Minneapolis	Northwest	80
6. Detroit	Northwest	80
7. Atlanta	Delta	74
8. St. Louis	TWA	72
9. Salt Lake City	Delta	72
10. Denver	United	70
11. Philadelphia	US Airways	63
12. Dallas Ft. Worth	American	61
13. Washington Dulles	United	54
14. Miami	American	54
15. Newark	Continental	53
16. San Francisco	United	51

Source: Jay Etta Z Hecker, *Aviation Competition: Challenges in Enhancing Competition in Dominated Markets,* US General Accounting Office, March 13, 2001, p. 6.

LOWER FARES ON HUB ROUTES THAT DISCOUNTERS PENETRATED

We have extensively discussed the fare premium the major airlines charge in their hub markets in comparison to other large markets. In 1999, the US DOT took a different approach in explaining the premiums charged by the major airlines in their hub markets. In prior studies, the DOT had presented information about fare premiums that airlines charged in hub markets dominated by major airlines, in comparison to more competitive markets. The 1999 DOT report examined how much more the major airlines charged in certain hub markets on routes without low-fare competition in comparison to routes with competition from low-cost airlines. Discount airlines such as SW, AirTran, and Frontier had been able to penetrate some of the major hub markets. The point of this study was to examine the savings that discount airlines provided in major hub markets.

For this study, the US DOT selected 10 cities where major airlines flew more than 65 percent of the passengers. The fare differential for 10 cities on routes flown with a low-fare competitor and comparable routes without a low-fare carrier are shown in Table 3.3. The major airlines charged 54 percent more on short-haul routes and 31 percent more on long-haul routes, where they did not compete with discount airlines. On average, the major airlines charged 41 percent more on routes where they did not compete with discount carriers in comparison to routes where they did. The potential savings from allowing discount airlines to compete in major airline-dominated hub markets amounts to billions of dollars a year.

The large fare premium the major airlines charge in hub markets where they do not compete with discount airlines, underscores a huge challenge to major hub airlines. Their costs are so much higher than the discount airlines that their future is threatened by the rapidly growing discount airlines that provide large savings to the flying public. During the fourth quarter of 2002, the domestic cost per mile of the legacy carriers was, on average, 60 percent higher than the low-cost airlines.[122]

Table 3.3: **Fare Differentials on Routes at Hub Markets without Low-fare Competitor vs. Hub Markets with a Low-fare Competitor (1999)**

Dominated Hub	Short-haul Routes (%)	Long-haul Routes (%)	All Routes (%)	Affected Passengers
ATL	49	28	41	4,796,380
CLT	75	23	54	3,590,790
CVG	78	35	57	1,936,020
DENVER	37	28	29	4,533,600
DTW	51	29	40	2,457,090
MEM	57	29	43	885,750
MSP	46	63	55	2,758,600
PIT	86	18	57	2,920,250
SLC	–6	6	2	1,041,780
STL	38	61	49	2,390,370
All Hubs	54	31	41	24,738,900

Source: Domestic Aviation Competition Series, *Dominated Hub Fares*, US Department of Transportation, p. 11.

The higher costs of the legacy airlines (American, Delta, United, Northwest, Continental, US Airway) are due to a number of factors reviewed in this chapter. These factors include frequent-flyer programs, travel agencies' incentives, and CRS, which enable major airlines to dominate their large-hub airports. However, a large portion of their higher costs are due to the higher wages they pay their unionized labor force. To avoid strikes that could imperil their operations, the major airlines gave into labor demands for higher wages and fewer hours of work per week. For example, pilots of some of the larger airlines work only seven days per month and senior pilots earn between $250,000 and $300,000 per year. Another factor contributing to the higher costs of the six legacy airlines is that they are flying much older airplanes than the discount carriers. Their older airplanes have higher maintenance costs and are less fuel efficient than the newer airplanes flown by many of the discount airlines.

Several government reports suggest that steps need to be taken to increase competition in the major airlines' hub markets to put downward pressure on price. Foremost among the recommendations is that discount airlines be allowed to obtain slots and gates in the major airline-dominated airports. The Federal government invested several billion dollars in building airports and landing strips, but the older airlines obtained long-term leases permitting them to control most of the slots at their major hub airports. The major airlines have also made sizable investments in the airports they dominate. So, for all practical purposes, they have been able to keep discount airlines from gaining enough gates and landing slots to have much of an impact. A minimum of six gates and landing slots is considered necessary for a discount airline to establish itself in a major airport.

The DOT has authority to allocate gates and slots at major airports to low-fare airlines. However, the DOT has generally refused to use its authority to increase competition in the hub markets of the major airlines. The clause permitting the DOT to allocate gates and slots states that the agency could withdraw slots from major airlines and allocate them to other airlines to increase competition. However, the DOT's response has been that it is not compelled to use its authority to increase competition at major airports. There is no question that the major airlines have used their substantial political influence to block entry by discounters in major hub markets. Presidents Ronald Reagan, George Bush Sr., and George W. Bush Jr. have all been recipients of large political contributions from several of the major airlines.

Building new airports in larger cities would provide access to discount airlines and could also increase competition. For example, there is only one airport in Atlanta that has long been ranked as one of the busiest airports (in terms of landings and take-offs) in the United States. Instead of building a new airport in Atlanta, a very expensive fifth runway is under construction. This tactic helps Delta to keep its stranglehold on airline traffic from Atlanta. Chicago O'Hare's Airport (a slot-controlled airport where entry is impossible) is ranked along with Atlanta's Hartsfield as one of the busiest airports in the country. A few years ago, a major effort was made to add a third airport to Chicago, but United was able to use its substantial political influence to keep this from happening. Therefore, Chicago O'Hare will continue to be monopolized by United and American airlines with no slots allocated to low-fare airlines. A related effort used by the major airlines to control slots at major airports is to refuse to support airport expansion unless the dominant major airline can control most of the new gates. Northwest used this ploy in the expansion of the single airport that serves Minneapolis, and several of the other major airlines have followed suit.

Summary

Several of the major airlines that emerged with deregulation in 1978 have been able to devise strategies to dominate most of the largest airports in the country. In turn, they have charged large fare premiums costing the flying public billions of dollars each year. The high cost of the hub-and-spoke system naturally has its shortcomings, indicated by the fact that the major airlines have been losing a great deal of money since 2001. Most of the major airlines experienced huge losses from 2001 through 2004, and the losses are expected to continue for several major airlines through 2008.

As discounters such as SW, AirTran, JetBlue, and Frontier continue to grow, they are eroding the sales of the major airlines and contributing to huge losses for the majors. Executives at Delta and Northwest predict that there may be only three major airlines in a few years, and this forecast seems likely. There may well be a parallel between the decline of department stores starting 30 years ago creating a rise of discount stores, and the decline in the costly major airlines creating the rapid growth in market share of low-fare airlines over the past couple of decades.

Predatory Pricing

AS EXPLAINED in chapter three, the six major airlines (American, United, Delta, US Airways, Northwest, and Continental) that existed before deregulation in 1978 developed 15 major hub markets dominated by one or two major airlines. The major airlines were able to dominate/ monopolize their hub airports based on a number of factors already discussed. They gained dominance over their hub airports by:

- mergers of major airlines,
- controlling most of the airline landing slots,
- purchasing most of the major feeder airlines,
- using frequent-flyer loyalty programs,
- giving ticket agent commission overrides (TACO), and
- using biased reservation systems.

These major airlines often charged fare premiums of 20–40 percent in the 15 hub markets which they dominated/monopolized, in comparison to the next 30 to 35 largest markets. This came unexpectedly following deregulation in 1978, when it was assumed there were no barriers to entry. At that time, it was anticipated that new discount airlines would enter high-priced markets and drive prices down to the competitive level.

All the costly methods used by the major airlines to dominate the large airports were still not enough to keep new discount airlines from penetrating their high-priced hub markets and driving down prices. Because discount airlines began penetrating their high-priced hub markets, the major airlines felt vulnerable and, as a result, developed the practice of predatory pricing to stop this, and in the process, drove many small discount airlines out of business. During the 12 years of Republican administration from 1981 to 1992 (eight under President Reagan and four under President Bush Sr.), little action was taken to stop predatory pricing because the Republicans tended to favor big business. Consequently, only one out of more than 150 new airlines survived. Many died due to poor financing and weak management, but a large number were driven out of business as a direct result of the major airlines' use of predatory pricing.

The term "fortress hub" came into use because the major airlines decided to reduce prices when a low-cost, discount airline entered one of the routes of their dominant hubs. In addition, the major airlines would generally add capacity on routes that the discount airlines entered, to ensure that the later could not attract enough price-sensitive customers and thereby operate profitably, forcing it to withdraw from the market. Furthermore, in some cases, the major airlines would even meet the price of the discount airline in markets which they did not previously serve. This was a more flagrant method used to drive the small discount airlines out of business. In summary, predatory pricing became a ruthless method of defending the major airline-dominated markets where they charged large fare premiums.

The major airlines argued there was nothing unfair about meeting discount airline prices and that this was merely fair competition. People considering this response need to recognize that the major airlines dominated/ monopolized their hub markets. As a result, they were able to raise their prices far above the competitive level. Moreover, the major airlines cut their fares only in a small portion of their markets, and were able to subsidize their losses from the vast majority of markets where they charged premium fares.

US anti-trust laws prohibit large firms from "bullying their smaller competitors", as was occurring in the airline industry. Furthermore, the DOT which oversees the airline industry has authority to stop unfair competitive practices in the airline industry. But it never used this authority to contest one case of predatory pricing. Big-business influence in Washington, D.C., is tremendous, and the major airlines had the size, money, and influence to keep action from being taken to defend fair competition.

When President Clinton took office in 1993, he and members of Congress and the GAO became concerned about the dominance of the major airlines and the monopoly fares they were charging. The Clinton Administration tried to stop predatory pricing and to "even the playing field". Members of the Administration met with the major airlines accused of predatory pricing, strongly urging them to cease the practice. For a while, this meeting appeared to have a positive impact, but that did not last for long.

In the hope of slowing the pace of predatory pricing, the DOT proposed a set of guidelines in 1998 that defined what would be considered predatory pricing. There were more than 5,000 responses to the guidelines, most of them from people associated with the six major airlines, and as would be expected, they opposed the new rules defining the practice of predatory pricing.

Following the responses, the US Department of Justice filed a lawsuit against American for predatory pricing in its Dallas hub where it succeeded in driving three small discounter airlines out of its dominance. Unfortunately, the judge refused to hear the case, indicating that the Justice Department had not demonstrated the occurrence of any illegal behavior. The Justice Department appealed against the decision, but was unsuccessful in convincing the judge to hear the case. The basic problem was that an old-school academic philosophy defined predatory pricing so narrowly that it was hard to provide grounds supporting these charges. Thus, few predatory pricing cases were filed and none of them won. However, over the last decade many economists and lawyers have grown to recognize that predatory pricing can and does occur in the airline industry.

ESTABLISHED AIRLINES CHARGE AMERICAN AIRLINES WITH PREDATORY PRICING

It was not just the low-cost airlines that complained about predatory pricing. After driving smaller firms out of business, the predator generally raises its prices back to, or above, the earlier high levels. Studies show that the predator recoups its losses and becomes stronger by engaging in further predatory pricing. Most of the predatory pricing charges since deregulation have been brought by new, small, discount airlines against the much larger, high-service, legacy airlines, which existed before the deregulation in 1978. However, it is interesting to note that two of the smaller and weaker major airlines at one time charged American, the largest major airline today, with predatory pricing.[123]

Northwest and Continental filed an anti-trust suit against American in the summer of 1993 in which they accused American of reducing prices and selling below cost with the purpose of driving them out of business. Continental and Northwest sought $1 billion in damages, which would be tripled if they won their case. In pre-trial documents, Continental and Northwest claimed to have found statements by American's CEO, Robert Crandall, stating that American was prepared to lose hundreds of millions of dollars in a program to drive the weaker major airlines out of business. The documents also allegedly claimed that American believed if the weaker airlines were eliminated, it would increase it revenues by $1.5 billion between 1993 and 1995. American's response was that it was doing nothing more than what companies in a "take-no-prisoner" industry always do.[124]

American introduced its Value-Pricing Program on April 9, 1992. The new plan had four basic fares in place of the dozens of fares it previously offered, and it reduced its top business fare by 40 percent from its previous level. Most of the major airlines met American's fares. Then, on May 26, Northwest announced its "Grown-up Fly Free" summer promotion. American's response was to slash its lowest advance-purchase fare by 50 percent, setting off a rush for tickets. While planes flew full for much of the summer, the fares were so low that the airlines lost a huge amount of money. American alone lost $251 million during the second and third quarters of 1992.[125]

The plaintiff's lawyers posited that American—then the second largest airline—had cut its prices far below cost and was employing predatory pricing to run Northwest and Continental (two of the smaller and weaker legacy airlines) out of business. American would then be able to expand its business and increase its prices to much higher levels, hurting consumer interests. American countered that it was simply trying to attract more customers. The two airlines testified that American's fare reductions and subsequent half-off cuts in May 1992 caused them to lose nearly $1 billion collectively.

American's Crandall countered that the fare cuts were only intended to increase volumes, and not to drive his weaker competitors out of business. The jury of nine men and three women deliberated for less than three hours. The jury concluded that American was not trying to monopolize certain markets through its price cuts in 1992. With the verdict in favor of American in August 1993, Crandall stated that American would continue to market aggressively and would match the fares of other airlines.[126] American has done exactly this over the years, even when lower-cost and lower-price new airlines attempted to enter its dominant high-price hub markets, such as the Dallas-Fort Worth Airport. Several studies have shown that the major airlines charge premiums of 20–40 percent in markets where they dominate in comparison to other large markets in which they do not dominate.

It is also interesting to note that after losing its case against American, Northwest began to use predatory pricing to defend its hub markets. Several small discount airlines then accused Northwest of using the same predatory pricing over which it had previously sued American. Northwest dominates three markets (Minneapolis, Detroit, and Memphis) where it has market shares of 70–80 percent, and charges some of the highest monopoly fares in the country. However, when small discount airlines attempted to enter its hub markets, Northwest met their prices and drove them out of business. These small discount airlines have made complaints to the Federal government about Northwest's predatory pricing practices. Northwest derives almost 95 percent of its business from its three hub markets, rigorously defended by the use of temporary low prices when it becomes vulnerable to the entry of small-discount airlines.

Majors Used Predatory Pricing to Destroy New Discount Airlines

An insightful article was published in the *Los Angeles Times* in 1989 called "How Consumers Pay for Airline Deregulation." It explained how the major airlines temporarily lowered their pricing to drive practically all new discount airlines out of business over the first 10 years after deregulation in 1978. The article stated:

> They (the small discount airlines) only had one weapon at their disposal: lower fares.... It seems that every time a new airline lowered its fares; the big airlines simply matched them. The mega-carriers knew that no airline could make any money in the severely discounted airfare markets. But they also knew a simple but painful truth: They could lose money much longer than the new airlines.... And they were right. The little airlines ... couldn't. And today eight giant airlines control 92 percent of the market. As a result, it is much harder to get a discount fare.

The author of the article went ahead to note that the major airlines were operating "Fortress Hubs" in the markets they dominated and the fares they were charging were "nothing less than skyway robbery."[127]

Chapter three presented a similar observation made by a United executive. He said that United could afford to lower its prices sharply to meet the fares of the new discount airlines and drive them out of business. This was possible since United has much higher fares in most of the other routes in its hub markets, permitting it to subsidize its temporary low prices.

NORTHWEST AIRLINES GAINS NOTORIETY

Northwest became a powerhouse in 1986, when the DOT allowed it (the eighth-largest airline) and Republic (the ninth-largest airline) to merge. The Department of Justice strongly opposed the merger on the grounds that it *would create monopolies in the major cities the two airlines served.* And that is exactly why the merger happened. But at that time, the DOT acted in an advisory capacity and approved all merger proposals it received. On August 20, 1986, the DOT approved the merger of Northwest and Republic. Thus, throughout most of the 1990s, Northwest had a 70–80 percent market share in Minneapolis, Detroit, and Memphis.[128] With little or no competition on most of its routes, Northwest was able to charge monopoly fares.

Northwest had learned the hard way about the power of predatory pricing when it came close to being driven out of business by United's below-cost pricing. Ironically, Northwest adopted predatory pricing to defend the high prices it charged in its three fortress-hub markets— Minneapolis, Detroit, and Memphis. The airline often charged premiums of 40 percent or more in its hub markets which were among the highest in the industry. Northwest once again *ruthlessly defended its monopoly, using predatory pricing to prevent the entry of new low-cost airlines*.

In 1992, Northwest CEO John Dasburg provided important insight into the airline's response to new discount airlines when he said:

> In the long run, predatory pricing will reduce the number of airlines, ultimately cutting the number of flights and choices available, particularly in smaller markets. This will leave the few surviving airlines free to price just as high as they want for just as long as they want.[129]

The new Northwest airline with market power led to numerous complaints being filed against it for predatory pricing. From 1993 through 2002, there were at least seven predatory-pricing complaints by small airlines which had been prevented from penetrating Northwest's three-hub markets. Their claims were similar in nature, charging that Northwest temporarily lowered its prices to meet the lower-cost discount airlines that dared to enter the monopolized, three-hub markets. In addition, Northwest substantially increased its capacity to gain new travelers, who were attracted by the lower price. In most cases, the small discount airlines were unable to attract enough passengers to operate profitably, and were forced to withdraw from Northwest-hub markets. Several of the smaller airlines that went out of business attributed their down-fall to Northwest's predatory pricing. After the discounters withdrew from its markets, the airline typically increased its price back to the same or higher levels than before the discounter entered the market.

When Bill Clinton became President of the United States in 1993, he effectively reversed the inaction re-garding aggressive pricing by the major airlines against small discount airlines during the 12-year Reagan–Bush era. Clinton's administration became very concerned about the dominance of a few major airlines that had been in existence before deregulation and the large fare pre-miums they charged.

A LEADER IN RAISING THE ISSUE OF PREDATORY PRICING

Professor Paul Dempsey of the Travel Law Department then at the University of Denver now at McGill University in Montreal and Vice Chairman and Director of Frontier Airlines has written extensively on predatory pricing. His studies suggest that Northwest used predatory pricing to defend its fortress hubs in Minneapolis, Detroit, and Memphis, more than any other airline. The following scenarios reveal that Northwest has, time and time again, used predatory pricing to protect hub premiums that were often 40 percent or more than other large markets without major airline hubs. This is the same Northwest that, along with Continental, sued American for predatory pricing.

Northwest vs. Reno Air

One of the first actions taken by the Clinton Administra-tion was to intervene in a response by Northwest to Reno Air's decision to start flying from Reno, Nevada, to Min-neapolis (Northwest's largest hub). Northwest's response to Reno Air was clearly a mismatch between a huge airline and a small start-up. Northwest was a global giant serving 240 destinations in four continents. In sharp contrast, Reno Air was a small start-up airline which went public in May 1993, and started flying in July to under-served markets or over-priced markets of the major carriers. At the time of its confrontation with Northwest, Reno Air served six west-coast cities from its mini-hub in Reno, employing 600 people and flying seven leased airplanes.[130]

Reno Air announced its plan to start three low-cost flights every day between Reno and Minneapolis beginning April 1, 1993. Northwest had abandoned the route in 1991, saying it was unprofitable. However, upon learning of Reno Air's plan, Northwest announced that it would restart its service from Minneapolis to Reno, and meet Reno Air's low price. In addition, Northwest also said it would begin providing service from Reno to three west-coast cities that Reno served. Reno complained of foul play by Northwest that was designed to destroy the small discount airline.[131]

A meeting was held in Washington, D.C. between Transportation Secretary Federico Pena and Northwest's Dasburg (see his statement above about how predatory pricing can be used to drive out small airlines to keep prices high in major dominated markets). Secretary Pena gave Northwest three days to decide whether or not to cancel its planned flights from Reno to cities Reno Air served on the West Coast. Northwest agreed to cancel its plans. However, it matched Reno Air's low price to Minneapolis and added enough capacity, forcing Reno Air to drop its flights from three to one per day and then to withdraw completely from the Minneapolis market.[132]

In 1997, Reno Air sued Northwest, charging that it had used predatory pricing to drive the discounter out of the Minneapolis market. The suit stated that Northwest had used similar predatory practices to drive People Express, Midway, and other new entrants out of Minneapolis. In 1999, Reno Air was sold to American, which dropped the lawsuit.[133] As was often the case, another major airline would pick up the pieces from a battle between a discounter and a major airline.

Northwest vs. Western Pacific Airlines

Western Pacific Airlines started flying from Colorado Springs in 1995. The airline rapidly expanded and by 1996, it was serving 16 cities from Colorado Springs, flying 15 Boeing 737-300 airplanes. The rapid expansion of the new airline caught Northwest's attention and it initiated flights to Colorado Springs from each of its hubs in Minneapolis, Detroit, and Memphis. According to Professor Dempsey, the message was clear. "Western Pacific would be unwelcome at Northwest hubs, would be met with fierce opposition, lots of seats and low fares." Western Pacific exited Colorado Springs in the fall of 1997 and was liquidated the following year. Northwest's interest in Colorado Springs rapidly dissipated, and it discontinued service from its Memphis and Detroit hubs.[134]

Northwest vs. Kiwi International Airlines

Kiwi International Airlines, based in Newark, accused Northwest of using predatory pricing to drive it out of business in the fall of 1998. Kiwi claims it was forced to withdraw its flights from Minneapolis to Detroit and Mineapolis to Newark when Northwest and Continental matched its prices on all of its flights. They first met Kiwi's $79 fare and when Kiwi lowered its price to $69, they matched that, too. Before long, Kiwi's flights were half empty, forcing it to exit the market after which Northwest and Continental sharply raised their fares.[135]

Delta Airlines' Response to ValuJet/AirTran

Northwest was not the only airline that used predatory pricing to protect its fortress hubs in Minneapolis, Detroit, and Memphis. All major airlines employed the same technique to varying degrees to defend their high-price monopolized markets. ValuJet/AirTran had a number of run-ins with Delta that threatened the discounter's future in its early days.

ValuJet began operating on October 26, 1993, flying two airplanes from Atlanta to three tourist destinations in Florida (Jacksonville, Orlando, and Tampa), all cities served by Delta. ValuJet had "peak" and "off-peak" fares (based on the day of the week) available on a one-way basis. This simplified fare schedule was quite different from those of the major airlines. Delta met ValuJet's "peak" and "off-peak" fares, but continued to require a 21-day advance purchase, a round-trip ticket, and a Saturday night stay-over. However, Delta maintained its higher-price business fare and did not flood the market with extra capacity.[136]

Had Delta initially reacted more aggressively to the small discounters as did Northwest and other major airlines, ValuJet would have been just another one of the small airlines driven out of business by the major airlines' temporary low prices. Instead, ValuJet/AirTran is today the third largest discount airline in the United States, with consistent profitability in recent years. Over the years, there has been much debate as to why Delta's initial response to the new low-price ValuJet was so mild in comparison to the responses of other major airlines. Rumor had it that the other major airlines were critical of Delta's mild response to ValuJet.

It was not long, however, before Delta began aggressively responding to ValuJet/AirTran's prices. ValuJet/AirTran did have several advantages. Many cities were disgusted with the high fares they had to pay Delta and the other major airlines. As a result, they paid substantial bonuses to ValuJet/AirTran to begin service to cities where passengers felt they were being gouged by Delta's high prices. To the extent it was able, instead of flying to Delta's hub in Cincinnati, it flew to two nearby cities and was able to establish profitable service because Delta did not meet its price to those locations.

However, ValuJet/AirTran was not immune to Delta's price cuts and additional seating capacity on routes that the discounter began flying. In 1997 and 1998, Delta reduced its price by more than 40 percent in 10 cities that ValuJet/AirTran entered (Washington [Dulles], Fort Lauderdale, Fort Myers, Jacksonville, Memphis, New Orleans, Orlando, Savannah, Tampa, and West Palm Beach), relative to what prices had been before the discounter began operating in the last quarter of 1993. ValuJet/AirTran complained to the DOT about Delta's unfair pricing and brought a lawsuit that was settled relative to this practice (the terms of the settlement remain confidential).

The second step involves forcing the small discount airline to withdraw from the market. The third step involves the major airline increasing its prices to, or above, the level before the discounter entered the market. Since the major airlines often raise their prices to above the level before the discounter entered the market, they can recoup their losses. Delta reduced its price, on average, by 40 percent when ValuJet/AirTran entered several of its markets. Then, when the discounter failed to attract enough customers to be able to operate profitably, its only recourse was to withdraw from these markets. AirTran was forced to abandon seven cities including Columbus, Ohio; Indianapolis; Jackson, Mississippi; Louisville; Mobile, Alabama; Nashville; and Pittsburgh. As was to be expected, Delta and other major airlines increased their fares after the withdrawal.

DEPARTMENT OF TRANSPORTATION TAKES A STAND

On April 7, 1998, the DOT issued a statement regarding "Unfair Exclusionary Conduct in the Air Transportation Industry." The statement noted that the DOT

has a mandate to foster and encourage legitimate competition.... Some of the responses we have observed, however,
appear to be straying beyond the confines of legitimate
competition into the region of unfair competition that ... we
have not only a mandate, but an obligation to prohibit.[137]

Many examples have described how small, low-cost
discount carriers were confronted with deep price cuts by
the major airlines when they attempted to enter the major
airlines' large hub markets. The DOT reached much the
same conclusion and stated:

In recent years, when small, new entrants have instituted
new low-fare service in major carriers' local-hub markets,
the major carriers have increasingly responded with strategies of price reduction and capacity increases designed not
to maximize their own profits but rather to deprive the new
entrants of vital traffic and revenues. Once a new entrant
has ceased its service, the major carrier will typically
retrench its capacity in the market (and) raise its fares to
at least their pre-entry levels or both. The major carrier thus
accepts lower profits in the short run in order to secure
higher profits in the long run. This strategy ... dissuades
other carriers from attempting low-fare entry. (This) can hurt
consumers in the long run by depriving them of the benefits
of competition.[138]

The DOT stated that it would take action to stop such
anti-competitive behavior when one or more of the following exclusionary practices occur:

(a) the major carrier adds capacity and sells such a large
     number of seats at very low fares that the ensuing
     self-diversion of revenue results in lower local rev-
     enue than would a reasonable alternative response;
(b) the number of local passengers that the major car-
     riers carry at the new entrant's low fares (or at
     similar fares that are substantially below the major
     carrier's previous fares) exceeds the new entrant's
     total seat capacity resulting, through self-diversion,
     in lower revenue than would a reasonable response;

or

(c) the number of local passengers that the major carrier carries at the new entrant's low fares (or at
similar fares that are substantially below the major
carrier's previous fares) exceeds the number of low-
fare passengers carried by the new entrant resulting, through self-diversion, in lower local revenue
than would a reasonable alternative response.[139]

The DOT charter gave the agency the power to take
actions against "Unfair Exclusionary Conduct in the Air
Transportation Industry." But instead of bringing lawsuits
against the major airlines involved in predatory pricing,
the DOT decided to issue the price guidelines to clarify
what it would consider unfair conduct. One could have
readily forecasted what the response would be. The wis-
dom of issuing the price guidelines when the DOT already
had authority to act, can be fairly questioned.

There were over 5,000 responses to the proposed guidelines. Most of these responses were negative, and came
from major airlines and those associated with them,
rather than from the low-price airlines. As a result, the
DOT did not implement its guidelines and the major
airlines continued to:

(a) sharply reduce their prices when small discount
airlines entered one of their high-price hub markets,

(b) drive the small discount airlines from the market as
they were unable to gain enough traffic to operate
profitably, and

(c) increase their prices to higher levels prior to the
discounter's market entry, after discounters were
forced to withdraw from the market.

Several of the small, low-cost, discount airlines experienced new aggressiveness by the major airlines when
the DOT withdrew the guidelines.

While the DOT was not going to take action to stop predatory pricing, the US Department of Justice had authority to stop unfair-pricing behavior by firms with monopoly positions. The attempt by the Justice Department to stop unfair pricing by the major airlines in their high-price hub markets is discussed in the next section.

JUSTICE DEPARTMENT SUES AMERICAN AIRLINES FOR PREDATORY PRICING

Free entry into markets by new airlines was widely argued as a major reason for airline deregulation in 1978. Supposedly, if a major established airline charged high fares, a new carrier would enter the market and thrive by offering the public a lower price. However, during the 1990s, the US Justice Department received numerous complaints from small discount airlines accusing the major airlines of predatory pricing in an attempt to deny them access to their high-priced hub markets. There were several charges of predatory pricing involving American in Dallas, Delta in Atlanta, and Northwest in Minneapolis and Detroit. The charges generally involved major airlines sharply dropping their prices on routes that small discount airlines entered.

The Justice Department studied numerous complaints and obtained documents from the major airlines accused of predatory pricing. After reviewing the facts of the various complaints for 18 months, the Justice Department filed a predatory-pricing suit against American on May 13, 1999—21 years after the airline industry was deregulated. American was charged with using predatory pricing to drive Vanguard Airline, Sun Jet, and Western Pacific out of the Dallas market it dominated, where it had a 70 percent market share and a 90 percent share of direct flights.[140] Government studies showed that Dallas was one of the hub markets that charged a large-fare premium associated with American's monopolistic market position.

Justice Department officials stated that the case against American was particularly compelling, based on documents they had uncovered during pre-trial discovery. According to the Justice Department, American (then the second largest airline and now the largest airline) had deliberately embarked on a strategy of selling below cost to drive three low-cost airlines—Vanguard, Western Pacific, and Sun Jet—from its hub in the Dallas/Fort Worth Airport. Joel I. Klein, Assistant Attorney General in charge of the anti-trust division, stated that "American quickly realized that these new carriers could be a significant competitive threat, estimating that as much as $1.5 billion of its annual revenues were at risk if they were to succeed." The Justice Department complaint discussed American's report, *Dallas/Fort Worth Low-Cost Carriers Strategy*, which indicated that the response to the low-cost carriers "could prove unprofitable in the short run." But it went on to conclude that "the short-term cost, or impact on revenue, can be viewed as the investment necessary to achieve the desired effect on market share."[141]

According to Klein, "American crossed a fundamental line. The anti-trust laws are there to police that line between competition on merits and predation." The suit charged that in a 1996 meeting, top executives at American met and agreed on a strategy to drive low-fare carriers out of business. The complaint states that American's Crandall, said that "If you are not going to get them out, then (there's) no point to diminish profit." Other memos from American were uncovered, indicating that the airline would like to "drive (Vanguard) from the market" and get (Western Pacific) out.[142]

The Justice Department, going into the case, recognized that it could be difficult to meet the more recent standard of proving predatory pricing. It would need to show that the alleged predator had reduced prices below variable cost that was very low in the airline industry. The variable cost on an extra seat on an airplane is a small portion of the total cost of providing that seat. However, the pre-trial evidence seemed to be very strong and showed that American had purposely lowered its prices far below its cost to drive three small discount airlines from the Dallas/Fort Worth Airport. Furthermore, it added new planes on the routes where it intended to deny entry to the new discount airlines. Once the start-ups were driven from the Dallas market, American sharply increased its prices often by 50 percent or more, and reduced the number of airplanes on the route.

US District Judge J. Thomas Martin dismissed the Justice Department suit against American on April 27, 2001 before the case was scheduled to be tried. The judge stated in a 142-page opinion piece that American played by the traditional rules. It competed with low-fare carriers on their terms. There is no doubt that American may be a difficult, vigorous, even brutal competitor. But here, it engaged only in bare, not brass-knuckle conduct.[143]

In a statement before the case was filed, John Names, Deputy Assistant Attorney General, said that the suit alleges "principles of hub economics that the department believes create barriers to entry." When the Justice Department brought the case against American, the airline flew 77 percent of the passengers nonstop to and from Dallas—one of the "fortress hubs" that the DOT identified as charging large fare premiums because of the monopolistic position of the dominant carrier. With its large fare premiums, it was easy for American to decrease its fares significantly on a handful of flights, when a small discount airline entered the Dallas/Fort Worth Airport, and then to raise them back to their prior premium level or above when the discounter exited the market.[144] It was clear that predatory pricing allowed American to protect its "fortress hub."

A spokesman for Vanguard (which had twice been driven out of Dallas by American) said that it found the decision "unbelievable."

The court has implicitly ruled that a monopolist or near monopolist may act intentionally to drive a small competitor out of the market.... We feel the ruling will result in higher airfares for the flying public.

The Chief Executive Officer of National Airlines, a Las Vegas start-up that was in bankruptcy court, stated that he believed predatory pricing by large airlines against small start-ups was widespread. He said that as a result of the decision, major airlines were likely to become more aggressive in shooting new entrants out of the skies.[145]

A thoughtful article in *Business Week* entitled "Predatory Pricing: Cleared for Takeoff", also questioned the judge's decision dismissing the Justice Department suit against American. The article stated, "The judge's ruling opens the door for dominant companies to wage bareknuckle price wars against pesky smaller competitors." The judge's decision was based on the fact that the Justice Department had not shown that American priced below variable cost. But in the airline industry, the cost of providing a seat for an additional passenger is low. The Justice Department had argued that the test for predatory pricing needed to be updated. The decision instead should have been based on whether there was "any business justification for American's aggressive pricing other than driving away competition."[146] Kahn, who played a major role in airline deregulation, said, "the Supreme Court has written predation out of the law."[147]

Summary

There is no question that economists and politicians expected competition to increase rapidly when the airline industry was deregulated. They expected prices to fall as new discount airlines entered high-price markets and drove prices down. However, the major airlines sharply lowered their prices to meet those of the discounters, while providing the public with a large number of costly services. When the discount airlines no longer had lower prices, most went of business.

It was not until the mid-1990s that the tide started to turn with some new discount carriers such as ValuJet, Frontier, Spirit, and Jet Blue starting to expand. SW, which existed before deregulation as an intra-state discount airline, continued to spread across the country, moving from Texas and nearby states to the West Coast, then to the upper Midwest and finally on to the Northeast. The discount airlines have generally prospered in the period 2000 to 2004, while all the full-service major airlines have incurred huge losses. The market share of the discount airlines has grown significantly since the 1990s and they account for close to 30 percent of all passenger traffic.

Chapter Five

Pacific Southwest Airlines: The First Large Discount Airline

PACIFIC SOUTHWEST Airlines (PSA) started flying in California in 1949. Being an intra-state airline, PSA was not under the direction of the CAB that regulated the major airlines flying across state lines. Instead, the California Public Utilities Commission (CPUC) regulated PSA, and provided intra-state airlines with more operating freedom. As a result, PSA had much greater leeway than the major airlines in selecting the routes it would fly and in deciding on the fares it would charge. PSA, in fact, charged fares that were often 50 percent less than the major airlines. Before the creation of PSA, customers of the major airlines were primarily business people or very wealthy individuals. The general public either traveled by bus, train, or automobile to cities that were located several hundred miles away. The problem with these land-based modes of transportation was that they required a great deal of time for people to travel long distances.

PSA started flying with one airplane in 1949, but in less than 20 years it grew to be the largest airline in California. The general public and business travelers responded positively to its low fares and highly reliable service between San Diego, Los Angeles, and San Francisco. Unlike the major airlines, PSA received no revenue from the US Postal Service which was a significant revenue source for them. PSA was initially known as the "Poor Sailor's Airline." It started with an emphasis on flying sailors who were on leave from San Diego to Los Angeles and San Francisco. The sailors' incomes were low, and so PSA designed an airline that had no frills and provided basic flying service at the lowest possible price.[148]

PSA continuously upgraded its fleet of airplanes and provided more frequent service. By the mid-1960s, PSA had the least expensive jet fares in the United States. For example, its fare between Los Angeles and San Francisco in 1965 was $14.18, and it dropped another $2.18 to an even $12 for standby passengers.[149] PSA's goal of providing low-cost and friendly airline service gained widespread acceptance by the flying public. While its initial target was sailors, business travelers and the general public rallied to its low fares and friendly service as well as its more convenient hourly service between major cities in California.

In a few years, business travelers outnumbered the general flying public and PSA became the largest airline in California. As can be observed from Table 5.1 (part A), the number of passengers between Los Angeles and San Francisco approximately doubled as low-fare air service became accepted. Part B of the table also shows that PSA flew almost half of its passengers between Los Angeles and San Francisco from 1962 to 65. It started providing service to more markets, and by the late 1960s it flew more passengers in California than any other airline.

While PSA started as an intra-state airline providing service between just three cities, it rapidly expanded and provided service throughout much of California. Then, following airline deregulation in 1978, PSA continued its expansion and began flying to many cities in the western part of the United States as well as operating international flights to Mexico.[150] Unfortunately, a leading authority on PSA notes that regardless of how successful and innovative PSA was, "very little was written about the

Table 5.1: Airline Passengers Flown between Los Angeles and San Francisco and Market Shares of the Respective Airlines

	United Airlines	Western Airlines	Pacific Southwest	Other Airlines	Total
A. Passenger Flown by Different Airlines					
1962	494,520	314,580	731,787	74,020	1,614,907
1963	394,530	641,281	949,000	91,400	2,076,211
1964	441,890	850,093	1,096,000	85,370	2,473,353
1965	1,000,000	608,000	1,330,000	200,000	3,138,000
B. Market Share of Airlines (%)					
1962	30.6	19.5	45.3	4.6	100.0
1963	19.0	30.9	45.7	4.4	100.0
1964	17.9	34.4	44.3	3.5	100.0
1965	31.9	19.4	42.4	6.4	100.0

Source: "Sky's the Limit—Despite Lower Fares, West Coast Airlines are Flying High," Barron's, June 13, 1966, p. 5.

(airline)" in the business press. One of the reasons for this was that it began flying more than 50 years ago when not much was written about airlines, particularly a discount airline, in California.

THE FOUNDERS OF PACIFIC SOUTHWEST AIRLINES

In 1946, Kenny Friedkin and Joe Plosser opened a flight-training school in San Diego's Lindberg field to train veterans under the G.I. Bill so they could obtain commercial pilot licenses. The school developed a national reputation with more than 200 students enrolled at a time. However, the following year the number of G.I. Bill applicants had fallen sharply and the founders brainstormed for a way to keep flying. The founders loved to fly and initiated several ideas, such as providing an aerial-banner-towing service. They even started flying 10,000 live mud suckers per flight from Mexico to Colorado where they were used as bait. But this effort to keep flying only lasted a short while. Their next venture was to offer charter service with a small four-seat Cessna aircraft.

However, this venture also failed to provide a sufficient livelihood.[151]

The founders kicked around ideas about what to do next and someone came up with the idea that they acquire a bigger aircraft, a DC-3 with 28 seats, instead of the familiar Cessna with just four seats. The idea initially scared everyone since they had only been flying the small airplane. It was also suggested that they might provide general flying service from San Diego to San Francisco, a city none of the founders had ever visited. They traveled to San Francisco and decided that flying from San Diego to Los Angeles and San Francisco was an idea worth trying. One of the members of the group stated:

> We've said many times that if we'd known anything about the airline business, we'd have never succeeded and probably never would have gotten into it. But flying was something we knew and we wanted to give people a good service. We weren't out to make a million dollars apiece; we just wanted to stay together and continue flying.

The fact that they had no background in the airline business turned out to be an advantage, since they could create a new and uniquely designed airline focusing on creating a reliable-and-fun flying experience.[152]

HUMBLE BEGINNING

PSA was born out of a DC-3 that was leased for $2,000 per month. PSA's first flight was on May 6, 1949 from San Diego's Lindbergh Field, and headed for Oakland just outside of San Francisco. Initially, PSA flew only on weekends, and with its low fares attracted a large number of military personnel. The philosophy behind the airline was that if fares could be kept low then passengers could be diverted from buses and trains. The ultimate goal was to provide service every hour to major cities in California in order to be competitive with bus and train service. Early service was barebones: PSA's first gate was a repainted military outhouse placed adjacent to the new terminal in San Diego. The upgraded latrine had a ticket counter and a set of bathroom scales to weigh passengers' luggage.[153]

Camaraderie in the early days established the tone for how PSA operated. Everyone worked together to do what was necessary to please passengers. Pilots loaded the luggage and flight attendants cleaned the airplane and, according to old-timers, everyone drew bathroom duty at least once. According to Mike Bogle, who became chief pilot in 1967, everyone helped out when there was a problem.

> When winter weather would hit all of a sudden, and air-planes had to have their deicing boots put on the wings, it was a massive, all night job. Pilots, mechanics, and baggage handlers—everybody would help put them on. There wasn't any extra pay involved.[154]

PSA experienced considerable competition as it started providing scheduled discount service. There were non-scheduled chartered airlines that flew when they were filled to capacity, and they offered rock-bottom fares on the same routes PSA was beginning to fly. Other major airlines such as United Airlines and Western Airlines also considered California their turf. The major airlines played hardball and tried to stop the small discount airlines from applying to fly in California. Initially, PSA charged $9.95 to fly from Los Angeles to San Francisco while the major airlines were charging $33. For a while, the large airlines ignored the discounter doubting that it would succeed, and then started matching its deeply discounted fares. But meeting the discounter's fare had a surprising beneficial consequence.

> People doubted we could do adequate maintenance if we were charging such low fares. They feared we weren't safe. Out biggest problem was establishing PSA as a legitimate,

safe airline. When United and Western came down to our fares, that did it. People realized that we could fly with the same degree of safety.[155]

PSA became the first airline to be hijacked, but this had comic overtones from the beginning. The plane's owner believed that the leased DC-3 would be flown 12 hours a month and thought that it was a good deal at a monthly rent of $2,000. However, in a few months the DC-3 was being flown 150 hours per month. According to Andrews,

> After several months ... the owner could stand it no longer. So we pulled into Burbank one day with a load of passengers, and I get a call from the captain: "Somebody just came in and took our airplane and all the passengers away." Apparently a 250-pound maintenance guy, acting on behalf of the owner, hand marched up to the cockpit, got in and said he was taking the airplane back.

The DC-3 was returned the next day after the lease was renegotiated.[156]

FRIENDLINESS: KEY TO PACIFIC SOUTHWEST'S SUCCESS

Early PSA frequent flyer Scott Newhall (former editor of the *San Francisco Chronicle*) used one word to describe the airline: friendly. He said, "Their business was to get you there feeling pretty good. Sometimes it was like a party, with a little band or guitar player. And they were on time and had good-looking girls." Carol Austin, a 23-year veteran of PSA stated, "We treated customers as if they were guests in our homes. We were never allowed to go into our work area and hide-out, talking among ourselves," as often occurs on the major airlines. The airline was dubbed "Personality Sells Airlines."[157]

The airline's first advertising agency credits PSA's management team with the relaxed and supportive nature of the flight crews. "They were a young airline and they had a lot of fun. Their competitors were big guys who were very stuffy, formal, terribly dignified. PSA was a bunch of gung-ho kids who wanted to build something." Everyone agreed that one of Friedkin's major traits was his belief that flying should be fun. Andrews, who succeeded Friedkin when he died, stated, "Life is tough enough. If we're not having fun, let's go do something else." A longtime flight attendant similarly stated, "We sought to make almost a sporting event of it by involving the passengers as well as crew members in the fun. The differentiating factor was that we got people to loosen up."[158]

A Symbol is Born

One day when ad man Len Gross was getting ready to board a PSA flight, he looked at the black radar dome on the front of the airplane. He observed "Gee, that looks like a nose." He thought that if the Flying Tigers during World War II could paint "Shark's teeth" on their planes to emphasize their ferocity, then why could PSA not, similarly, paint a "smile on the nose of its planes to stress its fun and personality. But when Gross suggested the idea to Andrews, the CEO, he thought it was a bad idea. He said "I thought flying an airplane with a big smile would be a putdown to the captain. It just wasn't right." However, everyone else liked the idea and in 1970 "a big smile" was painted on the front of all PSA planes. The "smile" became its central artwork in all advertising. The smile was also used in all collateral materials such as brochures and ticket folders. The "smile" was employed as a central theme when PSA became an interstate airline in 1978 with ads such as "Catch Our Smile to Portland" or "Smile to Phoenix." The smile became closely identified with the lightheartedness of PSA. The "big smile" was used until the airline was sold to US Airways in 1986.[159]

SEXY FLIGHT ATTENDANT UNIFORMS INTRODUCED

Like all other airlines, PSA's flight attendants were female and wore traditional two-piece military-style business suits. But in 1962, PSA changed the uniform their flight attendants wore. From that point on it is said that most male passengers wore smiles when flying the discount airline, and the uniform had a great deal to do with their pleasure. The first of the new uniforms introduced was called a "banana skin." This was not because of its color that was brown, but instead because of its form-fitting silhouette. One flight attendant recalls "It was very form-fitting with a zipper all the way up the front; you really had to peel it on and off. Everything showed. It was definitely ahead of its time ...." PSA even used the new uniforms in ads during the swinging 1960s, with print ads stating "PSA gives you a lift." Supposedly, as a result of the uniform, some men had to be tethered. An equally bold ad stated that aisle seats were the best on the airplane. This was based on the observation that many men watched the stewardesses walk back and forth on the aisle. "So we advertised that the aisle seats were the best on the plane at $13.50. Some customers actually thought due to the advertising that the price of the aisle seats was more expensive. But in fact all seats were the same price".[160,161]

Given the positive response of many male passengers to the one-piece skin-tight uniform, new and more revealing uniforms were introduced over the years. In 1967, two-piece, tight-fitting miniskirts were introduced, and over the years the skirts got shorter and shorter reaching five inches above the knee. But "orange ruffled pettipants underneath kept everything decent when they reached for the overhead racks". Andrews, the man responsible for introducing the miniskirts, was unrepentant and said "We didn't hesitate a moment to promote them. Sure it created a lot of talk, but that's fine. It promoted the airline."[162]

Competitors liked to insinuate that a discount airline like PSA had cut too many corners and might not be mechanically safe to fly. But employees informed Andrews that famous individuals were flying PSA on a regular basis. As a consequence, Andrews began to call on public relation firms in Hollywood and Washington that represented the famous and wealthy. The California news media started to report on celebrities who flew PSA and showed their pictures. This was good publicity for the airline and passengers were pleased to be on flights with prominent people. Furthermore, if the rich and famous flew PSA, then many felt that "so should I." Some of the politically famous people flying on PSA included US Senators Edward Kennedy, Hubert Humphrey, Margaret Chase, and Mrs Lyndon B. Johnson. PSA also carried Governor Nelson Rockefeller during the primary presidential elections. Press Secretary Pierre Salinger regularly flew between San Francisco and Los Angeles when he was running for a US Senate seat in California and past President Ronald Reagan also was a PSA passenger.[163]

Movie star Charlton Heston was photographed buying a ticket in Burbank, situated next to Hollywood. This airport was very convenient to people in the movie industry and major stars and their supporting casts flew the discount airline. A host of other movie and television stars who flew PSA included Jerry Lewis, Milton Berle, Bing Crosby, Bob Hope, Dick Van Dyke, Gregory Peck, Nina Foch, and others. Knowledge of such famous people flying the discounter helped PSA attract a growing number of passengers.[164]

Frequent and On-time Service

While PSA gained a lot of attention due to the startling and revealing uniform of their stewardesses and the elite who flew the discount airline, a more critical aspect of the discounter's success was its *frequent flights* and *reliable service*. After all, that is what most flyers are looking for and the rest are frills. PSA, over its first 15 years of rapid growth, attracted many customers because of its punctual departures, often arriving at its destination ahead of schedule. It provided hourly service between major cities in California including San Diego, Los Angeles, and San Francisco. Over the years, PSA regularly upgraded its airplanes from second-hand military prop engine airplanes to turbojets and then on to fleets of the most modern jet aircraft. Management made it a primary goal to provide frequent, fast, and on-time service that business travelers and general flying public could rely upon. In less than an hour, passengers could fly from San Diego to San Francisco.[165]

PSA's success formula included:

1. Highly reliable service
2. Low fares
3. Frequent flights
4. A good safety record
5. Attractive and friendly stewardesses

PSA also provided flights to more cities in California than any other airline.

SW AIRLINES STRATEGY: THE PACIFIC SOUTHWEST AIRLINES MODEL

Rowland King, a financial investor, and Lamar Muse, president elect of SW in Texas, met with PSA president J. Floyd Andrews and his other officers in 1969, indicating they were aware that PSA had been in business for 20 years in California and had been quite successful. The reason for their visit was to ask for help to start a similar intra-state discount airline in Texas. King and Muse said that they knew nothing about operating an airline, but felt that their marketing opportunities were similar: to provide discount airline service between major cities a few hundred miles from each other. They were interested in learning how PSA competed so successfully with the major airlines. Andrews was impressed with the Texans and requested that his officers and directors hold nothing back and explain everything that PSA did.[166]

SW subsequently sent its Chief Attorney, Herb Kelleher, and other officers to study every aspect of the flourishing PSA airline and the two airlines' relationship continued to grow. PSA agreed to sell SW its pilots' uniforms, train its pilots to fly Boeing 737s, sell uniforms for flight attendants, and train them. SW also studied the nature of PSA's marketing and finance departments and was so impressed with what it learned that it literally used PSA operating manuals and simply replaced PSA's name with SW. SW also tried to make arrangements to buy three of PSA's Boeing 737s in exchange for part ownership in the new airline. Unfortunately, they could not reach an agreement on some details, so instead leased SW one airplane on June 2, 1971, putting it into service on June 18, 1971. Thus, when SW began flying between three cities in Texas, 23 years after PSA had started, the Texas discount airline was closely emulating PSA's operating style.[167]

The irony is that SW, which was modeled after PSA, has been a big success, while PSA was forced to sell its business in the mid-1980s to US Airways. What SW did was to "keep the formula simple." The Texas discount airline flew one type of aircraft to cities located several hundred miles apart, landing and taking off from lower-cost secondary airports, and providing fliers the lowest airfares. Over time, SW expanded from Texas to nearby states on to the West Coast, back to the upper Midwest, and then on to the Northeast. The saying "that if it works, then don't mess with it" applies in the case of SW. It has consistently had near to or the lowest cost-per-seat mile flown in the airline industry. SW may not be fancy, but continues to provide reliable discount airline service to an increasing number of fliers in the United States.

Cloud over Pacific SW's Future

The best years for PSA were from the late 1960s to the early 1970s. As can be seen in Figure 5.1, the number of passengers flown increased from one million in 1962 to 6.4 million in 1972—an increase of over 500 percent. Eight years later, air traffic had not increased at all. Figure 5.2 shows how PSA's profit soared from 1962 to 1972, climbing from $1.4 million to $5.6 million—an increase of more

Figure 5.1: Soaring Number of Passengers Fly Pacific Southwest Airlines

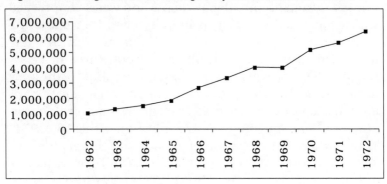

Figure 5.2: Rapidly Increasing Profits of Pacific Southwest Airlines

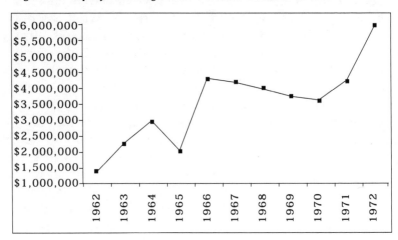

than 300 percent. In fact, the profit of $1.4 million in 1962 was close to the total amount the discount airline had earned since it started flying up to 1961. During its boom period from 1962 through 1972, PSA rapidly expanded service from primarily serving San Diego, Los Angeles, and San Francisco, to providing service to six other cities in California. It was so successful that it had more than 50 percent market share in the state in 1972.

Unfortunately, PSA was hit hard during the remainder of the 1970s and early 1980s (it was sold to US Airways in the mid-1980s). The airline's problems were largely of its own doing, though some of them were beyond its control.

Fly/Drive/Sleep Program

Andrews and the board of directors were convinced that the public wanted more than PSA's discount airline service. In 1967 they devised a Fly/Drive/Sleep program that entailed PSA to: (a) fly people; (b) rent cars; (c) provide hotel accommodation.

The first phase of the expansion program was initiated in 1968, when PSA bought a small car rental company called ValCar. The new PSA car rental business expanded rapidly and soon became one of the largest discount car rental agencies in the country. It leased top-of-the-line automobiles for at least 15 percent less than traditional auto-leasing companies. Car rental operations were established in most of the major cities PSA served in California and in 1969 it had nearly 2,000 cars to lease.[168]

ValCar sales increased from $2.4 million in 1969 to $5.8 million in 1970. Unfortunately, ValCar employees did not develop the kind of friendly customer service for which PSA was known. Analysis of the automobile rental business showed that while employees were efficient, they did not develop a friendly and close relationship with customers. During 1970 ValCar lost almost $1 million. An economic slowdown, higher cost of new cars, increase in automobile insurance, and a weaker used-car market contributed to the huge losses. The outlook was bleak for the car-rental business, and as a result, ValCar was shut down in October 1971.[169]

In 1969, as ValCar was being launched, the "sleep" portion of the program was also put into motion. In September, PSA purchased the Islandia Hotel on Mission Bay in San Diego. Then in November, it obtained leasing rights to the 475-room San Francisco Hotel adjacent to the Civic Center in San Francisco. Plans were made to remodel Islandia Hotel and increase the number of rooms from 105 to 266, and also add a convention center and a new marina. Coupled with reconstruction of the Islandia Hotel, in 1971 the hotel subsidiary lost $400,000 on revenues of $3.2 million. Even with this loss, PSA decided to proceed to modernize the San Francisco Hotel. It had been built in the early 1900s, and even though it had been renovated a few times it needed major improvements. The hotel was adjacent to the Bay Area Transit station and therefore attractive to the general public. With a sparkling lobby and new rooms, the airline expected the hotel to make money.[170]

PSA's hotel operation continued to grow in 1972 and 1973. It opened new hotels and completed the renovation and expansion of its first two hotels. In addition, PSA took over the *Queen Mary*, berthed in Long Beach Harbor in January 1973, and opened 400 rooms located on the three decks of the ship. In 1972, PSA's hotel operation lost nearly $600,000 on revenues of almost $3 million. Losses soared further in 1973 to more than $2 million on revenues of $6.76 million. The money-losing hotel venture was leased to Hyatt in 1974 and later divested. PSA also diversified into the radio business, believing that this initiative would provide exposure to the public and help build the airline's image and business. The radio subsidiary incurred a loss of $420,000 on revenues of $816,000 during 1973 and was sold off at the end of 1974.[171]

THE LOCKHEED L-1011 TRISTAR FIASCO

As PSA's management was always looking for ways to reduce its flying costs and provide faster service, the discounter regularly purchased new aircraft. PSA management became enamored of the possibility of flying 300 passengers per flight between its major destinations. The Lockheed TriStar carried 50 percent more passengers than the older Boeing aircraft which they intended to replace. They also expected this replacement to give PSA a further cost advantage over the competition. Thus, PSA ordered two L-1011s in December 1972 and began flying the new three-engine, high-capacity aircraft in August 1974. The two TriStars were used to fly between San Francisco, Los Angeles, Sacramento, and Burbank, where new boarding gates were constructed to handle the larger airplane. However, eight months later the two TriStars were removed from service and parked in the desert in the dry climate of Arizona.[172]

The economic recession reduced demand for flying and the Federal government reduced fuel supply. These factors doomed the future of the L-1011 TriStar. In addition, PSA's management failed to anticipate problems associated with the large aircraft. According to Scott Newhall, who shuttled back and forth for the *Chronicle* newspaper, it took nearly as much time to board and deplane passengers as it did to fly between Los Angeles and San Francisco. According to the newspaper writer, "The L-1011 was a fine plane to fly them between California and Czechoslovakia, but for the commuter run it was too big." Not only were the two TriStars stored in the desert, but PSA was also forced to cancel its order for three more of the same aircraft. During 1975, PSA reported an after-tax loss of $16.7 million (in comparison to a profit of $1.6 million the previous year) which was the first loss since the airline went public in 1963. Disposing the two aircraft and canceling the order for three more planes was responsible for $7.89 million of the loss.[173]

Pacific Southwest has a Major Airline Collision

PSA had a perfect safety record for 29 years from the time it was founded in 1949 and it was considered a very safe airline. But a major tragedy occurred on September 25, 1978, when a Boeing 727-200 was on a visual approach to landing at Lindbergh Airport in San Diego. The control tower warned the cockpit crew that a small Cessna 172 was climbing for take off and was at an altitude of 1,400 feet. Both PSA pilots and the pilot of the Cessna acknowledge having each other in sight. Nonetheless, at 9 a.m. the two planes collided about three miles northeast of Lindbergh Field. The Cessna, flown by a student pilot with an instructor, slammed into the underside of the right wing of the declining PSA airplane. Both planes crashed into a neighborhood and exploded. All 135 people on board the PSA airplane were killed as also the two persons in the Cessna. Twenty-six houses were damaged or destroyed, and seven people on the ground were killed. This crash had a demoralizing impact on PSA's flight crew and passengers.[174]

Some Good News—and more Bad News

Clearly, PSA had more than its share of problems during the mid-1970s. From 1973 through 1977, its profits were sharply lower than they had been in the past 12 years. The California Public Utility Commission (CPUC) had refused to permit PSA to expand its services to new cities in California since the early 1970s. Instead, the CPUC favored Air California, which was steadily losing money. However, with airline deregulation in 1978, PSA began to provide discount airline service from California to several cities in nearby states, and even to international destinations. In December 1978, it began flying from California to Las Vegas and Reno in Nevada, both popular gambling centers. Then in March 1979, it started flying to Phoenix, and in November it started service to Salt Lake City. The airline's friendly and courteous service, combined with low fares, resulted in positive customer response and good press coverage. PSA also started flying internationally, and in 1980 commenced flights to Mazatlan and Puerto Vallerta in Mexico.[175] From 1978 through 1983, PSA started service to 14 cities outside of California. The growing number of destinations served contributed to a major boost in profit in the late 1970s and early 1980s. From 1978 through 1982, PSA earned an average of $18 million a year, while it had low or negative profit from 1973 through 1977, when it was not permitted to fly new routes in California and to cities in nearby states.

While PSA was benefiting from flying to destinations in other states and internationally, the bad news was that PSA pilots went on strike on September 25, 1980. This was the first major strike in the history of the airline, and for 52 days PSA was completely shut down. Every plane was grounded and all flights were canceled while 3,000 employees were placed on leave. The pilots called the strike due to working conditions, pay level, and reduction in number of flights. They demanded pay increases of $100 million. Since the airline had only earned $23 million during 1979 and profits were hurt by skyrocketing fuel prices not expected to abate, management could not come to an agreement with the pilots. Lawyers representing the striking pilots said the airline could take a bank loan, but PSA said that was not feasible and was not going to happen. The striking pilots obtained only a few concessions. Fortunately, the strike occurred during the off-peak time of the year. Passenger count dropped from 8.6 million in 1979 to 6.1 million in 1980 and profits declined to $12.6 million compared to $23 the previous year.[176] However, there was good news toward the end of the year when PSA became the first airline to start flying the 153-seat Super 90. This was the "Quietest Commercial Jetliner" and it was 30 percent more fuel-efficient than the Boeing 727s it replaced.[177]

PSA had nearly recovered from the impact of the first strike when it was it hit by a second strike in 1981. The Professional Air Traffic Controllers (PATCO), a union consisting of men and women who direct air traffic and maintain safety, went on strike over wages and working conditions. President Reagan subsequently fired them, and this led to a personnel shortage causing the Federal Aviation Commission to order a large reduction in flights. According to PSA's Barkley, "We got depeaked. We had a lot of flights at 5:00 p.m. Because of the strike, the FAA limited the number of flights and made us spread our flights over the entire day." This was a disaster for PSA since it catered to business people who regularly flew up and down the coast. Furthermore, Barkley explained that the major airlines started what he calls "the crowding-out theory" which involved flying old airplanes while buying new ones and rapidly expanding. The major airlines gobbled up airport gates and saturated markets where there was limited business. Barkley indicated that the new game in town was: "I don't want it and I don't need it, but I'll take it before anybody else gets it."[178]

Deregulation Heralds Beginning of "Free For All Battle"

PSA began rapidly expanding service, flying from California to nearby states beginning in 1978, which initially increased profits. The airline had been stymied for a number of years in adding new routes in California which was contributing to PSA's abortive diversification effort. The first few years following deregulation, PSA reported record earnings from the growing number of routes it served. However, the established major airlines saw California as a rich underserved market and many began expanded flights in the state. While PSA reported record profits in the first few years following deregulation, a number of major airlines began flying in California, leading to intensified competition which began to take its toll.[179]

During 1981, increased competition coupled with recession affected the airline's operations, which lost $17
million (although it did report an overall profit due to its
profitable subsidiaries and sales of aircraft). United introduced a special subsidiary targeted at PSA and matched
the discounter's prices. The economic recession continued throughout 1982, and with still more competition
from the major airlines, PSA reported a loss for the second
year in a row. While the discounter had record passenger
revenues in 1983, it reported a net loss of $9.3 million
during the year. Due to its worsening financial condition,
in 1984 PSA was able to obtain a 15 percent cut in wages.
In turn, it established a 25 percent profit-sharing program
for its employees. Nonetheless, PSA, as well as its profitable subsidiaries, reported a profit of $2.2 million in
1984. This was down from a peak of more than $20 million
a year in the early days following deregulation in 1978
when the airline was rapidly expanding. The turf battle
continued during 1985, and PSA experienced more competition from new low-cost airlines as well as from established major airlines. PSA's airline division lost $648,000
during 1985, which resulted in four straight years of
losses, while its subsidiaries continued to make money.[180]

PSA Purchases part of Bankrupt Braniff Airways

Merger mania was sweeping the airline industry by 1986.
With all the new competition and financial problems, PSA
tried to expand through buying part of another airline. It
signed an agreement in late 1982 with the bankrupt
Braniff Airways to purchase its hub operation in Dallas-
Fort Worth Regional Airport. The agreement called for PSA
to purchase 30 Braniff Boeing 727s which would operate
from its hub in Dallas. The airplanes would be repainted
and decorated as PSA airplanes and serve 16 new cities
beginning late in the spring of 1983. But the agreement
was abandoned in early 1983 when PSA could not reach

an agreement with Braniff on what to pay for the airplanes.[181]

With its Back to the Wall, PSA Agrees to be Bought

Over the years, the owners of PSA had sworn they would never sell the airline. In 1984, CEO Barkley firmly stated that PSA could make it on its own "and I mean it." But merger mania was sweeping the country and PSA losses over the past four years were pushing the airline into a corner from which it had little chance of recovering. Smaller airlines that PSA had driven out of business merged with larger airlines and returned with vengeance.[182]

Republic Airlines, which PSA had driven out of major western markets, merged with Northwest Orient—an airline with strong financial resources—and decided to retake the West. The same happened when Delta Air Lines purchased Western Airlines, the airline PSA had driven out of its territory. Delta, like PSA, was a short-haul specialist, and it helped Western Airlines to devise a strategy to regain its territory in California. Similarly, Continental Airlines purchased the Denver-based Frontier Airline. This made Denver an unfriendly airport to the grinning discount airline. Another big challenge to PSA was American Airlines' purchase of AirCal in November 1986. Given its advanced computer system, American/ AirCal was able to battle PSA on its North/South flights along the coast—its prized turf.[183]

Faced with its profitability problem and new competition, CEO Barkley said, "It was inevitable we would have survival problems and we would be bought." Large carriers eyeing the huge California market had two choices. They could either spend billions on purchasing new aircraft for the already heavily saturated West Coast market, or they could buy one of the remaining regional carriers, which already had $1 billion of airplanes and facilities, as well as increasingly important landing slots. The choice was obvious. Within an hour of the announcement of one of the major airlines' purchase of a West coast carrier, PSA received a call from another major airline. Shortly thereafter, it was announced that PSA, once the largest California airline, was being sold to US Airways. Bonnie Johnson, a 27-year veteran of the accounting department, said "When the planes are painted and the smile is no more, it will be a sad day for California and a sad day for me. But things go on. US Airways is a good company." Founder and former CEO Andrews was distraught that the airline he had nurtured was no more, and said it was "like pulling out my arm and beating me with a bloody stump."[184]

Requiem for a Dream

Even though it is no longer in business, there is no question that California's PSA had a major impact on the airline industry. It has been properly credited for helping to create the discount airline business that experienced many challenges in its early days. PSA proved there was a large market for quality discount airline service, even while the United States was dominated by major high-cost, full-service airlines. Had PSA not openly shared its operating strategy and working manuals with SW, would the Texas discounter have got off the ground and become so successful? Furthermore, over the first decade following airline deregulation in 1978, SW was the only successful discount airline.

SW, discussed in Chapter six, adopted the fundamental operating procedures used by PSA. While the major airlines tried to drive PSA out of business, the low-cost formula worked so well that the major airlines have largely ignored SW, allowing the discount airline to expand over much of the country. Furthermore, SW developed a "point-to-point system" that involved flying shorter routes directly from one city to another, in contrast to the major airline's hub-and-spoke system where its subsidiaries flew passengers to major cities and on to another. Major airline executives have openly stated that they cannot compete with SW, whose success helped spawn other successful discount airlines so that today the vast majority of the flying public has an alternative to flying the major airlines and paying their high fares.

Chapter Six

Southwest Airlines: Deregulation's Biggest Success Story

SOUTHWEST IS the most successful discount airline, consistently profitable for 32 years, and new discount airlines have been modeled after it. From its humble beginnings flying a few airplanes serving three cities in Texas, SW now competes with the major full-service airlines in most states across the country. It also flies more passengers than any other airline. SW's discount operation was copied from Pacific Southwest Airlines (PSA) in California, which no longer exists. The die-hard spirit and perseverance of everyone involved with running and managing SW is what made this airline extremely successful.

It all began as what appeared to be a hare-brained scheme by Rollin King, a Texas entrepreneur who operated a small commuter airline. In the mid-1960s, King had been studying the success of the point-to-point model of PSA in California. He began to think that if PSA could establish a successful discount airline in California, then why could they not do the same in Texas? After discussing the idea with his banker, King began to envision a new discount airline that would provide service between Dallas, Houston, and San Antonio—which later became known as the Golden Triangle in Texas. These three cities represented a large underserved market that commuters used to drive to because of the high airfares of the major airlines. Looking back today, providing service between the three Texas Triangle cities does not appear extraordinary, but given the humble beginning of SW, it was quite a unique business move for the time.[185]

Prior to deregulation in 1978, SW operated solely in Texas, learning not just how to make money but, more importantly, how to survive. The climate of the airline industry during the 1970s was such that small airlines like SW were forced to find ways to keep from getting squashed by the major carriers of the time. SW only served routes in Texas that kept the airline from being regulated by the CAB. The CAB regulated the fares of the major airlines and required that the airlines charge the same fares for routes with different distance also, fare discounting was not allowed. However, the Texas Aeronautical Commission (TAC) regulated SW and provided a high degree of flexibility, both in pricing and in the nature of its operation. The TAC provided SW the flexibility it needed to overcome the difficulties faced in building a successful intra-state discount airline—the same airline that became a nemesis to the major airlines after deregulation.

HERB KELLEHER—THE GUIDING LIGHT OF SW

From the very beginning, Herb Kelleher was the driving force that made SW what it is today. As one of the original founders of SW, Kelleher is a true fighter determined to succeed, no matter how hopeless things may appear. In his own words, Kelleher is a born revolutionary. He said, "I love battles. I think it's part of the Irish in me ... I've never gotten tired of fighting."[186] His perseverance, flamboyant attitude, and sheer will-power truly define Kelleher as a leader who simply does not know how to quit. Moreover, it is this underlying resolve which has left a lasting impression on the entire culture of SW.

Kelleher graduated from law school and became a practicing attorney in San Antonio, Texas. In 1966, he met Rollin King, and after a few drinks, King sketched out a plan to create a new discount airline on the back of a cocktail napkin. It would be a three-route triangular airline flying between Dallas, Houston, and San Antonio. Kelleher's initial response was that the idea was absurd. Starting such an airline would mean getting into a head-to-head competition with the other entrenched major Texas carriers. Nonetheless, they forged ahead to create the new discount airline. Kelleher made a small personal investment of $10,000 in the venture, and his share in SW is now worth over $200 million. Acting as legal counsel for the new airline, Kelleher filed the articles of incorporation on March 15, 1967. This began an enduring series of restraining orders and appeals that dragged on for more than four years as Herb Kelleher vehemently fought his way through the courts for the right to get SW flying.[187,188]

During the four-year span prior to beginning air service, these two entrenched carriers sought to protect their market in Texas by every means possible. SW found itself involved in battle after battle and case after case. SW filed for permission from the easily accessible Texas Aeronautical Commission to begin flying and soon was granted permission. However, the very next day a state district court issued a restraining order to stop the airline from beginning service. The long legal battle was well underway. SW filed an appeal to lift this restraining order, but the order was initially upheld. However, the Texas Supreme Court overturned the restraining order. Braniff, Texas International, and Continental took their request for a restraining order to the US Supreme Court, but were turned away when the court ultimately refused to hear the appeal. Next, Braniff and Texas International petitioned the CAB to issue a restraining order, but this effort too was unsuccessful.

Two days before SW's first scheduled flight, the same two major airlines convinced an Austin judge to issue a restraining order against SW. Kelleher had had enough— before he left Dallas to seek relief from the Texas Supreme Court, he told Lamar Muse, then CEO of SW, to proceed with the inaugural flight no matter what. Muse asked what to do if the Sheriff showed up and tried to stop the flight. Kelleher advised him to "leave tire tracks on his shirt. We're going come hell or high water." Fortunately, Kelleher again found relief from the Texas Supreme Court the day before the inaugural flight. Finally on June 18, 1971, SW took to the sky for the very first time. However, soon Kelleher would once again find himself inside the courtroom. These hard-fought battles paved the way for Kelleher and the other founders to develop a strong passion for the start-up airline, which in turn affected how the SW culture came to be.[189]

Kelleher was adamant about pioneering unique ways of taking care of his people, including both customers and employees. It is this innovative spirit that helped SW win a heated fare war that broke out in early 1973 against Braniff. Attempting to increase passengers on flights between San Antonio and Dallas, SW cut the normal $26 fare in half to $13, and a week later, Braniff retaliated by cutting its price on the lucrative Dallas-to-Houston route in half, from $26 to a mere $13. An obvious game of predatory pricing had begun as Kelleher knew Braniff was not planning to maintain the low fares as they had dubbed them special "get acquainted" prices. To match the fares would have led SW into bankruptcy. Instead, Kelleher and his gang did something unique—or in other words, they did it the SW way. They decided to offer the customer a choice, take the flight at the cheap $13 price or pay the regular $26 dollar fare and receive a free bottle of liquor. Amazingly, the idea was a hit and the two-page ads that read "Nobody's going to shoot SW out of the sky for a lousy

$13" worked like a charm as 76 percent of SW passengers initially paid the higher fare.[190]

Kelleher knew that for SW to deliver exceptional customer service it needed good people, and once those people were in place, he understood the importance of taking care of them. Reflecting on this idea in 2001, Kelleher commented, "You have to treat your employees like your customers. When you treat them right, then they will treat your outside customers right."[191] This simple concept has become a defining characteristic of SW's culture and certainly represented a major competitive advantage for the new airline. To maintain this advantage, Kelleher ensured that the "people always come first." He points out "Nothing kills your company's culture like layoffs. Nobody has ever been furloughed here, and that is unprecedented in the airline industry."[192] Through his relentless drive and unwavering commitment to both customers and employees, Kelleher has become a leader of almost mythical proportions, one who put in place the necessary components that have enabled SW to attain the success it continues to enjoy to this day.

THE SW PHILOSOPHY: MAKING FLYING A FUN EXPERIENCE

The question on everybody's mind is "what exactly is it about SW that all these people are buying into?" The answer is not difficult to determine; almost everyone who has interacted with the company has become a true believer in the SW philosophy. And, in the end, this cult-like mindset really boils down to just two factors, the first of which is good planning with well thought-out processes. Ultimately, however, these processes are organized and put into action by the second factor, which is people helping people. The latter of these two has been in place since the onset of SW's operations as Kelleher set and enforced that standard through the various positions he held while working with the airline.

One of the driving forces for most SW employees is a culture that not only inspires employees to have fun while doing their jobs, but also demands it. This attitude truly comes to life as pilots and flight attendants are notorious for cracking jokes while making the required safety announcements. In the early years, SW wanted to stand out, so they dressed the stewardesses in brightly colored hot pants and high-heeled go-go boots.[193] The gimmick was to help customers feel more comfortable while flying on SW, and the sexily-styled uniforms kept the flight attendants from acting too serious or stuffy. Everything revolved around working together to improve customer service and flying enjoyment. However, as soon as the flight attendants began to feel silly and out-of-date in their hot pants, management immediately provided an alternative: a wrap-around skirt. This sort of teamwork that occurs between management and employees at SW, and its willingness to adjust to each other's needs, is a hallmark of the airline.

The team atmosphere that Kelleher and other managers have been able to accomplish is nothing short of extraordinary in the context of an airline, especially since SW is almost 80 percent unionized.[194] It is not uncommon to see a pilot helping to load luggage or a stewardess stopping to pick up trash in the terminal. These are certainly not duties listed in their job descriptions; instead, these are motivated employees willing to do what it takes to get a job done while providing the best possible quality service. A good illustration of this service came in January 1995 when the pilots' union willingly signed a 10-year contract, and agreed to freeze their wages for the first five years in return for stock options.[195] These types of concessions from employees only come about when they trust the leadership at the top to treat them fairly and take care of them in times of need. This "people-helping-people" concept seems to grow stronger every day, reinforcing the overall SW philosophy.

BE LEAN, DISCOUNT AND RESPOND QUICKLY

Without a well-orchestrated plan of attack, even the most dedicated employees with the best of intentions will come up short. This is where the initial guiding principles that Kelleher instilled so many years ago have become one of the airline's greatest advantages, representing the process-driven side of the SW philosophy. The underlying principle of this philosophy is the simplicity and flexibility of the business model which has allowed SW to remain lean and provide customers considerably lower fares than the major airlines.

This flexibility has proven invaluable at times, especially when SW has been able to move quickly to take advantage of opportunities created by the ever-changing landscape of the airline industry. One such example was SW's unexpected expansion into the California market. American Airlines and US Airways pulled out of multiple California cities at one point, and instead of wasting time thinking about it, SW simply reacted. Kelleher put his people into action, snatching up the abandoned gates and then quickly purchasing new airplanes.[196] Where larger or more structured airlines have to deal with internal bureaucracy and hierarchical politics, SW is able to keep it simple and adapt to the situation at hand.

The motto at SW is "keep it simple," exemplified in many of the day-to-day operations of the airline. For instance, SW does not offer assigned seating. A passenger with a ticket does have a reserved seat, but no guarantee as to which seat he/she may get. Passengers are boarded on a first-come-first-serve basis in groups of 30. Better still, until recent security measures forced them to change, SW had specially colored plastic reusable boarding passes and had never instituted any form of paper ticketing. These measures helped instill efficiencies throughout the system, which saved time and ultimately bolstered the bottom line for SW.[197]

There are other factors also that have contributed to SW's efficiency and low cost. It is the management's philosophy of keeping debt to a minimum and reviewing the overall cost structure on a continuous basis. In keeping the balance sheet clear of unnecessary debt, SW has avoided the pitfalls of overreaching on its obligations. The airline flies one type of aircraft, the Boeing 700 series, which reduces training, spare parts, and overhaul costs.[198]

SW's commitment to the low-cost, point-to-point strategy helped the discounter to maintain a high level of efficiency. In contrast, the major airlines built up centralized hubs, funneling passengers into big cities in order to fill up huge aircrafts for long-haul flights. This created an inherently high-cost system of flying. SW also concentrates on short-haul routes and carries, on an average, less than 100 passengers per flight. This emphasis stresses the high frequency and low fares based on the point-to-point model it employs.[199] All this is put into practice by "people helping people"—the principal SW philosophy. Furthermore, for the most part, SW flies to secondary, instead of major, airports. There are two primary advantages of its point-to-point system of flying to secondary airports. For one, the cost of landing and take-off is lower at the smaller airports and results in substantial savings. Second, landing and take-off times are less at the smaller airports. This permits SW to keep its airplanes flying more hours per day than the major airlines, and is a further factor contributing to its lower cost and prices.

SW Emerges from Deregulation and Never Looks Back

With the passing of the Airline Deregulation Act in October 1978, the entire airline industry was poised to change. In theory, airlines would no longer operate as huge utility providers with government-controlled pricing. Instead, the industry was to become a model of economic efficiency with full-scale competition driving down prices.

As the CAB relinquished its authority over ticket pricing, SW knew it was time to spread its cheap fares outside the borders of Texas. In 1979, SW did just that and began an expansion effort that 28 years later in 2006 has the airline flying to 61 cities in 32 states.[200] This expansion effort started with a single route outside of Texas in 1979 when service was offered between Dallas and New Orleans, hallmarking SW as an interstate airline.[201] The next few years brought further growth, and in 1980, SW was servicing the neighboring states of New Mexico and Oklahoma.[202] Pressing further westward, SW started flying to Phoenix, Arizona, as well as Las Vegas, Nevada, and by early 1982 reached its first destination in California by servicing San Diego.[203]

However, the airline remained "geographically shackled" by its position in Love Field and its implications under the Wright Amendment. The Wright Amendment was instituted in 1979, immediately after SW's first interstate route was added, but its entire creation is tied to the history of SW's "home" airport at Love Field.

Love Field was purchased by the city of Dallas from the Army in 1928 for $350,000. However, in 1968, Dallas and Fort Worth responded to pressure from the Federal government and agreed to build a regional airport to replace Love Field. The existing airlines at the time all agreed to move to the new airport. When SW commenced its intra-state operations in 1971, it did so from Love Field and, not being a party to the previously mentioned agreement, chose to keep Love Field as its headquarters airport when the new one opened in 1972. This action prompted the cities of Dallas and Fort Worth, as well as the Dallas-Fort Worth Airport Board, to sue SW.

After a long appellate process, the Federal courts allowed SW to continue intra-state operations from Love Field. Unfortunately for SW, its battle was far from over. With the passage of the Airline Deregulation Act in 1978, many new markets were opened to the start-up airline.

However, 1979 brought the announcement of SW's first interstate flight to New Orleans and Dallas-Fort Worth Airport, and the cities of Dallas and Fort Worth tried another avenue to block the growth of SW. To do this, they turned to US House Leader, Jim Wright. He subsequently passed the Wright Amendment to the International Air Transportation Competition Act of 1979 which effectively restricted interstate air service to and from Love field to the states of Louisiana, Arkansas, Oklahoma, and New Mexico. Later, Alabama, Mississippi, and Kansas were added to the list of restricted cities.

This amendment seriously limited SW's interstate expansion from Love Field and shaped its development as a whole. It meant that if SW wanted to expand, then it would either have to hop from Love Field to another of its Texas markets and then on to its final destination, or it would expand only within a predefined set of states. It also protected DFW Airport and the airlines serving it, allowing those airlines to charge higher fares and be safe from the brutality of low-fare competition. This bubble of higher fares in and out of Dallas was so widely felt that, in 2004, Tennessee introduced legislation to open Tennessee markets to Love Field. SW currently denounces the Wright Amendment as outdated and anti-competitive. These developments are discussed later in this chapter.

In the early days after deregulation, SW was still the small fish in a very big pond. On paper, the discount airline had the ability to fly anywhere at any price, but as the industry wavered and competitive forces came to bear, SW was often forced into an absolute game of hardball. One such instance of industry disruption came on August 3, 1981 when 12,000 union members of the Professional Air Traffic Controllers Organization (PATCO) went on strike, causing the FAA to step in and limit the number of flights allowed in and out of most airports. Carriers would partici-pate in a bi-monthly drawing for available slots and then trade with each other as they saw fit.[204] Kelleher put the situation in perspective:

> It was a huge crisis. Whether or not you got the right to fly your new airplanes was determined by a lottery in Washington. We were actually picking Ping-Pong balls—like a bingo game—out of a big container. We had new airplanes coming in, and airplanes don't do very well if you just put them against the fence and plant geraniums in them.[205]

It is situations like these that stretched the innovation and flexibility factor of the SW philosophy. Being a lawyer by profession, Kelleher knew something had to be done, so remaining ever mindful of the law, he found a creative way to play within the system and get his planes in the air.

During this time, it seemed that new airlines were afforded preference in assigning available slots. To take advantage of this, SW used a non-operating subsidiary called Midway SW Airlines to draw in a preferred position, and then simply transferred the slots from Midway to the parent firm, SW. Of course, when the FAA realized what SW was doing, they changed the rule so that only operating airlines could participate in the lotteries. Not to be beaten that easily, Kelleher sold the subsidiary to a one-plane airline, making Midway operational. The owner of the airline would get the slots and transfer them to SW.[206, 207] This was certainly not what the FAA administrators in Washington had intended, but it was legal and truly representative of the "never-quit" attitude instilled at SW from those early court battles of the 1960s and 1970s.

The decade of the 1980s was a real roller-coaster ride for SW beginning with the shaky situation created by the air traffic controllers' strike that lasted until the end of 1982. After Kelleher fought his way through that battle, SW enjoyed several years of rapid expansion and favorable dealings. In 1984, again following the SW philosophy, the airline was able to reap huge concessions in employee wages in exchange for a profit-sharing plan. This plan was not just for show either; it effectively provided a 13 percent ownership stake back to SW personnel.[208] Kelleher felt that if the employees actually owned a piece of the airline, no matter how small, this would provide the incentive to push everyone to increase their personal output for SW. These happy employees fueled further expansion in the mid-1980s. Although it would eventually leave the congested Stapleton airport, SW began serving Denver in 1984.[209] Then, in 1985, SW spread to St Louis, Missouri, and Midway Airport in Chicago.[210]

This aggressive expansion program would come back to haunt SW when it purchased a small-time competitor called Muse Air. As the brainchild of Lamar Muse, a former CEO of SW, Muse Air was rumored to have been created solely for the purpose of opposing SW and was even called Revenge Air by many. In its short four years of existence, Muse Air never turned in an operating profit, so as the airline was on the verge of collapse, Kelleher stepped in and bought the failing operation. Muse Air was structured as a direct competitor to SW in Texas, and the expanding western markets actually offered what appeared to be a good entrance for SW into the Florida markets. On the face, the deal seemed like a logical move, but Kelleher would find out soon enough just how big of a mistake he had really made.[211]

In late June of 1985, after the merger had finally received all regulatory approvals, SW took control of Muse Air as a wholly owned subsidiary and put in place a plan to run the airline as a completely independent operation. Oddly enough, the business model for the newly acquired Muse Air was almost opposite to that of SW. Whereas SW prided itself on the no-frills, low-cost, short-haul model, Muse was positioned as a non-smoking, upscale, long-haul carrier.[212] Muse was operating with a fleet of 14 McDonnell Douglas jet aircraft including a few DC-9s with a primary focus on using the newer MD-80s, neither of which matched up with the familiar Boeing 737 upon which SW relied.[213]

To try and boost awareness, SW renamed the airline TranStar and kept the upscale model in place. Everyone, including Wall Street, thought that TranStar's longer flights and all-leather seating would provide a perfect complementary product for the existing SW service. However, the airline industry was changing—as people became more price-sensitive, they were unwilling to pay the higher fares that TranStar needed to charge in order to provide the higher class of service. TranStar simply could not keep up with the constant price competition from Texas Air. After the subsidiary had to borrow more than $15 million from SW just to make payroll, Kelleher knew it was time to throw in the towel.[214] Although the airline had 18 planes and accounted for 20 percent of SW's total traffic, TranStar's last flight was on August 9, 1987, and within a few months, most of the unit's assets were liquidated.[215,216] In his usual style, Kelleher did not let arrogance and pride get in his way. Once he realized the acquisition of Muse Air was a mistake, he openly admitted the failure and shut down the operation. This flexibility and decisive action has always been, and still is, emblematic of SW and its dynamic leader.

By the end of 1987, TranStar was out of the picture, and having survived this bump SW was primed once again for explosive growth. Grow is just what they did—expansion to the east had begun and by 1988, SW was serving Detroit and Birmingham.[217] After that, service to Oakland's International Airport was added in 1989.[218] Then, in 1990, SW passed a phenomenal milestone, having been in operation less than 20 years, the "little airline that could" reached the billion-dollar mark in revenues. This officially earmarked it as a "major" airline, and never again would the title "start-up" or "small" be used to describe SW.[219]

This was just the beginning of the dominant footprint SW would create within the airline industry. With the demise of PSA in the late 1980s, the early 1990s saw SW solidify its lead position in the California markets.[220] Stretching in the other direction, SW finally reached the east coast in 1993 when service began to Baltimore/ Washington International Airport.[221] Just about the same time, a new player came on to the scene that would ultimately boost the growth of SW.

Late in 1992, Morris Air began operations with a fleet of four Boeing 737s based out of Salt Lake City, Utah. The Morris family had no intention of competing directly with SW as they set up a small route structure in the Pacific Northwest.[222] At that point, SW had not entered these markets which led Kelleher to recognize another merger opportunity. Having failed so miserably with the acquisition of Muse Air, it was expected that the managers at SW would have approached this situation with a great deal of caution. But, in fact, the exact opposite happened. Kelleher was a risk-taker and a true visionary: he saw that Morris Air was a perfect acquisition target. The airline flew routes that SW did not cover and, best of all, it only used 737s, the same aircraft on which SW relied. Kelleher pounced on this opportunity and, in December 1993, Morris Air was merged with SW as part of a deal valued at more than $130 million.[223] This immediately created new routes and provided new aircraft. In 1994, SW extended services to seven new cities including Seattle, Spokane, Portland, and Boise.[224]

The acquisition of Morris Air turned out to be a huge success, paving the way for new innovations and even further expansion during the mid to late 1990s. SW had always been a leader in using technology to help run the business, and in 1995 it was the first major airline to introduce a ticketless travel system throughout the entire process. This was the first major action ever taken by a big airline to eliminate the major reservation systems in use at the time. With the ticketless travel system, a customer would receive a confirmation number directly from SW and simply show up at the time of the flight.[225] Building on this concept, SW revealed further innovation when, in 1996, it established online ticketless travel through its website, www.southwest.com.[226] This form of booking was so successful that, in 2003, SW was forced to close its call centers in Dallas, Salt Lake City, and Little Rock. True to its employee loyalty, SW offered all displaced employees jobs in other cities, but by the beginning of the following year, half had declined the invitation.

The growth continued, and 1996 brought new service to the lucrative Florida market, where SW's low fares sent Delta Express packing. Later that year, service to Providence, Rhode Island began as the east coast became more accessible to SW.[227,228] In 1997, Jacksonville, Florida became the 50th city to receive the low-fare treatment from SW, quickly followed by Jackson, Mississippi. Manchester, New Hampshire, was picked up in 1998, opening the gates to the Northeast. From there, SW was able to connect with Islip, New York and Bradley Airport in Hartford, Connecticut, along with beginning service to Raleigh-Durham International—all during 1999.[229]

SW's expansion since deregulation has been quite systematic. As its name implies, SW first expanded into the states of the southwestern portion of the nation. It began with westward expansion into nearby states. By the mid-1990s, SW had spread its coverage to several states in the Midwest as well as the Pacific Northwest. Finally, by the year 2004, SW had reached the Northeast, where it continued to enjoy booming business despite the oxymoron of its name and its service.

More recent innovations include an online tool called "SWABIZ," introduced in 2000 to assist "company travel managers in booking and tracking trips made through www.southwest.com."[230] In 2002, SW partnered with IBM and began investing in self-serve kiosks that led the

airline gradually to begin a process of retiring the old
plastic boarding cards still in use.[231] In 2004, SW operated
2,900 flights a day to 60 airports in 59 different cities with
32,000 employees, and it has plans to continue expanding.
In 2004, the airline also flew 70.9 million passengers in
its fleet of 417 Boeing 737 jets. More importantly, as SW
expanded its service to cover much of the country, it
continued to make money. Year 2004 marks its 31st
consecutive year of profitability, an amazing feat no other
airline can claim. SW's net income in 2004 was $313
million.[232] By comparison, Delta Air Lines flew approximately 110 million passengers with its 60,000+ employees and lost over $5 billion in the same year.

Figure 6.1: States Served by Southwest Airlines, 1984 and 1994

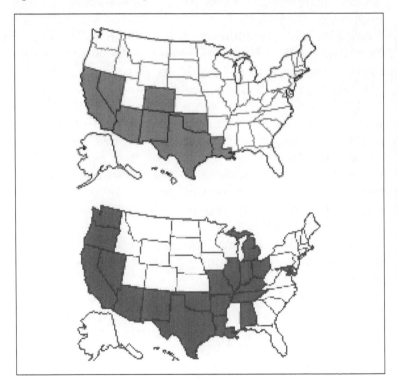

Figure 6.2: States Served by Southwest Airlines, 2005

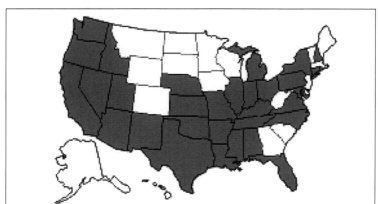

The success of SW is nothing new. The early 1990s was a tough period for the entire airline industry. However, SW was the only airline to post both operating and net profits in 1990. It has remained profitable through both good times and bad. As can be seen in Figure 6.3, SW has been profitable for 32 years from 1971 to 2003.

One of the driving forces behind the continued profits has been SW's ability to predict future market conditions and act to mitigate future risks. A perfect example of this is SW's oil futures hedge against rising fuel prices. As of August 28, 2004, SW was 80 percent hedged on oil at a price of $24 per barrel, helping it maintain profitability as oil prices skyrocketed to over $50 per barrel following the invasion of Iraq in 2003.[233] Delta, on the other hand, sold its oil hedges to free up cash. Analysts predict that without financial hedges to help maintain fuel costs, SW would have lost money in three of the last eight quarters.[234]

Over the past decade, SW has outpaced its competitors not only by turning in profits when everyone else was posting losses, but also by increasing its traffic at a much faster rate than the legacy carriers. Since 1994, SW has more than doubled its revenue passenger miles. One revenue passenger mile (RPM) is equal to one passenger

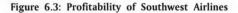

Figure 6.3: Profitability of Southwest Airlines

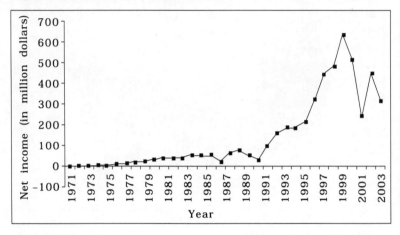

flown one mile. In 1994, SW flew 21.6 billion RPMs and 53.4 billion RPMs in 2004. This amounts to a growth of 147 percent since 1994, which is tremendous when compared to its competitors. American Airlines increased its traffic only 26 percent during the same period, and United Airlines only showed a 6 percent increase in traffic.

Like all airlines, SW has seen a downturn following the terrorist attacks on September 11, 2001. It is also struggling with the loss of Kelleher, who stepped down in June 2001, as well as the abrupt retirement of his replacement, James Parker, in July 2004.[235] The industry environment in the years of Parker's reign made his time in office quite turbulent, forcing him to deal with a downturn in the economy, high fuel costs, and trouble with labor. After a rare labor dispute, he hastily resigned, turning rule of the company over to former CFO, Gary Kelly, and a woman who worked her way up through the ranks starting as Keheller's secretary, Colleen Barrett. Barrett is credited with much of the development of SW's unique corporate culture.

Kelly now sits at the helm as CEO and has to battle growing competition from other low-cost airlines such as JetBlue and even major legacy airlines that have sharply reduced their prices even while experiencing huge losses.[236] SW currently provides service from Dallas Love Field and a smaller airport just outside Dallas. An outdated law passed in 1979 restricts SW to providing service to only seven adjacent states. With SW's operations vastly restricted, American charges high prices on many of its flights to cities where it does not compete with SW. With Delta dropping Dallas as one of its hub markets in 2004, SW could benefit from flying more passengers from Dallas.[237]

SW is faced with the option of moving a portion of its operations to the large DFW airport dominated by American Airlines. SW is hesitant to move its operations to DFW or to split its operations for more than one reason. The airline avoids major hub airports as they charge higher fees and often experience delays due to heavy air and ground traffic. Kelly is calling for the repeal of the amendment, which he claims every Congressman to whom he has spoken agrees is a bad law. He speaks out strongly against it, claiming the amendment is "protectionist, anti-competitive, and anti-consumer." Analysts estimate that the repeal of this law would free up approximately $500 million in potential revenue for SW.[238]

In the wake of losing its eccentric founder, and looming industry problems, no one knows for sure if SW will remain profitable. Kelly is shaking things up at SW headquarters. Inside the company, Kelly is focusing on restructuring management for more accountability and cooperation between departments. Because SW's typically warm labor relations were recently frayed by bitter contract negotiations, Kelly created a new department focused on labor relations and now meets regularly with union leaders to discuss finances and strategy. Kelly made his boldest moves yet—the acquisition of six gates at Chicago's Midway Airport from the bankrupt ATA Holdings Corp. and the signing of a code-sharing agreement with ATA.[239] Now, SW customers can easily connect with ATA flights to cities such as Boston, Denver, Minneapolis, and Honolulu. Before this move, SW was one of the few airlines not to offer service through code-share partnerships. In 2005, SW planned to expand its fleet by 10 percent with the acquisition of 29 more planes, keeping to the belief that a main key to its future is a focus on continued growth.

Skeptics have criticized SW for years claiming that one day the start-up airline would get too big for its britches and finally start to falter, even if just a little bit. What is certain is the lasting impression that Kelleher and SW have left behind. Kelly plans to continue the tradition of Kelleher's business model. He recently announced that SW would not initiate any programs to sell meals or in-flight entertainment on board its aircraft, as many of its low-cost competitors do. Kelly says that charging passengers for additional services does not fit the SW business model. The low-cost, no-frills, fun, and flexible model is the one that works for SW.

SW's many years of profitability have been credited to its business formula of maintaining low costs and providing low fares with friendly customer service. It has the lowest costs per passenger mile in the US airline industry although its labor force is 80 percent unionized. SW has been able to achieve and maintain its low cost by: (a) flying only one type of aircraft, (b) achieving high worker productivity with employees assisting each other with routine duties, (c) flying point-to-point service to smaller and less costly airports, and (d) flying its airplanes more hours per day than the competition.

It was the only major US carrier to maintain a full flight schedule after September 11, 2001, and has not laid off any employees. The fact that employees own stock in the company also helps create employee loyalty, which translates to better customer service. SW plans to combat increasing competition in the industry through growth, not through changes in its proven business model. SW plans more expansion in the Northeast, evident by the recent move to start flights to Philadelphia and Pittsburgh.

Campaign to Repeal the Wright Amendment

The Wright Amendment was passed in 1979, restricting SW Airlines operations to the four states adjacent to Texas (New Mexico, Oklahoma, Arkansas, and Louisiana) from the Dallas Love Field Airport. It was later amended to include Kansas, Alabama, and Mississippi. The law was originally passed to protect the new Dallas-Fort Worth, Texas, airport from competition because of the high cost of building the new airport.

A campaign to repeal the Wright Amendment started in early 2005. SW's Kelly stated, "I don't care how long it will take, we'll keep after it until it falls under its own weight." SW rejected the option of moving its operation and headquarters from Love Field to the new Dallas-Fort Worth Airport. The new major airport did not fit its model of flying to small secondary airports with lower landing fees, less congestion, and faster turnaround times, all important aspects of the discounter's strategy. Since the September 11, 2001 tragedy, SW's business from Love Field has been shrinking as more people travel by car to nearby states. In contrast, the discount airline is rapidly expanding to other cities like Philadelphia and Chicago.[240]

SW created a new website, www.setlovefree.com, explaining that the Wright Amendment had long outlived its usefulness. The website claims that the restrictions imposed by this amendment is stifling competition and costing the public hundreds of millions of dollars per year in higher airfares. The website further explains that American Airlines is free to serve any market it chooses from the nearby Dallas-Fort Worth Airport. In fact, it flies to 49 cities from here, carrying over 6.5 million one-way passengers each year.

American Airlines has a virtual monopoly at Dallas-Fort Worth airport where it provides more than 80 percent of the flights. The website states that given American's monopoly position at Dallas-Fort Worth, the average business fare is 48 percent higher than at other airports in the United States, making it one of the most expensive airports in the country to fly from. The website explains that the public would save hundreds of millions of dollars per year if SW was permitted to fly to other states from Love Field. Repeal of the Wright Amendment would also attract new businesses to Dallas and increase visitors to the city.

Campbell-Hill, an aviation consulting firm, was hired to study the impact of the Wright Amendment on competition and public welfare. The report issued, called *The Wright Amendment Consumer Penalty* and dated June 7, 2005 stated that the

> Wright Amendment imposes an economic cost on travelers and communities throughout the United States by prohibiting competition from Dallas Love Field in air travel between North Texas and any point outside a seven-state perimeter.

The report further stated that if the Wright Amendment was repealed, permitting SW Airlines to make three daily roundtrip flights to 15 prohibited airports, the following benefits would be realized:

- 3.7 million more passengers would travel in the 15 markets each year due to new competition and lower fares.
- Passengers would save nearly $700 million annually compared to airfares charged by American at Dallas/Fort Worth Airport without competition from SW from Love Field.
- North Texas would reap an additional $1.7 billion in economic activity annually due to increased air travel to the region.
- The total Wright Amendment Burden on Passengers, North Texas, and cities beyond the seven-state perimeter exceeds $4.4 billion per year.[241]

The Dallas-Fort Worth Airport is the fifth-largest airport in the world. American's monopolistic position at the airport is clearly contrary to public interest, while competition from SW from Love Field would create huge public benefits. In fact, if it was not for American's monopoly position and premium fares from Dallas-Fort Worth, the carrier could be in a serious financial situation, as are most of the major airlines.

EXPANSION IN EXISTING MARKETS AND MOVEMENT EASTWARD

SW has recently expanded its flights from Chicago's Midway Airport, located just 10 miles south of downtown Chicago instead of the very busy and more distant Chicago O'Hare International Airport. O'Hare is one of the biggest airports in the world and is dominated by United Airlines and American Airlines. SW is in the process of shattering the duopoly of United and American at O'Hare. SW expanded its position at Midway through the purchase of six gates from the bankrupt ATA in December 2004, giving it a total of 25 gates from Midway. In addition, SW purchased a 27.5 percent share in ATA and developed a code-sharing agreement with it.[242]

Hawaii is an important recreational destination and one that has helped separate the major airlines from the discounters. Competitors have often belittled SW's frequent-flier program for not providing service to Hawaii. SW has studied the possibility of using its longer-range 737s to fly to Hawaii, but the airline was not large enough to compete efficiently on more distant international flights. However, ATA, with which it developed a code-sharing agreement, flies the larger 160-passenger Boeing 737-800 airplanes to Honolulu from Los Angeles, San Francisco, Phoenix, and Seattle and to Maui from Los Angeles, San Francisco, and Seattle. Through its code-sharing agreement with ATA, SW is now able to offer connecting flights from Midway to two cities in Hawaii. For example, customers can purchase a ticket in Baltimore on SW and fly to Midway, and then change to ATA's Hawaiian flights and have their baggage automatically transferred.[243]

Historically, SW tried to fly under the radar of the major airlines. Under the guidance of Kelleher, the discounter had avoided direct competition with the long-established airlines by flying to secondary airports. However, under the direction of Kelly, SW has been willing to go after weaker network carriers at major airports. According to an industry consultant, "SW's stated goal is to attract more business travel," and to "Serve businesses, you need to reach all the nation's largest cities."[244] Through the code-sharing agreement with ATA, SW is now able to provide service from Boston, Denver, Minneapolis, Newark, San Francisco, and Washington Reagan National.[245] ATA flies from Midway to New York's LaGuardia Airport 10 times a day and five times a day to Newark. It also flies five round trips daily to Boston and four to Washington, D.C.'s Reagan National Airport.[246]

With the purchase of the six gates from ATA in July 2005, SW increased its number of flights from Midway to 192 a day, boosting Midway to the discounter's third largest airport. SW is considering further expansion of its flights from Midway, which would make it the airline's largest hub in the country. This would shatter the duopoly that United Airlines and American Airlines have long held in Chicago, and would lower fares and attract a portion of its lucrative business-traveler base. SW is also consider-ing increasing its Chicago flights by another 30 percent to close to 250 daily departures. This would be close to the capacity of United and American at O'Hare International Airport. According to SW's Mr Sweet, the company plans to fill its planes with people who have not flown before as well as business travelers drawn by its prices, and Midway's proximity to downtown Chicago. He adds that "The Chicago market in itself is just very inviting," and, "It doesn't hurt that the industry is in the state that it's in and we're in

a good financial position to actually grow."[247] Furthermore, if ATA folds, SW could purchase its eight remaining
gates and become an even more powerful force in the
important Chicago market.

The two newest markets in SW's eastward march are
Philadelphia (its 60th city) and Pittsburgh (its 61st city),
both of which used to be strongholds of US Airways. SW said
it was entering Philadelphia because of the unusually
high fares fliers were paying. The discount airline started
providing service from Philadelphia on May 9, 2004 with
13 flights to six nonstop destinations. Table 6.1 compares
the fares and traffic from the third quarter of 2004 (the
first full quarter SW operated in Philadelphia) to the third
quarter of 2003 in the discounter's top ten Philadelphia
markets. The table shows that fares dropped sharply on
several of the routes while the number of passengers
flying rapidly increased. This is known as the "SW Effect"
with many business and general-public passengers flying
when the discounter offers sharply lower fares in new
markets.

Although the government report cited in Table 6.1
focused on the 10 markets directly served by SW, the
impact of the discounter entering Philadelphia was far
more extensive. Several other markets, such as Oakland,
St Louis, Sacramento, Nashville, and San Diego, that SW
served indirectly also experienced a sharp decline in
fares. As a consequence, the overall fare premium in
Philadelphia declined sharply relative to average domestic fares—from more than 20 percent during the third
quarter of 2003 to –2 percent during the third quarter of
2004.[248] Given the positive response SW received, it
rapidly expanded its flights to 41 per day to 18 destinations
by February 2005. By the end of 2005, SW increased the
number of its flights to 51 a day, making Philadelphia one
of its fastest growing markets in its history.[249]

SW continued its expansion to the East when it began
service to Pittsburgh in May 2005 following its successful

Table 6.1: Change in Air Fares and Passengers on 10 Major Routes from Philadelphia Serviced by Southwest

Market	3rd Qtr. 2003 Average Fare ($)	3rd Qtr. 2004 Average Fare ($)	Percentage Change in Average Fare	3rd Qtr. 2003 Passengers per Day	3rd Qtr. 2004 Passengers per Day	Percent Change in Passengers per Day
Providence	328	57	-83	50	546	1002
Manchester	309	56	-82	43	473	1012
Raleigh/Durham	213	61	-71	201	731	264
Chicago	210	113	-46	992	1,512	52
Los Angeles	253	161	-36	623	1,002	61
Las Vegas	186	137	-26	538	911	69
Tampa/St. Pet.	127	105	-18	485	692	43
Orlando	118	102	-13	1,018	1,394	37
West Palm Beach	120	105	-12	225	355	58
Fort Lauderdale	107	104	-3	670	726	8

Source: *Southwest Expands to Philadelphia—Third Quarter 2004,* Office of Aviation and International Affair, Aviation Analysis. Domestic Aviation Competition Issue Brief No. 26.

penetration of US Airways' "fortress hub" in Philadelphia. Both Philadelphia and Pittsburgh were ideal cities for SW since most of its flights were 700 miles or less. SW started with ten flights a day:

- four flights from Pittsburgh and Philadelphia,
- four flights to Chicago Midway, and
- one flight a day to Orlando, Florida, and Las Vegas, Nevada.

Before SW started the service, US Airways had a monopoly on the heavily traveled route between Pittsburgh and Philadelphia. SW's one-way fare of $79 represented a 65 percent savings in comparison to the average fare offered by US Airways. Kelly said the sharp cutback in Pittsburgh flights and the "high-fare environment" made Pittsburgh a "perfect opportunity" for SW.[250]

According to SW's spokeswoman Whitney Eichinger, "Pittsburgh is performing outstandingly. It's been so strong for us, that we'll be adding service by the end of the year. We've had outstanding load factors."[251] Contributing to SW's success in quick penetration of both Philadelphia and Pittsburgh has been the high quality of its service in comparison to the bankrupt US Airways. US Airways, as it struggles to survive, has laid off thousands of employees and sharply reduced its routes in western Pennsylvania. Its quality ranking in early 2005 fell 9 percent to 57, the largest decline and the lowest level of the seven largest airlines. In contrast, SW, which had just started flying to Pittsburgh International Airport, had a 1 percent increase in its customer satisfaction score with an overall rating of 74. That was the highest in the industry for the seven largest airlines, and considerably above the average score of 66.[252]

Chapter Seven

The Resurrection of Frontier Airlines

EARLY HISTORY OF FRONTIER AIRLINES

FOR 40 years, Frontier Airlines served as Denver's hometown airline. Following its acquisition by upstart carrier People Express in 1986, it became one of the first experiments with low-cost, low-fare travel post deregulation. After the demise of People Express, Frontier was dormant for 7.5 years until it was restarted by a group of former Frontier executives in 1994. This new version of Frontier incorporated many elements of the low-cost discount airline model. Although it has seen many tough times in its 12 years of operation, it currently operates as a solid carrier with an emphasis on markets in the western two-thirds of the country. At the beginning of 2005, Frontier operated 48 aircrafts providing service to 42 destinations.

The word most commonly associated with Frontier is "resurrection." It is not often that a carrier that gets wiped out of the sky by financial turbulence can come back in any form, but Frontier has proven to be an exception. Over the years, Frontier has experienced a great deal of change in the airline industry. Although it has changed hands and has operated as several different corporate entities, the executives running Frontier today consider the "Spirit of the West" of the original Frontier to be a vital part of the new Frontier Airlines.

At first glance, Frontier does not appear to meet the standard model of a start-up carrier. The original Frontier was started in 1946 under the name Monarch Airlines. It flew as a full-service regional carrier based in Denver, and mostly served western cities. However, this version of Frontier encountered deep financial trouble in 1984 and lost $31.4 million during the year.[253]

The airline was forced to evaluate its options to stay alive and, in 1985, an employee buyout was seen as the answer to the airline's financial woes. However, the labor union was outbid first by Texas Air Corp, and then by People Express, one of the original low-cost carriers to develop after deregulation. People Express bought Frontier as part of its coast-to-coast expansion and hoped that its acquisition would open new western markets to the carrier. A year later, however, Frontier continued to lose money. This prompted the management of People Express to reduce airline services and costs so it could sharply lower its fares. Since a low-cost, low-fare approach had appeared to work for its parent company, Frontier simplified its price structure and cut costs wherever possible. It began to offer three tiers of pricing: premium, economy, and discount, which ranged from $29 to $119 and charged for meals and checked baggage. These modifications allowed People Express to boast that it offered low-cost travel to 43 states due to its merger with Frontier.[254]

Despite these adjustments, People Express faced dire financial circumstances, almost half of which were due to Frontier, which accounted for $28 million of People Express' $51 million first quarter losses in 1986.[255] In order to avoid a buyout by Texas Air Corp, People Express decided to sell Frontier to United Airlines for $146 million. However, when no agreement could be reached between Frontier's pilot union and United's executives, the deal was called off and People Express shut down Frontier. All 4,700 employees were furloughed and 42 planes grounded.[256] In late August of 1986, Frontier filed for

Chapter 11 protection, and a few weeks later, Texas Air bought People Express and all of Frontier's assets.[257] Under the new plan, Continental would operate all of Frontier's assets, the planes would be repainted, and the "Frontier" name would disappear.[258]

"I don't think they're ever going to come back now," noted Conrad Blomberg, president of the Rocky Mountain Chapter of the American Society of Travel Agents. "Once you stop an airline, it's pretty hard to start it up again," but Blomberg added that Frontier was just "too good of a company to die."[259] Seven and a half years later, a group of former Frontier officials headed by former Frontier President and Chairman, Hank Lund, announced that they had decided to resurrect the airline. "We'd like to think it has been sleeping for seven and a half years," said Bob Schulman, Vice President of Corporate Communications and the old airline's Public Relations Director. He also said that Frontier's name, coupled with pure jet service, would be a selling point of the airline.[260] The company wanted to fill a "ready-made niche," the service gap at the small and medium cities left when Continental phased out its Denver hub.[261]

THE REBIRTH

"What we've done is to resurrect the spirit of the old Frontier Airlines—not the company itself. We are a new company. We will be a little guy and look for modest growth," stated Schulman. He went on to explain some differences between the new Frontier and the old Frontier:

> The former Frontier Airlines was known for its elaborate dining service. Steak and lobster were served on many flights, with free bottles of imported wine. We'll be several notches below that. We'll offer some nice hors d'oeuvres, pastry services, and some good snacks. But don't expect steak and lobster.[262]

Even with his detailed strategy, Lund needed capital to launch his new airline. For this reason, he turned to friend and former business partner Sam Addoms. Lund was convinced that Addoms' strong leadership and financial skills would be an asset. As it happened, Lund had earlier invested in one of Addoms' start-ups, Rio Grande Produce, which closed after just nine months and lost all of its investors' money. "I figured I owed him a favor," Addoms remarked. He admitted he knew nothing about the airline industry but said he had always had the heart of an entrepreneur.

At the start of his career, Addoms saw that the life of an entrepreneur was fraught with financial risk, and he informed his wife that they had to plan to be able to live on $25,000 per year. So she was not terribly surprised when, after a meeting with Frontier's executives around their kitchen table, he told her that he would be working with them for a while; he also added that he would not receive a salary to begin with. So, with a background in banking, meat-packing, and groceries, Addoms went into the $100 billion US airline industry.[263] The small, start-up airline seemed to suit him. Six months after the original announcement, Addoms had raised $8.7 million—including a $6.9 million public-stock offering and $500,000 of the founders' own money.[264] The launch of the airline demonstrated the commitment and dedication of its founders; none of them took a paycheck during the first year.

On July 5, 1994, Frontier began operating with 175 employees and two Boeing 737 twin-jet airplanes. To give the illusion of a larger fleet, the company painted different 21-foot animals on each side of the tail of its airplanes. The tagline, "Spirit of the West," was intended to convey the carrier's attitude of being open and friendly in the way it conducted business.[265] "This company was founded with basically the same goodwill and the people's spirit of the old Frontier, which was like a good neighbor and a friend."

While some people thought of the tagline "Spirit of the West" as a geographic connotation, it was actually intended to convey the attitude of the new airline and its employees.[266] It was the goal of Diane Willmann, Director of Advertising, to create a friendly personality for the fledgling airline.

In the beginning, Frontier provided service between four cities in North Dakota and Denver: Grand Forks, Fargo, Bismarck, and Minot. The original plan was to enter into an agreement with either Continental or United to transfer connecting passengers to destinations across the country on one of the other airlines. However, Continental almost completely pulled out of Denver just after Frontier began operations. Faced with almost no competition, United saw no need to cooperate with Frontier.[267] Predictably, without easy connections in Denver, few passengers were interested in Frontier's service.

In 1995, Addoms became CEO when Lund returned to Arizona to be with his ailing wife. Due to the lagging traffic in the small markets that Frontier served, 1995 also marked a shift in strategy by flying to larger markets, including Chicago and Phoenix. This new strategy of providing lower fares to people flying from Denver to other large cities posed a direct challenge to United Airlines. To keep from being wiped out of the sky by the dinosaur airline, Frontier avoided antagonizing United by pricing only slightly below United's fares, flying at different times, and flying only a few trips per day to each city, leaving United feeling less threatened.[268]

This strategy also meant that the airline would cut its service to smaller markets. "The economics just weren't there for continued service to smaller Montana and North Dakota markets," Schulman advised.[269] The shift in philosophy from "providing low-cost jet service to small- and medium-sized western markets" to "fly to big cities with low fares"[270] proved to be a good idea by the first half of 1996, when the fledgling company of 675 employees and nine 737s reported a profit of $2 million. Frontier attributed its increased earnings to "concentration on mainstream routes from the airline's Denver hub rather than on secondary markets." This transition marked a move from being a default carrier for travelers when the major airlines were booked to a "carrier of choice." It also allowed the airline to connect passengers through its Denver hub. A passenger could fly from Chicago to Denver on a Frontier flight and then to Phoenix on another Frontier flight, without the hassle of switching airlines.[271]

THE WESTERN PACIFIC AIR FIASCO

The leadership of Sam Addoms proved invaluable. In 1997, Western Pacific Airlines moved its operations from Colorado Springs to Denver International Airport. Realizing there was not room enough for two discount carriers at Denver airport, Frontier and Western Pacific agreed to merge. This new airline would challenge United on multiple routes and create new demand by offering lower fares. Addoms would also retire, and the Frontier name would once again disappear. "Nobody on our side felt good about it. But it was for the survival of our employees," Addoms said.[272]

However, Addoms took a close look at Western Pacific's finances and realized that the company was consistently missing its targets. He called off the merger one week before Western Pacific declared bankruptcy. Although the reports that came out of the final meeting accredited the termination of the merger agreement to be due to "differences in operating style," it was actually the signs of looming disaster that led Addoms away from the deal. His successor, Jeff Potter, later wrote, "Sam is the most astute businessman I've met. Once it hit him that it was not going to work, he made a quick decision." This ordeal reflects the business style that Addoms employed to guide his company—he used conservative business principles to do what was best for the company, yet he was bold enough to make big decisions in order to pull his airline out of danger.[273]

STRATEGY AND MANAGEMENT

Frontier shook free of the Western Pacific fiasco in time to post a $2.5 million profit for the third quarter of 1999. Addoms attributed this success to improvements in schedules, new aircraft, new major markets, and execution of its own ground handling at Denver, which was expected to result in $1 million in annual cost savings. In 1999, Frontier had succeeded in building a strong niche in Denver (which was a prime market), had an adequate $25.1 million in cash, and was virtually debt free. These assets made Addom's annual growth plan of 20 percent seem entirely feasible.

In fact, it was Addom's legendary frugality that was a major factor in the airline's success. Although mocked at times for the extent to which he cut costs, Addom's tight cost structure got results. For example, Addoms insisted that workers at the company headquarters receive his personal permission before using the color printer. Similarly, his low-cost mindset also extended beyond the office. He diligently sought to maintain excellent relationships with his employees, and it paid off. A partly non-unionized workforce and strict budgeting resulted in Frontier's costs to be 25 percent less than United's.[274] In order to achieve more cost efficiency, Frontier decided to purchase 20 narrow-body jets from Airbus Industrie. These A319 jets had greater fuel efficiency and lower maintenance costs than the old Boeing 737s they replaced. They also had 45 percent more overhead bin space and a wider fuselage, meaning wider seats and a wider center aisle.[275]

Other reasons for success also include the solid management behind the airline. Aviation consultant Terry Trippler praises Frontier's pricing strategy thus:

> Frontier will not price below break-even. They came into
> Minneapolis, and they were way below Northwest fares.
> Then Sun Country came in and offered rock-bottom fares.
> Frontier stuck it out. Sun Country went belly-up, and
> Frontier is still thriving. It is established, well-run, and
> profitable.[276]

Addoms' business plan was one of steady growth with an
emphasis on customer service and employee relations.[277]
In order to build employee loyalty, he embraced an "open
and candid" management philosophy. "In the context of
the tension-filled relationship between employer, shareholders, and employees, employees have to be the key,"
said Addoms. According to Potter, "Sam has a policy of no
secrets. He says for people to feel part of something
special, there can't be secrets." Addoms insisted on building meeting-room space and company headquarters without walls. He added, "You never know when an employee
might hear something that can benefit them personally
or improve company operations in some way." In 2002,
Addoms received the Daniel L. Ritchie Award, one of four
Colorado Ethics in Business Awards given to individuals,
businesses, and nonprofit organizations committed to
ethics, social responsibility, and community service.[278]

When Addoms retired, Potter learned a great deal from
Addoms, but brought his own passion to the industry. He
quit college in the mid-1980s to clean airplanes for the
original Frontier in Spokane. From there, he became a
station manager, ticket agent, and worked at the company
headquarters where he discovered scheduling, pricing,
and route planning—the heart of the airline industry.
After the original Frontier shut down in 1986, his career
included stints at Pacific Southwest, Continental, Northwest, and McDonnell Douglas Corp. He returned to the new
Frontier in 1995 as Vice President of Marketing and
helped Frontier get on track. Potter was attracted by
Frontier's working environment, which he believes differ-
entiates it from other airlines: "I like the culture and

atmosphere at Frontier. With Addoms as my mentor, we set out together on a plan to grow and focus on what we are here to do."[279]

THE WAR WITH UNITED

The growth and success of Frontier is seen as a remarkable phenomenon. Not only was it built from the ground up and started with only two aircrafts, but it has also been successful in the shadow of United at one of its stronghold hubs, Denver International Airport. It is one of the few start-up carriers to compete successfully head-to-head with a major carrier in one of its hub airports.

How has Frontier managed to survive and grow in an environment dominated by United? In the beginning, Frontier was designed to serve markets that United did not, therefore reducing tension between the carriers. However, when Frontier changed its focus to larger markets, United started paying attention. As soon as United started taking note of Frontier and restructuring prices and routes, Addoms began complaining to anyone who would listen about United's "predatory pricing." He accused United of practices such as switching to bigger airplanes on overlapping routes, selling more seats below cost, and even undercutting Frontier's low fares.[280] Frontier claimed that United undercut already-low prices to drive out new airlines and then increased them as soon as the newcomer left the market.[281] Although the Justice Department never found United guilty of these charges, United backed off once the noise got too loud. Addoms had made another good play.

Some analysts attribute Frontier's improbable success to its business philosophy that "owes something to Cold War-style propaganda and espionage." Frontier uses its cleverness to chip away as much business as it can get away with by anticipating United's moves and counter-moves. For example, instead of trying to swamp a market with flights, Frontier learned that if it flew only two times a day to a city, then United was not likely to cut its price and increase its capacity. In addition, Frontier timed its flights to arrive and depart outside United's banks of connecting flights. Another way that Frontier "outsmarted" United was through timing. For instance, when Frontier was ready to announce an increase in service to Portland, Oregon, the discounter waited until United had already loaded its summer schedule into its computer system to make the announcement. Consequently, after the announcement, United's flight schedule remained unchanged.[282] In this case, Frontier's flexibility and anticipation enabled it to stay one step ahead of United.

The other weapon Frontier used against United was price. Frontier priced below, but not too far below, United's fares. The fares were set high enough so that United would not retaliate and abandon its higher fares. Potter claims that:

> We understand United as well as United does, and what sets them off. We can coexist. There's never been any agreement over competitive boundaries, but we learned where to fill in. Frontier doesn't offer as many nonstops as the majors do, but we are a bit more aggressive on price.[283]

Frontier's tight cost control is what allowed it to price successfully below United. Whereas United has multiple hubs and many different types of service, Frontier has one hub and one class of service. The simple nature of its operations contributes to its lower operating costs. Data from Roberts, Roach & Associates for 1999 showed that Frontier's 737 operating costs beat United's but were higher than SW's for distances up to 950 miles. Above that distance, the difference between the two grew rapidly in Frontier's favor. Frontier's cost structure continued to become more efficient as it gradually built its all-Airbus fleet, made improvements in schedules, and found other ways to cut costs. All these factors helped to create a lower cost structure that allowed Frontier to sell its tickets cheaper than United. Aviation specialist Andrew Watterson observed that "It costs more for United to fight them than to leave them alone, which has allowed Frontier to get great margins and flourish in a market that United dominates."[284]

The dynamics between Frontier and United changed when United launched Ted, its discount airline-within-an-airline in February 2003. Ted, an effort to speed United's emergence from bankruptcy, was created specifically to compete for leisure-travel dollars with other discount carriers such as Frontier. The day Ted was launched, Frontier executives personally served donuts and coffee in front of Frontier's gates to thank and greet passengers and show that it was still the friendliest airline. However, Frontier did not seem terribly concerned about the new competition. "United has always matched our fares, so it's not really anything different," Joe Hodas, a spokesman for Frontier, noted.[285] Ted illustrated its price-matching ability when it matched Frontier's cap of $299 for every one-way fare.[286]

POST SEPTEMBER 11 STRATEGIES

Frontier executives breathed a sigh of relief when all eight Frontier planes that were in the air on the morning of September 11, 2001 landed safely. Frontier then turned its mind to the task of protecting its airline from the expected turbulent times ahead. "We're going to start at the top with pay cuts," Addoms announced. Senior executives agreed to pay cuts ranging from 20 to 40 percent. In addition, Frontier decided to ground four planes and cut its flight schedule by 20 percent. A total of 393 employees were furloughed, and the pilots' union took an 11 percent pay reduction to avoid further job cuts. To make it brutally simple, all executives were told they had 24 hours to cut their department budgets by 20 percent.

Frontier's small size, flexibility, and conservative financial approach gave it an advantage over the competition. In the months following September 2001, Frontier came up with some creative ideas to handle the decline in sales. It determined that if it was going to lose money flying nearly empty planes around the country, it might as well drum up some goodwill. So, it started a program called "Seats for Sharing," which offered free tickets to worthy Colorado organizations that applied by October 31 and demonstrated how the travel would benefit the community.[287] One group to use this deal was a fifth-grade class that had the opportunity to fly to Kansas City and visit the Negro League Baseball Museum while they were learning about the Negro Leagues in class. Other groups to apply included religious organizations and non-profit organizations.

In June 2002, Frontier asked the Federal Air Transportation Stabilization Board (ATSB) for $59.5 million in guarantees to back a $70 million line of credit it was trying to arrange. This application was filed under the loan-guarantee program that Congress approved after the September 11 terrorist attacks, to help stabilize the airline industry.[288] In December 2003, Frontier became the first airline to repay its federal loan under the program. Frontier made a required payment of $10 million in July 2003 with its federal tax refund and a second loan payment of $48.6 million in September 2003 with the proceeds from the company's common stock offering. According to Democratic Representative Diana Degette, "Everyone at Frontier Airlines should be proud of being the first airline in the nation to pay off its federal loan. It is a testament to the current and future success of the airline and all its employees."[289]

SHIFT FROM BUSINESS TO LEISURE MARKETS

Frontier's initial strategy focused on attracting a large base of business passengers by developing contracts with corporations that would provide air service at attractive prices. However, after September 2001, Frontier noticed a significant decline in business traffic and an increase in leisure customers. As a result, Frontier decided to offer nonstop flights to top Mexican resort cities in December 2002.[290] These routes proved to be extremely successful, and in many cases, Frontier was the only airline serving these routes. Frontier now flies to Cancun, Cabo San Lucas, and Mazatlan—none of which previously had daily nonstop service from Denver. Of course, it did not hurt that the Denver International Airport offered Frontier $25,000 in marketing subsidies for each Mexican market it served.[291]

At the same time, Frontier cut back on traditional business routes. In August 2002, it canceled its two daily flights between Denver and Boston. This redistribution of routes seems to be an industry trend, at least in Denver. Sean Donohue, Vice President for United's mountain region, observed, "We're all fine-tuning our schedules and redeploying aircraft into markets where we're going to be more profitable." This ability to alter strategy and re-allocate resources is what enables airlines to stay afloat in the dynamic airline industry.[292] The Mexico expansion was part of a broader effort by Frontier to start flying beyond continental US. It also established flights to Anchorage in May 2004.[293]

CODE-SHARE AGREEMENTS

One method used by Frontier to reach smaller markets was to sign code-sharing agreements with small feeder airlines. In September 2001, Frontier signed an agreement with Mesa Air Group, under which Frontier would market and sell flights operated by Mesa as Frontier JetExpress. Initially, Mesa flew five 50-seat jets to eight new destinations, expanding the possible routes that Frontier customers could fly. However, in July 2003, Mesa was forced to end its agreement with Frontier due to its new contract with United, which carried a non-compete clause.[294]

To compensate for this loss, Frontier extended its code-sharing agreement with Great Lakes Aviation to cover 36 markets.[295] However, Great Lakes did not operate regional jets, but instead offered service on turboprop planes. Although the substitution of a turboprop for a jet added only just 15 minutes of flight time, many passengers perceived the flights to be much slower and less reliable. It became such an issue that a customer in Wichita, Kansas, almost rioted when Frontier replaced its regular jet service with turboprop service to cut costs and allocate its jets to larger markets.

To overcome the objection to turboprop service, Frontier signed an agreement in September 2003 with Horizon Air, a subsidiary of Alaska Air, which operated a fleet of regional jets. The service provided by Horizon Air is called Frontier JetExpress, and permits Frontier to offer jet service to many smaller markets. These flights are booked through Frontier and used primarily to serve markets in the Midwest and Western United States. Meanwhile, Great Lakes' turboprop planes have been re-allocated to serve still smaller markets in North Dakota, South Dakota, Texas, and the states immediately bordering Colorado.

LOSSES AND NEW PRICING STRATEGY

Despite numerous cost-cutting measures, Frontier began sustaining losses in the first quarter of the fiscal year 2003.[296] Frontier's CASM, or cost per available seat mile, fell 11.3 percent to 8.28 cents (including fuel). However, the losses were attributed to diminished demand due to the sustained economic downturn, global uncertainties, and an extremely competitive industry environment.[297] These factors, combined with high fuel expenses, low fares, and the entry of other low-cost carriers into the marketplace, created a tough operating environment for Frontier in 2003.

Frontier responded to these losses with a new pricing strategy that simplified its fare structure to offer six fares levels. It also eased restrictions by eliminating the requirements of advance purchases, Saturday-night stayovers, or round-trip ticket purchases to avail lower fares. These fares were all capped at $499 each way. A two-week test of this new fare structure showed that the airline was able to draw more business travelers. Although on average, they paid lower fares, the net effect was a boost in revenue.[298]

This strategy paid off by June of 2003 when Frontier rebounded with increased traffic, filling up to 75.6 percent of its seats. It continued with this program in January 2004, slashing fares further to a cap of $299 each way. However, Frontier continued to post losses. The airline cut its costs by 7 percent compared with the previous year, but high fuel prices wiped out most of that gain. In fact, Frontier's unit costs, excluding fuel were, for the first time lower than SWs.[299]

In an effort to cut costs further in the wake of losses, Frontier decided to institute a fuel-hedging program similar to SW's to combat the rising fuel costs. It also continued its transition to an all-Airbus fleet, which significantly cut operating costs.[300]

Frontier's overall strategy was to maintain a low-cost structure while differentiating its service and continuing to grow. CFO Paul Tate explained:

Since September 11, this company has significantly reduced its unit costs relative to others in the industry. We took out a lot of overhead costs that have not come back. Our strategy post September 11 is to continue our growth plan. We have really utilized our economies of scale as we ratcheted down our overhead costs.

However, Frontier was not forced to cut labor costs. The airline continued with its growth plan of 15 to 18 percent per year despite its losses.[301] Although the losses continued into 2004, analysts agreed that strong cost control was an encouraging sign for an airline.[302]

Potter summarized the airline's dilemma when he commented,

> We tried to develop a plan for this company that even in the worst of times would be at least break even, and I think we have. Our only problem was no one, *no one*, ever could have contemplated what the worst of times would bring.[303]

STRUGGLE FOR GATES

In August 2003, Frontier leased 10 gates at Denver International Airport to facilitate the airline's pressing need to maximize usage of its growing fleet of airplanes. United, which was at the time trying to emerge from Chapter 11 bankruptcy, refused to give up any gates on Concourse A, which Frontier claimed it was not fully using. Thus began a three-way struggle between Frontier, United, and the Denver International Airport. United wanted a regional jet facility and refused to give up its gates on Concourse A which Frontier desperately needed. The airport—young, deeply in debt, not wanting to upset United, had no option but to increase its gates on Concourse A.[304]

In December 2003, with the situation in Denver deadlocked, Frontier decided to expand beyond its Denver hub to maximize the use of its expanding fleet of airplanes. In a decision marking a major strategic shift, Frontier made plans to connect Los Angeles directly to Kansas City, St Louis, and Minneapolis. However, the airline made it clear that Los Angeles was a "focus city," not another hub.[305] In the beginning of 2004, Denver International Airport decided to spend a $137 million on expansions, making concessions to both Frontier and United. This agreement resulted in Frontier obtaining 16 new gates and United gaining a new regional jet facility.[306]

By June 2004, Frontier operated 49 point-to-point departures from Los Angeles. But with more gates available in Denver and incredibly intense competition in Los Angeles, in August Frontier decided to reduce the frequency of its flights to and from Los Angeles by 60 percent.[307] Frontier claimed that its increased frequency to and from Los Angeles was merely seasonal, and the schedule changes were anticipated for the fall and winter months.

MARKETING EDGE

From the launch of the new Frontier in 1994, the airline had sought to differentiate itself on the basis of its culture. When Frontier hired Genesis, a marketing firm, to develop an identity for the fledgling company, it did not have much money, and Genesis actually charged Frontier less than its normal rate because it believed in the airline. Genesis gave them the idea to paint animals on the tails of Frontier's planes, an idea embraced by the airline because it "encapsulated the spirit of the company Addoms had created," according to Genesis director James Adler.

Frontier hired a new advertising agency in late 2002 that was a division of Grey Worldwide. The goal was to build a stronger national profile as a carrier that offers quality service along with lower fares. Ian Arthur, Frontier's Director for Marketing and Brand Management, noted, "The airline industry is in turmoil right now, and we're one of those airlines well-positioned to redefine what the industry can be. Our new advertising will be a vehicle to communicate what our difference is." The new advertising campaign was designed to stress Frontier's quality service, 35-route network, Airbus fleet, and personal TV sets on new planes.[308] The seat-back TV sets were installed in Frontier's new Airbus fleet in October 2002 in the hope to emulate JetBlue's success with a similar program. Frontier's program, however, charges five dollars for use of the DirecTV programming, while JetBlue charges nothing.

In the middle of 2003, Frontier launched its "Whole Different Animal" ad campaign to replace the older "Spirit of the West" campaign. This campaign gave new life to traditional aspects of the airline, such as the 21-foot animals that adorn the tails of the aircraft. The biggest hits were the TV commercials where the animals talk to each other and joke around. In one, Larry the cougar chides the dolphin for not getting the desired route to Florida, despite Frontier's extensive schedule there. The commercials gave the animals unique personalities while working in different ways to exhibit the less well-known features of the airline, such as its coast-to-coast capabilities.[309]

In 2003, the ads contributed to a 50 percent leap in brand recognition. They created a sensation, especially in Frontier's hometown of Denver. Parents say that kids get excited when they fly, and ask which animal they will get on their plane, and people call the airline with the express purpose of commenting on how much they like the ads. However, the success of the ads is not solely due to the fact that the animals are cute and cuddly, said Grey Worldwide creative director Graham Button. He added:

> They resonate on a deeper level than that. When the animals line up at the airport gates and catch up with each other like friends do, it creates a sense of community and bringing people together, which is what the airline industry is about. This is a new way of doing airline business.

He went on to reveal the psychology behind the ads:

> The secret to the airline is that every plane has an individual, different animal. It shows the airline recognizes the difference between flights and the difference between planes,

and therefore, it translates into "the airline recognizes the difference between individual passengers." People are fed up with being treated like cattle.[310]

In conjunction with the ads, Frontier initiated several new promotions to attract travelers. In 2003, it signed agreements with many of Denver's professional sports teams and all of the major universities to sponsor sporting events and arenas. Although most of these promotions are aimed at Denver travelers, Frontier also started programs to attract out-of-state travellers. One such agreement with Vail Resorts allows skiers to buy a season pass that enables them to fly any number of times to Colorado during the winter season.[311] In 2004, it joined Intrawest Corp. in a similar market partnership that gave skiers at Winter Park and Copper Mountain discount airfares and frequent-flyer miles, with Frontier flyers also getting good deals on the slopes.[312]

In early 2004, Frontier also launched a program designed to attract valuable customers from other airlines. Frontier's Quick Ascent program gave preferred seating, priority check-in, and a waiver of the 15,000-mile requirement to join the Ascent level of its frequent-flyer program, Early Returns, to target customers who travel at least 25,000 miles annually. These travelers are the most prized in the industry, and Frontier's attempt to target them posed a direct challenge to United.[313] Under the normal Early Returns program, travelers earn a round trip ticket to any destination in the country for every 15,000 miles they fly on Frontier.

As another strategy of its rebranding effort, Frontier redesigned its in-flight entertainment in 2004. It had a three-fold approach. First, it replaced its in-flight magazine with a "lifestyle" magazine called *Wild Blue Yonder*. Similarly, it launched its own channel of onboard movies, also called *Wild Blue Yonder*. These movies are not just short films; they are part of Frontier's "Cloud 9 Short Film

Festival," in which passengers judge the short films. In order to vote for their favorite films, buy gifts, or enter contests, passengers can visit the related website, www.gowildblueyonder.com. A Denver marketing firm, Mphasis Integrated, spent nearly $1.5 million to develop the magazine, TV channel, and website. In exchange, the marketing firm splits advertising revenues with Frontier; still a money-maker for Frontier since the airline formerly received no revenue at all from its old in-flight magazine.[314]

Vice President of Marketing and Planning, Sean Menke, summarized his vision of Frontier's image:

> We are not the 'old' Frontier, an airline acquired by People Express in 1986. We are not the Frontier of 1994. People have to understand that we are a coast-to-coast carrier. We are a niche carrier, but we now provide new Airbus aircraft, DirecTV on board, a good product, including food service, good fares, and we are a friendly airline.

Figure 7.1 illustrates Frontier's financial data over its years of operation through the third quarter of the fiscal year 2005. The first few years of operations represented

Figure 7.1: Profitability of Frontier Airlines

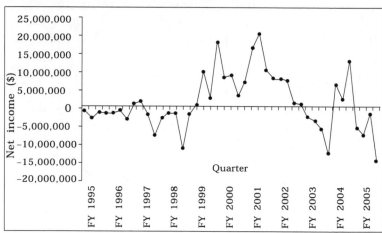

a period of sustained losses. However, the leaders of Frontier, Addoms and Potter, orchestrated a strategy to make the young airline return a profit by reassessing the markets it served and constantly evaluating Frontier's cost structure.

When analyzing Frontier's financial data, it is important to remember that the airline's fiscal year ends on March 31 every year. Therefore, the effects of the terrorist attacks of September 2001 can be seen only in the second quarter of Frontier's fiscal year 2002. Despite turbulence in its early years and also during the early part of the millennium, Frontier has managed to make forays into the realm of profitability after each drop in income. Frontier's ability to rebound from its serious losses demonstrates sound management. Although its profits have fluctuated, Frontier has remained on a steady path of well-planned growth.

In fact, the company grew from 180 employees in 1994 to 4,200 in 2004.[315] Frontier also increased its traffic from 22.9 million revenue passenger miles in December 1994 to 567.3 million revenue passenger miles in December 2004.

During the same time period, Frontier's load factor increased from 49.8 percent to 70.6 percent. This represents not only a vast expansion of service, but also an increase in the extent to which Frontier has been able to use its aircraft. The airline currently operates 48 aircrafts to 42 destinations. However, as Frontier expands, it is adamant about not losing its friendly neighborhood culture.

"We're more structured these days, but our heart is still intact," said Dianne Willmann, Director of Advertising. Eberwein, Frontier's Vice President of Communications, noted that the airline's philosophy has always emphasized that customer service must go hand-in-hand with low fares, and not to be inhibited by them. She added, "We offer low fares, but we don't crowd people in our planes like cattle. Our philosophy has always been to keep it simple."[316] Frontier plans to continue to grow while providing its customer good service and affordable fares.

Something about this two-pronged approach has seemed to work for Frontier. On the one hand, the company focuses on cutting costs and maintaining a tight cost structure, thus allowing it to slash fares. On the other, the airline emphasizes customer service; it focuses on making the Frontier travel experience as attractive as possible. While executing these objectives, Frontier projects its image in the marketplace by stressing both these aspects. This image appeals to both the budget traveler as well as the traveler looking for a comfortable flying experience. The result is a thriving start-up airline in the hub of a major competitor.

It helps that United has been in bankruptcy for three years. As part of its plan to emerge from bankruptcy, United is looking for ways to reduce its costs and has indicated that it might reduce its service in Denver and concentrate on its other hubs. Accordingly, Frontier would be the likely primary beneficiary if United cuts back its operations in Denver as Delta did in Dallas.

Chapter Eight

AirTran Airways: Overcoming Tragedy to Become an Industry Leader

VALUJET AIRLINES: PREDECESSOR TO AIRTRAN AIRWAYS

FLORIDA'S TOURISM industry attracted tens of thousands of travelers a year in the early 1990s. Most of the tourists flying from Atlanta to Florida had little choice but to fly Delta Air Lines, although its fares had sharply increased in recent years. As Delta's fares climbed, tourists began looking for other means of traveling to their Florida retreats, and some opted either to drive or fly small charter airlines. The under-served price-sensitive segment of the market provided an opportunity for a small discount airline to come in.

Four industry veterans founded ValuJet in 1993: Robert Priddy, Lewis H. Jordan, Tim Flynn, and Maurice Gallagher. Priddy had 11 years of experience with airlines, including eight years with Atlantic Southeast Airlines of which he was a co-founder.[317] Jordan had 30 years experience in the industry, including a term as president of Continental Airlines.[318] Flynn and Gallagher were two of the co-founders of WestAir, a California-based regional airline. The four originally planned to set up a charter service airline, but after observing the operations of Morris Air, a low-cost carrier later acquired by SW, decided to offer scheduled air service instead.

ValuJet marketed itself to leisure travelers who would otherwise drive to their destinations in Florida. In Jordan's words, the airline sought to lure "some of the 20-million vacationers who drive to Florida every year out of their cars and into a DC-9 for less than $100." To help keep costs low, ValuJet acquired two inexpensive old DC-9s from a fleet of jets retired by Delta Air Lines.[319] To attract leisure passengers, the airline cultivated a laid-back cabin atmosphere with flight attendants wearing golf shirts, khakis, and tennis shoes. Leather flying jackets were part of the pilot's uniform. ValuJet offered free soft drinks and peanuts, and hard drinks could be purchased.[320] Like SW, it allowed passengers to seat themselves on a first-come-first-serve basis.[321]

The airline started operating on October 26, 1993 with two old DC-9s making eight flights a day from Atlanta to three Florida destinations.[322] Its $49 fare was much less than what the major airlines charged to these destinations. Delta, the largest carrier flying from Atlanta's Hartsfield International Airport, initially matched ValuJet's fares hoping to drive the fragile start-up airline out of business, as was the practice of the old established airlines. However, Delta raised its fares after finding it was losing profits from lucrative connecting traffic through its Atlanta hub. Nor did Delta increase its capacity on ValuJet's routes, as other major airlines often did, to keep the small discounter from gaining enough traffic to make a profit. As ValuJet gained popularity in the following years, the consequences of these decisions began to plague Delta in the form of decreased business and leisure traffic.

ValuJet capitalized on an unmet demand of leisure travelers seeking low-fare flights to Florida. The airline generated a profit in its second full month of operation, bolstered by the southward winter travel rush. In documents filed with the US Department of Transportation prior to starting operations, the founders projected ValuJet would make an initial annual profit of $142,000.[323]

Instead, it produced a $20.7 million profit in its first year, a feat that took SW eight years to achieve.

ValuJet grew extremely fast and increased its fleet to 29 DC-9s by June 1994. The average age of the planes—all retired jets from Delta—was 20 years.[324] By November 1994, a week after its first anniversary, ValuJet had extended its service to 17 cities in the Southeast, including three new Florida destinations: Fort Lauderdale, West Palm Beach, and Fort Meyers. Its other 11 destinations were distributed such that it served, at most, two cities in each state.[325] ValuJet's second-year fourth-quarter profit topped $20 million.[326] Growth continued at a very rapid pace, and in June 1996 ValuJet flew 51 DC-9s to 31 destinations.[327]

ValuJet was able to expand rapidly since its service and fares met the needs of a large under-served leisure market. In December 1995, Jordan estimated that 75 percent of ValuJet's business came from its target market of leisure travel and 25 percent were business passengers. Business travelers were a major target market of the large airlines and they were upset to lose these customers to the discount airline. ValuJet closely monitored its expenditures, especially labor costs, so that it could provide low fares to attract price-sensitive leisure travelers. Its pilots earned between $42,000 and $45,000 a year, plus a maximum bonus of $20,000 and stock options. Its pay system was also time-based, so pilots and flight attendants were paid less if their flight was cancelled.[328]

ValuJet had acquired nearly all the available used DC-9s by the end of 1995, but this very successful discounter wanted to continue to expand and needed to acquire more airplanes. Thus, ValuJet placed an order with McDonnell Douglas for 50 MD-95-30ERs, which flew longer distances than its existing fleet of old aircraft. The $1 billion order included options for 50 more aircraft and made ValuJet the launch customer for the MD-95 program. The airline planned to begin receiving the new jets in mid-1999, but perhaps this was not quite soon enough.[329]

Disaster Strikes: The Crash of ValuJet Flight 592

On June 10, 1995, ValuJet Flight 597 was taxiing in preparation for takeoff when one of the DC-9's fuselage-mounted engines burst into flames. Pieces of a compressor disk penetrated the passenger cabin and seven people were injured in the incident. The Federal Aviation Commission carefully studied the incident. FAC officials announced that they had observed no shortfalls in ValuJet's maintenance practices, and the airline continued business as usual. Almost a year later, the airline was in the news again, and this time for a much more serious failure that would have far-reaching consequences.

On May 11, 1996, ValuJet Flight 592 crashed into the Florida Everglades, killing all 110 people aboard. Investigators determined that the DC-9 was carrying 119 supposedly empty oxygen generators in its forward cargo hold. The generators are commonly used on passenger aircraft to produce oxygen for air masks.[330] However, ValuJet was not authorized to carry the generators as cargo.[331] During the flight, oxygen gas was released in the cargo area, generating heat in excess of 500°F that created an explosion sending the plane into a fiery crash. None of the oxygen generators carried by Flight 592 had safety caps, which could have prevented them from heating up due to turbulence during the flight. ValuJet was shipping the generators from a Florida maintenance shop to Atlanta for refurbishment. Following the crash, the airline contended the canisters were indeed mislabeled "empty" by one of its maintenance subcontractors.[332]

Even before the crash occurred the Federal Aviation Administration (FAA) was investigating ValuJet. A 120-day re-certification inquiry had been prompted by an internal memo dated February 1996 that stated that 20 of the 48 violations ValuJet had incurred since 1993 were still unresolved. In the wake of the Everglades crash, the FAA increased its scrutiny of the carrier and made some disturbing discoveries. For example, the weather radar system of one airplane had been reported defective over 30 times before it was repaired. Another airplane had been flown seven times with a defective windshield, creating a risk of sudden decompression.[333] Investigators also reported deficiencies in the airline's quality control of the work performed by its numerous maintenance subcontractors. In addition, they found the airline's own maintenance operation was not appropriately staffed.

Although the FAA did not determine inadequate maintenance to have been a factor in the crash of Flight 592, it required ValuJet to shut down in June 1996. This shutdown was due to evidence showing the airline had knowingly flown aircraft with maintenance problems. The management agreed to suspend operations, since the FAA could have shut it down without its consent.[334] The once rapidly growing and highly successful discounter announced plans to lay off all but a few employees. Jordan still remained optimistic that ValuJet would begin operating again within a month. ValuJet's stock dropped 35 percent the day after the announcement.[335]

The FAA stipulated specific changes that the airline had to make before resuming operations. Before the accident, ValuJet used 60 maintenance subcontractors and 14 heavy maintenance contractors, prompting critics to call it a "virtual airline." The FAA directed ValuJet to reduce the number of contractors under its employment to 43 and 9, respectively. Because it had procured used planes, ValuJet operated aircraft with 11 different cockpit configurations. Thus, the FAA required that cockpits be redesigned so that each airplane would have the same layout. ValuJet was also asked to increase its oversight of the maintenance performed by contractors. In order to ensure it began performing industry-standard maintenance, the FAA assigned four more inspectors to the airline, bringing the total number to seven.

Unfortunately, ValuJet took slightly longer to get back on its feet than Jordan had hoped. The airline obtained recertification after a 58-day review on August 29, 1996.[336] At the end of September, ValuJet returned to the air with $19 fares and limited service from Atlanta to Fort Lauderdale, Tampa, Orlando, and Washington, D.C. Over the following three weeks, it reintroduced flights to 12 more cities. ValuJet's network included 26 cities before the crash. The airline's records showed that on April 30, 1996, it had $254 million in cash, a cushion it used to offset the losses incurred by offering such low introductory fares.[337] In the months since the incident, the public had come to associate the age of ValuJet's fleet (which had increased to an average of 25 years by May 1996) with the crash of Flight 592. Although unfounded, this connection would prove to be the greatest obstacle to ValuJet's comeback efforts.

After the crash, the airline's bookings dropped 42 percent below their prior level. As a consequence, ValuJet incurred a loss of $41 million in 1996 and began looking for another airline to merge with that would provide an opportunity to change its name. The carrier twice attempted to merge with Indianapolis, Indiana-based American Trans Air, but was rebuffed by ATA founder George Mikelsons.[338] A little more than a year after the crash of Flight 592, ValuJet successfully negotiated a merger with AirTran Airways, a Florida-based airline launched in October 1994.

AirTran initially provided service from Orlando International Airport to Hartford, Connecticut; Huntsville, Alabama; Knoxville, Tennessee; Newburg, New York; and Providence, Rhode Island.[339] The airline started with two 737-200s.[340] "Our whole business plan is targeted at Orlando and the leisure traveler," said John Horn, President and CEO of AirTran, in late 1995.[341] The airline's model was to provide non-stop service between Orlando and major cities that did not then have non-stop service to

Orlando.[342] Like ValuJet, AirTran contracted out its maintenance in order to keep costs down; it also contracted with larger carriers for baggage handling and ticketing, perhaps making it more of a "virtual airline" than ValuJet.[343] Its low fares caught the attention of vacationers, and by its first anniversary, AirTran had expanded to 17 cities and a seven-plane fleet.[344]

ValuJet acquired AirTran through a $61 million stock swap and the two airlines' combined network included 46 destinations and 238 daily flights.[345] ValuJet announced it would change its name to "AirTran Airlines." In October 1997, the new AirTran introduced itself with a fresh marketing slogan "It's something else."[346]

In the Shadow of ValuJet

After the merger, AirTran had difficulty maintaining its 60-percent break-even load factor and was forced to discontinue service to its most unpopular destinations. A preliminary FAA report published in January 1998 alleged it had uncovered new safety infractions within the airline. As a result, AirTran's stock dropped, traffic slowed, and its attempts to win back passengers along ValuJet's former routes were hurt.[347] AirTran increased its 1998 advertising budget by nearly 100 percent over the prior year, but it had little effect.[348] After the crash, it reported 11 consecutive quarterly losses before reporting a profit in the second quarter of 1998.[349] But that was only a temporary improvement and AirTran reported a $40 million loss for all of 1998.[350]

Part of the airline's difficulties stemmed from its operations out of Atlanta's Hartsfield Airport, Delta Airline's home turf. After ValuJet established itself and began attracting a following, Delta started matching its fares and continued to do so after the merger with AirTran. According to a Department of Transportation study, fares at Hartsfield dropped an average of 43 percent when AirTran started flying. Delta's network was big enough to allow it to take a hit on certain routes from Atlanta, while it made money on most of its other routes where it did not compete with AirTran. AirTran filed a complaint with the Department of Transportation, charging that Delta was using predatory pricing to hurt its recovery and stop its expansion.[351]

Some outside observers blamed AirTran's management for the airline's poor performance, and most agreed changes were needed. In early 1999, AirTran's board hired airline veteran Joseph Leonard as President and Chairman of the company, replacing Dr Joseph Corr and Robert Swenson, respectively.[352] Before joining AirTran, Leonard had held executive positions with American Airlines, Northwest, and AlliedSignal.[353] He had worked outside the airline industry for 10 years, but his most recent experience with the airline business was as Vice President of Operations for Eastern Airlines, just before and during its bankruptcy.[354]

Leonard, in his new job, had the tough assignment of winning concessions from unions, and Eastern declared bankruptcy when Leonard could not reach an agreement with striking pilots and machinists.[355] He could have appeased the unions and kept the airline afloat for a time, but he decided this was the wrong thing to do. Meeting the strikers' requests would have only allowed Eastern to stay in business long enough to go bankrupt from high costs. Leonard brought this certainty and fidelity to the bottom line with him when he became president of AirTran. Robert Fornaro succeeded him as president in March 1999, and Leonard became Chairman and Chief Executive Officer of the airline.[356]

AirTran's Comeback: Market Expansion, New Planes, and Lower Costs

AirTran needed to define itself as being distinct from ValuJet. On August 8, 2000, the cockpit of AirTran Flight

913 filled with smoke. The plane, a DC-9 built in 1970 for Turkish Airlines and later acquired by ValuJet, had to turn back.[357] On November 29, 2000, smoke entered the forward galley of AirTran Flight 956, forcing it to make an emergency landing. With the National Traffic and Safety Board (NTSB) officials out of view but still on site, AirTran employees cleaned the soot off the DC-9's fuselage after the crew and passengers had been evacuated. NTSB Chairman James Hall alleged this constituted tampering with a federal investigation and noted that the incident had similarities to the crash of ValuJet Flight 592.[358] Such incidents threatened to make the name of the floundering airline synonymous with that of its predecessor.

AirTran implemented a number of changes to assist in its recovery. It started reaching out to business travelers who are the most lucrative segment of the airline business. It developed cost-saving contracts with smaller businesses that were more price-conscious than larger firms. But AirTran was also able to develop favorable travel agreements with some larger Atlanta-based businesses including Home Depot, Coca-Cola Company, and BellSouth. To further assist its comeback, AirTran introduced its A-Plus frequent-flyer program which allowed its customers to earn free tickets more quickly than its competition. With its A-Plus Rewards program, its customers earned a free roundtrip ticket for every six business flights or twelve coach flights.[359] To make the program even more attractive, AirTran customers could redeem their frequent-flyer miles to fly on other airlines serving markets where it did not provide service.[360] The airline also began a marketing campaign targeted at the business community. As a consequence of several new programs, AirTran's business traffic doubled in 1999 from the previous year. A side effect of serving more business passengers is that it helped rebuild the airline's image.[361]

In 1999, AirTran started taking delivery of one new Boeing 717 a month. The Boeing 717s helped AirTran distance itself from its old DC-9 fleet whose reliability had been hurt in the wake of the Everglades crash and other smaller incidents. The purchase of the new jets reduced the average age of its airline's fleet from 22 years in the late 1990s to three years in 2003. AirTran then had one of the newest fleets in the industry, a fact that it proudly promoted and which helped rebuild its image.[362] The new fleet of Boeing 717s proved tremendously useful in lowering costs and strengthening the airline. The fuel consumption of the 717 was 24 percent less than the old DC-9. In addition, the 717s were much cheaper to service, and maintenance costs decreased by 37 percent.[363]

To lower costs further, AirTran became one of the first airlines to develop online ticketing, and by September 2000, the airline was obtaining one-third of its revenue through its website. In late 2000, a ticket booked online cost the airline 40 cents while one booked through a travel agent cost it over $9. The difference arose from the processing costs and commissions paid when booking a flight through a travel agent.[364] To lower reservation desk costs, the airline began investigating an automated telephone reserve system that would use voice recognition to handle calls, allowing a reduction in the labor necessary to run the system. The automated telephone reserve system was implemented and it not only reduced costs, but provided customers quicker service as well.[365]

One of the most important moves made by Leonard and Fornaro was to develop a hub at Hartsfield International Airport. AirTran reduced routes that did not fly through Atlanta, like Chicago–Washington, Boston–Washington, and Boston–Philadelphia, and added flights from Atlanta to Newark, Gulfport-Biloxi, and Myrtle Beach. The strategy worked, and by mid-2000, flights from Atlanta accounted for over half of AirTran's business. The discounter become the second largest carrier behind Delta, providing flights to and from Atlanta. In the coming years, AirTran would use its hub at one of the world's busiest airports to fly routes that would not be as viable on a direct basis.

While many of its cost-cutting moves took place behind the scenes, some of them were quite obvious to passengers. For instance, AirTran kept costs low by installing used furniture at its gates. This practice prompted passenger Jim Hightower to remark,

> If Atlanta's Hartsfield is their main hub—and they'd like to woo business travelers—they need to rethink their gate accommodations. Their waiting area is sparsely populated with what appears to be various styles of uncomfortable seats given away at dead-airline yard sales.[366]

But under the new management team, AirTran had renewed its dedication to providing travel at a low price. As Leonard said in 2001, "We have a very simple product. We don't try to pretend that we are an in-flight dining room."[367]

Riding out the Recession

From early 1999 to late 2001, AirTran posted 10 consecutive quarterly profits. According to a government report, the discounter saved Atlanta passengers $700 million in 2000 alone.[368] Due to the recession in 2001 and the terrorist attacks on September 11, 2001, airline demand fell sharply and remained sluggish in 2002. The six major airlines all reported large losses due to the weak demand for airline service, and major carriers like United Airlines and US Airways declared bankruptcy. However, AirTran continued to grow at rates comparable to those before the slowdown, due to its low-cost operations model.[369]

A major component of AirTran's discount model is lower labor costs. For example, in 2002 AirTran paid experienced pilots an annual salary of $136,000 as against $203,000 at American. Similarly, experienced AirTran mechanics received $56,000 per year while American paid $72,000.[370] AirTran also cross-trains its employees so they manage tasks in different areas, which also increases worker productivity.[371] Nonetheless, AirTran maintains good relations with its workforce, allowing it to secure temporary concessions after the 2001 downturn. AirTran negotiated an agreement with the National Pilots Association for a reduction in minimum guaranteed flight times and salaries. In exchange for the agreement, which provided for a 22 percent reduction in pilot-related costs, AirTran promised not to lay off any pilots. Mechanics also took a temporary 20 percent cut.[372] In contrast, the legacy carriers released thousands of personnel in order to cut their losses.

AirTran has also reduced its operating costs via less expensive Internet reservations, which have continued to grow with fewer flights booked through costly travel agents. By the end of 2002, Internet business accounted for 56 percent of its overall bookings.[373] Since then, AirTran has continued to increase its online business presence. In an effort to reduce fuel costs, AirTran installed carbon-fiber seats that weighed 80 pounds less per six-seat row than the standard seating.[374] While major airlines like United tried and failed to hedge fuel purchases, AirTran's strong financial situation allowed it to hedge a large percentage of its fuel at rates below market value in 2002.[375]

The airline also introduced broad changes to appeal to all its passengers. By April 2002, AirTran had set up curbside check-in service at Hartsfield and planned to expand the service to Orlando, Baltimore, and other high-traffic departure points.[376] In early 2004, in an apparent response to low-cost rival JetBlue's addition of satellite radio and DirecTV to its aircraft, AirTran reached an agreement with XM Satellite Radio for the installation of 100 channels of service in each seat of its aircraft, and offered the service to its passengers free of charge.[377]

Major airlines continued to support their inefficient business practices with loans from the newly established Air Transportation Stabilization Board and from suppliers of major airlines. The four major bankrupt airlines have continued to operate with government assistance. In 2004, Leonard testified before the US House of Representatives Aviation Subcommittee on the industry's health. He stated:

> [through] some actions, the government is postponing the day of reckoning for aviation business models that no longer work. We should keep the exit doors open and let the inefficient carriers (low or high cost) fail. No revival of the economy, no dip in fuel prices and no waiver of restrictions on mergers and alliances will save the day. The best thing Congress can do to improve the health of the industry is to encourage business efficiencies, refrain from targeted subsidies, and level the competitive playing field.[378]

According to Leonard, AirTran's business model was successful because it was efficient and low-cost while providing quality airline service. It was the right way to do business at the right time.

RAPID NETWORK GROWTH

Spurred by the transition to the Boeing 717s, its increased capacity, and the stumbling of its competitors, AirTran entered a stretch of swift development between 2001 and 2004. Over these four years, the airline restructured and expanded its east coast operations, developed agreements with feeder airlines, grew into the Midwest, began flying nonstop across-country, and placed an aircraft order that could double the size of its fleet. And all this happened while the major airlines were running losses of $30 billion.

In 2001, US Air shut down MetroJet, its low-cost "airline within an airline", causing its total daily departures from Baltimore-Washington International to drop from 154 to

26.[379] AirTran moved in and took over five of MetroJet's old gates, making Baltimore its third new city in 2001. By mid-2003, AirTran was flying 26 flights a day out of Baltimore.[380]

In 2002, AirTran began to expand into the Midwestern leisure travel market. The airline had begun serving Akron-Canton Regional Airport in 2000 with one weekend flight to Orlando, but in 2002, it began flying that route daily while adding four daily flights to Atlanta.[381] In the spring of that year, AirTran added Saturday-only service from Flint, Michigan, to Orlando.[382] That summer, the airline announced it would start flying from Milwaukee to Atlanta and Orlando. It also planned to add flights to Tampa and Fort Lauderdale in the fall.[383] The flights to the Midwest, which were much longer than AirTran's east coast routes, pushed the upper range of the B717. To provide more flights to the west coast, the airline would either need to build a new hub airport to refuel its airplanes, or it would need to acquire airplanes that flew longer distances.

In May 2003, AirTran began two daily nonstop flights from Denver to Atlanta using its Boeing 717s, the longest flight the airline could serve with its B717s.[384] When it began nonstop service from Atlanta to Las Vegas and Los Angeles later that year, AirTran leased two Airbus A320s from Ryan International Airlines of Wichita, Kansas.[385] Realizing it would be costly and unreasonable to continue expansion into the West with leased aircraft, in mid-2003, AirTran placed an order with Boeing for 50 B737s, with options for another 50, and also ordered another 14 B717s.[386] The B737s have larger capacity and fly longer distances than the B717s. AirTran took delivery of its first B737 in June 2004, just in time to pick up the traffic on some of the longer B717 routes. The B717s removed from those flights were deployed to carry traffic formerly served by its one-time feeder airline, JetConnect. The new aircraft order could double AirTran's fleet by 2008.

AirTran's last major expansion into the Midwest occurred when it began to fly to Dallas-Fort Worth International Airport, the fortress hub of the venerable American Airlines. In the summer of 2003, Continental Airlines moved its operations at Dallas-Fort Worth so that its four gates would be closer to those of alliance partners Delta Airlines and Northwest Airlines.[387] AirTran picked up three of those gates later that year, enabling it to increase its flights per day out of Dallas-Fort Worth from six to 24 between 2001 and 2004.[388] New routes included daily service to Las Vegas, Los Angeles, Baltimore, and weekend service to Fort Lauderdale.[389]

When AirTran began service to Dallas, American Airlines serviced 70 percent of Dallas-Fort Worth's traffic. Dallas was also one of the smaller hub airports of Delta Airlines. Both airlines had been charging high fares due to the lack of low-fare competition. In response to AirTran's route additions, American dropped fares on all destinations from Dallas that were served by AirTran. American described the reduced fares as a new structure, dissuading any perception that the airline was offering a temporary fare sale.[390] In October 2004, Delta Airlines, which had been operating 254 flights a day to 66 cities from the airport, announced it would reduce its Dallas operations to 21 flights per day to three cities. Delta executives admitted that AirTran's entry was a factor contributing to the discontinuation of service to its hub operations in Dallas.[391]

PUBLIC–PRIVATE PARTNERSHIPS, SUBSIDIES, AND TRAVEL BANKS

During its Midwest expansion, AirTran had been entering new markets dominated by the major airlines. When this happened, the incumbent carrier usually slashed fares and added capacity to prevent AirTran from succeeding. Having given up on filing complaints to the Department of Transportation regarding predatory pricing, AirTran began asking cities with especially high fares to provide financial support for two years until it became established. AirTran used the additional funds to help sustain its operation long enough to develop a reputation in the new cities. If, after two years of subsidized service, AirTran was unable to develop enough business to sustain its new service, it would withdraw from the market.[392] Leonard explained in 2002: "We don't go into a partnership unless we think we'll be successful. We're just protecting ourselves against cities saying they want us—a lot of cities do—but then don't fly us because the Majors match our fares." The airline deployed this strategy in multiple cities; among them being: Tallahassee, Newport News, and Wichita.

AirTran began flying to Tallahassee in November 2001 when the city, beleaguered by high fares from existing carriers, offered a $1.5 million revenue guarantee. Tallahassee also paid $600,000 in advertising and granted AirTran preferred airline status for government employees. It was the airline's first foray into subsidized service. Upon AirTran's entry into the market, Delta slashed fares to compete. AirTran ran a deficit of $2.4 million in the first two and a half months and requested the entire $1.5 million guarantee. In April 2002, a city audit found that only 16 percent of Tallahassee business travelers were flying AirTran. The audit also showed that city employees were not consistently submitting written justification for flying other airlines.[393] Tallahassee renewed AirTran's revenue guarantee for the second year. In mid-2003, the *Tallahassee Democrat* newspaper reviewed the travel records of high-ranking city officials and found that they traveled AirTran for just over half of their flights.[394] AirTran did not request for subsidy in the third year; traffic declined, and it pulled out of the city citing excessive operational costs. During AirTran's nearly three years of operation in Tallahassee, it was estimated that the airline saved local travelers $75 million, much more than the $3.6 million in subsidies paid by the city.[395]

In early 2002, AirTran began flying from the high-fare hot-spot Newport News, Virginia, to destinations in New York and Florida.[396] The airline had secured a revenue guarantee of up to $1.6 million for the first year. The terms of the guarantee stipulated that the city cover all daily shortfalls on AirTran's two round-trip flights to New York. AirTran reached a new agreement with Newport News for its second year of operations—the maximum aid was capped at $975,000 with an additional $225,000 available should AirTran add a third flight to New York. Instead of continuing with the old system, the new agreement guaranteed daily average revenue.[397] AirTran added the third flight to New York in April 2003.[398] As of mid-2005, the airline has served four cities from Newport News.

AirTran's began its first flight from Wichita on May 8, 2002. It initially flew three daily nonstop flights to Atlanta, and two daily nonstop flights to Chicago. Before it arrived, Wichita's fares were among the highest in the country. AirTran began service as part of a program called "Fair Fares," a local effort to eliminate excessive fares for service from Wichita. Wichita offered AirTran a first-year subsidy of $3 million, a second-year subsidy of $1.5 million, and $600,000 for advertising. It collected non-binding pledges of $3.7 million from local businesses.[399] Fares at Wichita's Mid-Continent Airport dropped significantly when AirTran began service. One major airline sharply reduced its fare by $1200 on its Wichita–Tampa route and another cut nearly $1000 from its round-trip walk-up fare to Chicago.[400]

AirTran lost $732,000 in its first month of operations, and by August it had used almost the entire first-year subsidy.[401] AirTran cited start-up costs and light passenger response for its large losses.[402] More people were flying, but they were taking the reduced rates offered by the major airlines. By December 2002, business travelers had spent only $885,000 of the $3.7 million they had pledged during the first year. Due to an insufficient number of passengers, AirTran dropped its Chicago routes in January 2003, and withdrew its mid-day Atlanta flight in March 2003.[403] As AirTran began its second year, it lamented the lack of business travelers: "There are always people wanting to fly to Florida for $99, but we need more than that," said AirTran spokesman Tad Hutcheson.[404]

AirTran used its entire second-year subsidy as well, although at a slower rate than in the first year. The city determined that, as of May 2004, only 40 percent of the companies that had offered pledges actually honored them. Due to the presence of AirTran, it was estimated that traffic increased 33 percent and fares declined by 30 percent.[405] Wichita renewed AirTran's subsidy to the tune of $2.5 million, with the provision that it increase its number of Atlanta-bound flights to three.[406] The city calculated that in its first year and a half of operations, AirTran saved Wichita travelers $67 million.[407]

In order to expand into the most lucrative markets dominated by the major carriers while still maintaining its competitive edge, it was necessary for AirTran to seek backing to compensate for competitors' fare-slashing, capacity-adding tactics. Out of 40 cities serviced by AirTran in 2002, nine of them had revenue agreements with the airline.[408]

In early 2004, having added 10 cities over the past three years, AirTran slowed its expansion to new cities in order to focus on building point-to-point connections within its existing network. Point-to-point service without flying through major hub cities was a key to AirTran's success, but also contributed to a decrease in AirTran traffic through its main hub in Atlanta. For instance, 90 percent of AirTran's flights passed through Atlanta in 2001, while only 69 percent did so in 2005. However, AirTran resolved to continue flying a significant number of flights through Atlanta. Vice-President of Planning and Sales Kevin Healy said that, "no matter how far down the road you look,

Atlanta will still be our biggest hub and our biggest presence." Hartsfield International Airport was one of the country's least expensive airports at which to land; its passenger-landing fee was $2.50—much less than that charged in Baltimore, Los Angeles, and Miami.[409]

In 2004, AirTran withdrew from Piedmont Triad Airport in Greensboro, North Carolina.[410] At the same time, it cut its Myrtle Beach service to provide service only from March to August.[411] Watchful of overextending itself, the airline also decided not to expand in some of the areas it had earlier considered. In 2004, business leaders in Charleston raised $4.4 million in travel pledges and secured a $1 million federal grant to bring AirTran to the city, but the airline declined to add the service.[412] By this time, AirTran was serving 45 cities through its 531-flight network.[413]

AIRTRAN TODAY

In the late 1990s and early 2000s, AirTran's low-cost business model gave it an advantage over all the major airlines. And, as a result of its expansion, AirTran increasingly heightened competition with other low-cost start-up and established airlines. For instance, in 2004, Independence Air—the successor to Delta and United's regional carrier Atlantic Coast Airlines—began operating as a separate low-cost airline. The regional jet operator entered some markets with walk-up fares up to 70 percent below AirTran's; it offered $59 fares from Atlanta to Washington, one of AirTran's most profitable routes. "The $59 fare is one of the silliest things I have ever seen," declared AirTran President and Chief Operating Officer Fornaro, although AirTran's predecessor, ValuJet, had entered the Atlanta-to-Washington market with $59 fares. As it had forced its competitors to do so often in the past, AirTran matched Independence Air's rate, spoiling profits on the route.

AirTran also began to face revitalized competition from the major carriers.[414] Biggest rival, Delta, imposed a 32.5 percent pay reduction on its pilots and a 10 percent cut on its flight attendants in November 2004. Between 2002 and 2004, it had reduced operating expenses by $12 billion in order to compete more successfully with the rising number of low-cost carriers.[415]

AirTran's network expansion has also led it to compete against SW, the established low-cost market leader. In the fall of 2004, ATA filed for bankruptcy protection. AirTran offered $90 million for ATA's 14 gates at Chicago's Midway Airport in November of the same year. SW already operated a sizeable number of gates at Midway and made a last-minute bid for ATA's properties. The bankruptcy court ultimately approved its $117 million code-sharing deal over AirTran's proposal.[416] AirTran had been flying in SW's markets for some time, but usually via larger and more congested airports than those SW used. If approved, AirTran's deal with ATA would have allowed it to make Midway into a miniature hub under SW's nose. Instead, SW's acquisition of ATA's gates allowed it to add 18 flights to its Chicago operations.[417] Both airlines were hesitant to confront the other because in doing so, they would lose their low-price advantage. However, the two will surely meet in other battlegrounds as they expand their networks in the coming years.

Since its establishment in 1993, AirTran has helped usher in a new era for the airline industry due to the revamped competition it faced from major airlines such as Delta. It has strengthened its position as a discount-travel icon. At the beginning of 2005, AirTran had lowered its costs for 12 consecutive quarters. However, things have changed at the airline over the years. In a move to appeal to corporate travelers, both SW and AirTran have begun offering hotel-booking and car-rental services through their websites.[418] Now, unlike with ValuJet, business passengers account for half of the airline's business.

The airline's nonstop flights from Atlanta to San Francisco, Las Vegas, and Los Angeles demonstrate its expanded service for leisure travelers while also luring business passengers. The airline continues to depend on its Florida leisure business, as evidenced by 2004's especially active hurricane season, causing AirTran's 2004 fourth quarter earnings to drop 95 percent from the previous year, even with hedges in place to counteract rising fuel prices.[419]

The airline has successfully emerged from the shadow of ValuJet. At AirTran's behest, an FAA representative sits in on its morning operations meeting so problems may be addressed before they cause difficulties in the field.[420] Although some observers of the industry have continued to remark on its "past life", AirTran's safety record has significantly improved. Today AirTran is mostly known for its execution of the low-cost model changing the face of the airline industry.

Chapter Nine

JetBlue Airways: The First Luxury Discount Airline

IT IS hard to believe that a luxury discount airline exists in the industry that consumers continually rate as one of the most loathed businesses in America. But JetBlue's founder and CEO David Neeleman has created a first-class discount airline with all-leather seats, individual seat-back monitors with satellite televisions, XM digital radio, spacious leg room, and large overhead storage bins. Its new fleet of airplanes is flown by flight crews who genuinely enjoy serving their customers. The airline also has one of the best on-time performance records and has received the highest customer satisfaction rating. All of these frills come with a standard JetBlue seat at half the price that legacy airlines were charging five years ago. Peter Greenberg of NBC's Today show sums it up in his comment that JetBlue "embraces two words that most airlines don't: common sense."[421]

Although there is a stark contrast between Neeleman of JetBlue and Kelleher of SW, they seem to share "an uncanny knack for knowing when an opportunity is right."[422] JetBlue's strong balance sheet and continued profitability after the airline started in 2000 serve as proof of Neeleman's successful innovative skills. When asked about Neeleman and JetBlue's success, CEO Dave Barger explains, "Neeleman takes notions that others dismiss outright and implements them... impeccably."[423] In a hated industry where losses of legacy carriers continue to soar, JetBlue has broken the mould with its low costs, unmatched flying experience, and sustained profitability.

THE MAKING OF AN AIRLINE GENIUS

Much of JetBlue's unparalleled success in the airline industry can be attributed to Neeleman's strong service philosophy that permeates every level of the airline. His background and experience provided him with a philosophy that has contributed to JetBlue being the start-up airline sensation it is today. Neeleman's childhood sheds light on a personal trait that would later become an integral part of his business savvy: focus on people.

David Neeleman's parents described him as being a person eager to please others. His first job was working at his grandfather's convenience store, and he described David as one who did everything possible to please customers. Neeleman was raised as a devoted Mormon, and one of his first successful and most fulfilling social interactions came while working as a missionary in Brazil. Despite his eagerness to learn and work with people, Neeleman became easily bored and struggled in school.

Neeleman's struggle in school, however, did not hinder his entrepreneurial drive. In 1982, he read an article in *The Wall Street Journal* discussing airline deregulation and the potential it presented. He seized an opportunity tossed out by one of his college classmates and purchased some condominiums in Hawaii and started advertising them as an inexpensive getaway to an attractive tropical island. To fly customers to his tropical retreat, Neeleman began looking for a low-cost alternative to the main airlines that charged high fares. He started advertising trips to Hawaii that included accommodation and airline service provided by a small charter airline called Hawaii Express. Neeleman's first business venture grew rapidly, producing $8 million in sales in 1983—while he was still a junior in college.

Hawaii Express then unexpectedly declared bankruptcy, and Neeleman lost all of his personal money as well as that of many travelers who had paid in advance. His Hawaii getaway business venture was over, and so was his first business undertaking. Neeleman contended that if he had more cash to allow him to find a new air service, then his travel business could have been salvaged. However, he learned a valuable lesson from his first business experience—he must have sufficient capital to take care of unexpected costs and financial blows. This lesson would prove to be invaluable for Neeleman and later help build JetBlue.

After the initial bad taste of business subsided, Neeleman was approached by June Morris, a family friend, who was in the travel industry. He eventually agreed to join Morris at her Utah-based travel agency, and within no time, he was back selling discounted package tours with a charter airline service. While working for a branch of Morris' travel agency (a division of Morris Air), Neeleman decided that he wanted to get into the airline business. He used his new colleague, Harvard Law graduate Tom Kelly, as a sounding board for potential business ideas. Neeleman was more interested in trans-continental routes and selling for less, than he was in becoming involved with the major airlines. Kelly explains, "If you want to know where the whole idea of JetBlue really got started, it was with our flights between Salt Lake and Los Angeles."[424] Neeleman initiated the service for Morris Air from Salt Lake and this new airline service proved to be very successful.

As Neeleman helped Morris Air grow, he began testing some of the business strategies that would later be employed at JetBlue. He implemented a program to eliminate much of the tedious paperwork involved in buying a ticket and boarding the plane. Drawing on his Mormon background, Neeleman saw an opportunity to cut costs while improving both employee and customer satisfaction. He also decided to use stay-at-home moms to make reservations and created a highly motivated, loyal group of "agents in fuzzy slippers."[425] Another change he made with Morris Air was to introduce a version of electronic ticketing to lower costs even further. Neeleman devised a way for customers to pay in advance with a credit card, show up at the airport, identify themselves, and head to the gate. Upon arriving at the gate, passengers were given reusable plastic color-coded boarding passes—a cost-saving technique out of Kelleher's playbook.[426]

Neeleman openly admits that he idolized Kelleher for his business know-how. He liked Kelleher's point-to-point service because it produced faster turnarounds and more flying time compared to major airline hub-and-spoke systems. Neeleman used only one type of airplane *a la* the SW model. The point-to-point techniques contributed to minimizing costs and maximizing efficiency. However, Neeleman had no desire to copy everything from the SW model; he wanted to build a model that would also provide better customer service. Before Morris Air became a scheduled carrier in 1992, it was evident that Neeleman was determined to create an organization dedicated to providing superior customer service.[427]

Morris Air fought its way through the courts and became a scheduled carrier rather than a charter carrier, in 1992. Shortly thereafter, Neelman decided to try to sell Morris Air. While business continued to do well, the company still needed to raise more capital. In addition, June Morris was sick and wanted to get out of the business. Since the airline was modeled after SW, it began negotiations with Kelleher of SW to buy Morris Air. The two airlines had a great deal in common—they operated the same airplanes and both provided point-to-point service. Furthermore, they competed in different markets and both had a "customer-focused culture."[428] The deal was done—Morris Air was sold to SW in late 1993 for $129 million in stock. In addition, "Neeleman was promised a prominent role in the future of the airline he'd long tried to emulate."[429]

It was not long before Neeleman's dream job at SW turned into more of a nightmare. The rambunctious Kelleher-inspired SW culture did not mesh well with the conservative Mormon culture of Morris Air employees. Moreover, Neeleman's hyperactivity and progressive thinking clashed with SW's regimented operations. Within six months, the Neeleman–SW marriage was dissolved to the benefit of both parties. Neeleman signed a five-year non-compete agreement to complete the exit. When Neeleman abruptly left SW, he claimed that he immediately began to think about starting a new airline. He stuck to the terms of his non-compete agreement, but his entrepreneurial drive continued to keep him occupied in different sectors of the airline industry.

After several failed attempts at being a venture capitalist, Neeleman again found business success in the airline industry when he incorporated a small company called Open Skies. Open Skies licensed electronic ticketing and reservations software that he developed with Dale Evans at Morris Air. Open Skies was performing well when he sold the company to Hewlett-Packard. Neeleman then decided to get back in the airline business. Since he signed an agreement not to work in the domestic airline business for five years, Neeleman joined some Canadians to form a no-frills carrier to compete with Air Canada. In early 1996, the new Canada-based airline, WestJet, began making low-cost flights from Salt Lake City to western Canada. While the new airline was prospering, Neeleman still had his eyes fixed on June 1999 when his non-compete agreement would expire. After selling his share in WestJet, Neeleman took his profits and started making plans to launch a new discount airline. He planned to include all the characteristics he thought would make the venture distinctive and highly successful. JetBlue was ready to be launched and it would have far-reaching consequences for the airline industry.

BREAKING NEW GROUND AS A LUXURY DISCOUNTER

Neeleman was looking forward to the day when he would again be able to compete in the domestic airline industry. In the meantime, he was formulating his strategies to create an innovative airline that would prove worthy in an industry where so many start-ups had failed. Neeleman was working with Tom Kelly on the idea for the new airline when he found the hook for distinguishing his new endeavor from the many failures since deregulation. Neeleman and Kelly decided, "the key was to start out *big*. He set out to create 'the first mega-start-up in aviation history'."[430] Neeleman learned from his failed Hawaii Express vacation packages that having sufficient capital was critically important.

One of his important initial decisions was to determine where the business would be based, and what would be its primary market area. After doing his homework on the location of the airline, he said the decision was easy. Neeleman opted for New York City to start his airline dream because the city had no discount airline since Donald Burr's People Express went belly-up in the mid-1980s. In addition to the lack of discount airline services, Neeleman's rationale to base his new airline in New York City was "that's where all the people are"![431]

The next decision for Neeleman was which New York City airport he would use to build his airline. To the surprise of many, he selected John F. Kennedy Airport. This decision seemed radical since JFK had been on a downward slide for nearly 20 years. Furthermore, it was regularly voted by fliers as one of their most hated airports.[432] Author James Kaplan describes JFK as "unwelcoming, unaesthetic, and next to impossible to drive to and from," also drawing attention to the growing

and organized crime problem, and sizable homeless population near the airport.[433] However, Neeleman only had
his eyes on one key aspect of Kennedy—the airport represented opportunity to create something big that could
not be done at the other two airports. He saw Kennedy as
an underused airport located in New York City, bustling
with travelers who longed for reasonable airfares.
Neeleman's research led him to believe that his airline
would succeed if it could serve the five million people who
lived near JFK and also draw some customers from the 18
million people who lived in the tri-state area.[434]

With the airport and location decision made, Neeleman's
next big task was to find investors to make his dream
airline a reality. He set the preliminary fund-raising goal
at an ambitious $200 million. He had learnt the hard way,
after the failure of Hawaii Express, of the need to have
adequate capital. The $200 million was nearly ten times
what most start-up airlines raised. The goal was later
changed to $130 million but it still meant raising quite
a large amount of capital.

Another distinguishing characteristic of Neeleman's
plan was to avoid the operating cost of flying older planes
and rely on drastically lower fares to fill seats. He knew
this tactic had failed before when big carriers used predatory pricing and bullied the start-ups out of business.
Instead, Neeleman decided to use the huge amount of
capital he raised to buy new planes with good fuel efficiency and low maintenance costs. Neeleman also decided to buy only one type of airplane, taking another page
out of Kelleher's SW playbook. To keep costs as low as
possible, he acquired more labor-saving technology than
SW employed. All unnecessary paperwork would be eliminated, and all reservations would be electronic. He also
planned to test fly at night to maximize the number of
flight hours per day and lower travel costs. Another innovative concept Neeleman implemented was one he had
first worked with at Morris Air: the use of at-home

reservationists. He created a "virtual call center" that reduced the cost to customers of making reservations and also created a happier and more productive group of workers. JetBlue's at-home reservationists have a turnover rate of less than one percent.[435]

Neeleman's research showed that an updated version of the SW model with point-to-point flights would be more cost-effective and would provide further savings in comparison to the hub-and-spoke system of the major airlines. Keeping planes in a hub-and-spoke system in the air and on time is a logistical nightmare, according to *Forbes'* writer Melanie Wells.[436] Neeleman's theory has proven to be correct with JetBlue airplanes staying in the air an average of 13 hours a day, compared to nine for many major airlines. These two strategies have helped Neeleman minimize his flying costs.[437]

Along with the low costs and low fares, another important feature of Neeleman's business plan was his commitment to provide customers a luxurious flying experience. This included seat-back monitors on all planes with free satellite TV programming.[438] Continuing on the trend of luxury service, he decided to install all-leather seats in place of the common cloth seats. The leather seats were inherently more comfortable and enticing to customers. Neeleman contends that, although they were more expensive initially, the leather seats were more cost-effective because of their durability and ease of cleaning. His commitment to exceptional service also included providing more overhead storage space. Given the success JetBlue experienced with leather seats and seat-back live TV programming, other carriers such as AirTran and Frontier emulated this model and upgraded their airplanes.

BUILDING DAVID NEELEMAN'S DREAM TEAM

Neeleman stayed in close contact with Michael Lazarus, a principal investor in Morris Air. Although he was originally skeptical, Lazarus eventually came on board to serve as the lead investment backer for Neeleman's airline. Continuing the capital campaign, Neeleman attained financial backing from many big names in the industry, including Weston Presidio, Chase Capital, and George Soros' Quantum Fund. Combined with his personal financial contribution, Neeleman's two-year fund-raising drive raised $130 million, making JetBlue the best capitalized new airline in aviation history.[439]

With the investors in place, Neeleman knew that to "build the best coach product in America with the lowest cost," he must assemble a top-notch management team.[440] He began building this team by cherry picking (business policies of picking out customers from a large base) from old friends and other airlines. Neeleman's old friend and sounding board, Tom Kelly, was with him from the start and helped make his mega-start-up idea a reality. Kevin Murphy, a senior airline analyst for Morgan Stanley and friend of Neeleman, joined his operations to help recruit the right people. The ambitious Alex Wilcox was one of the executives at Virgin who joined Neeleman after receiving a proposal for New Air Airlines (the original name of JetBlue) in the fall of 1997. Following the lead of Wilcox, Amy Curtis-McIntyre, a native New Yorker and marketing genius at Virgin, resigned and became part of Neeleman's management team. Neeleman also recruited old friends and top management from SW, starting with the treasurer of SW, John Owen, who has been described as being "brilliant with a balance sheet."[441] Neeleman's next recruitment from SW—Vice President of People, Ann Rhoades—was aimed at creating a people-centered approach. After Rhoades came on board, Neeleman still had to fill one of the most crucial spots in the company—the number two spot of President and Chief Operations Officer. The name Dave Barger kept coming up in conversation; Barger was a Continental Airlines executive who had done wonders for the airline's day-to-day operations.

After some extended discussions, Barger agreed to accept the new job and completed what Neeleman described as "kind of the dream team of airline management."[442]

Investors who had made tentative commitments were impressed with the notable management team and committed to provide financially for the new airline. After the investors and management teams met in August 1998, all things were set to go and New Air would be incorporated later that month. With an unprecedented $130.2 million in capital and a top-tier group of management professionals, Neeleman was only a few steps away from breathing life into New Air.

Getting New Air in the Sky

Neeleman seemed to be putting all the right pieces together for his mega-start-up luxury discount airline, but a few things remained to be done. He had no planes, no name for the new super-discount airline, and no gates from which to fly. With the capital campaign completed, Neeleman turned to purchasing aircraft. After initially going along with the choice of the industry, the Boeing 737, he went to Europe-based manufacturer Airbus to discuss alternatives to Boeing and its monopolized pricing of the 737.

After hearing the pitch from Airbus, Neeleman made the surprising decision to purchase the A320 rather than the Boeing 737. He was convinced that the 162-passenger single-aisle aircraft provided more seat and leg room while using less fuel, than the Boeing 737. The newer technology of the A320, combined with its higher passenger capacity and greater storage space, made it an obvious choice for Neeleman. He was convinced it was the best option to help him provide low-fare service. To get the best plane at the best price, Neeleman placed an order for 82 new A320 aircraft on March 4, 1999 at a considerably lower cost-per-seat mile than if he had bought Boeing 737s.

Neeleman's next task turned out to be a more complicated and lengthy ordeal than he and his management team had anticipated—naming the new airline. He knew he wanted a strong brand identity like Starbucks, Heineken, or GAP, that would imply a high-quality product at a low price.[443] Neeleman hoped that through superior service and low fares, the airline would be able to bring a refreshing change to a tired industry: "It's like a Starbucks thing: They built the brand by building the experience first."[444] After many failed suggestions and much deliberation, the team of top executives finally selected the name JetBlue.

After purchasing the aircraft and naming the airline, Neeleman began taking steps to gain government approval and to select the airport from which JetBlue would start flying. The airline chose JFK Airport in New York City. While navigating governmental "red tape" in the way of becoming an established airline, Neeleman and his crew made an extraordinary move for a start-up airline by requesting 75 landing and take-off slots at JFK. Prior to this move, the largest number of landing slots ever granted at one time was 11. But Neeleman believed he would have to obtain all the slots to have a chance of surviving against the three majors already at JFK—American, Delta, and TWA. Despite strong opposition from the major carriers, Neeleman received encouraging news that the Transportation Authority would give him the approval to fly in and out of JFK if JetBlue was granted the slots at JFK's Terminal Six. After some added help from several prominent New York politicians, Neeleman's airline was granted all 75 slots in September 1999, setting a new record and cutting the last of the red tape before it could start flying.

With government approval, new technology-rich aircraft, and a catchy name for the airline, it was time to announce JetBlue to the public. On July 14, 1999, Neeleman and his team held a widely attended press conference. In preparing for the pivotal press conference, he commented that he "could talk only from his heart about what he wanted the airline to be."[445] During the press conference, he explained, "We're going to bring humanity back to air travel."[446] Besides providing a superior flying experience, JetBlue would also strive to offer airfares that were half the price of the major airlines. The goal was to attract "frugal yet style-conscious" consumers.[447]

After introducing JetBlue to the public, Neeleman had the huge challenge of building the quality flying experience he envisioned. He began hammering out some of the "details of the new discount airline that would provide the flying public an excellent flying experience."[448] Neeleman announced details that would put JetBlue in a class of its own. The new discount airline would provide only one class of service, which was unusual in the airline industry. His goal was for JetBlue to provide an extraordinary experience to everyone. The tickets were non-refundable to "minimize accounting time to further help control costs, thus keeping fares low."[449] Moreover, customers could exchange JetBlue tickets for a flight on another day. In order to create a high level of customer satisfaction, JetBlue would not overbook flights. While all the other airlines overbooked their flights in an attempt to increase load capacity, Neeleman believed that the reasonable fares and customer loyalty would keep JetBlue's load capacity higher than that of its competitors. Continuing with his customer-oriented philosophy, Neeleman implemented a system that kept customers informed about any delays or cancellations. Furthermore, if any of his flights were delayed for more than an hour, customers were compensated for the inconvenience.

Neeleman knew that deplaning quickly would minimize delays, which in turn would ensure his planes were quickly back in the air and making money. To achieve this goal, JetBlue deplaned passengers from both ends of the plane, rather than using just one exit like most airlines. Another twist to his model for minimizing turnaround time and cutting costs was to have no formal cleaning crews. Instead, regular crewmembers, consisting of flight attendants and pilots were responsible for cleaning the cabin. Finally, Neeleman and Barger eliminated the frustration associated with the final step of the flying experience: the baggage claim. JetBlue's goal was to have the first bags at the luggage carousel within 10 minutes of arrival and the last bag within 20 minutes. He explained,

> It's the last thing you remember about JetBlue. You could have a flawless experience. Everything could go wonderfully perfect. And you go to the carousel and wait 45 minutes and ... screw up the whole thing. So that is one metric that we think is very, very important.[450]

It seemed that Neeleman and his team had put some great ideas together and were only one crucial step away from having JetBlue in the air. The final step was securing the right type of crewmembers to successfully implement the high service and low-cost strategy of JetBlue.

WANTED: THE BEST "PEOPLE" PEOPLE

Because of her success and experience with SW, as mentioned earlier, Neeleman recruited Ann Rhoades to manage the recruiting process. He explained his philosophy of hiring the right people to bring humanity back to air travel. He stated:

> We're in a service economy, and a service economy means that you rely on people. If you're going to rely on people then you better select the best people and you better train them well, and you better stand by them.[451]

Neeleman contends that JetBlue crew members and their dedication to customers is what really set JetBlue apart from other airlines, rather than the TVs or leather seats. Therefore, his goal was to hire the best people possible who cared about providing friendly customer service. However, how was JetBlue going to hire exceptional crewmembers when its starting salaries were lower than the industry average? Neeleman's response was that JetBlue's culture and its commitment to taking care of people would attract caring employees. Neeleman contends that of JetBlue's genuine commitment to its workers JetBlue flight attendants are non-unionized workers. JetBlue also offered its crewmembers perks such as a profit-sharing program, organized social functions to build camaraderie, and it even had a crisis management fund to which Neeleman donated his yearly salary.

An even tougher task was recruiting and retaining pilots for JetBlue's new A320s. Even though its pilots' salaries were below the industry average and they were not unionized, yet Neeleman was able to keep his commitment to respect every JetBlue crewmember. He provided them with perks such as stock options, good severance packages in case of merger or bankruptcy, and seniority rules in the cockpit. In addition, pilots used laptop computers in the cockpit instead of having to manually complete a number of forms. The paperless cockpit further contributed to efficiency and decreased the cost of updating manuals.

Neeleman believed that "the more you can make your employees feel that they have a huge impact on how the operation goes, the more they'll take ownership of their duties."[452] Neeleman further contended that his commitment to his employees was what makes his crewmembers "strive for flawless execution" in their daily duties of customer satisfaction.[453] All in all, JetBlue takes excellent care of its crewmembers and pilots, and in return, they take care of their customers. This philosophy builds brand loyalty and keeps customers coming back.

JETBLUE TAKES FLIGHT

JetBlue's first flight was from JFK airport in New York to sunny Fort Lauderdale, Florida, on February 11, 2000. The promotional one-way price was an unthinkably low $49 to $79 for the area. Ten weeks into its history, the $79 flight to Florida with the JetBlue experience received strong praise from passengers and good publicity from the media, and New York to Florida would remain one of JetBlue's most lucrative routes. Another primary route came about in May 2000 when Tower Air stopped operating, opening the doors for JetBlue to begin a route from New York to the west coast. Within weeks of JetBlue's announced route from JFK to Ontario, CA, the flights were selling out, and Neeleman added a second flight. By August 2000, JetBlue was operating 48 flights a day, a record for a new airline. In October, JetBlue was ranked first in on-time performance in every market it served.

As the company's first anniversary approached, Neeleman stated that its success was due to JetBlue's employees' commitment to maintaining a customer-friendly environment. This success was highlighted when crunching the numbers showed JetBlue coming close to breaking even in its very first year of operation—a remarkable feat for a start-up airline. As the summer months came, Neeleman ordered more A320 aircraft from Airbus, increasing the total number on order to 131. As demand continued to soar, JetBlue took over the rest of Terminal Six at JFK airport.

With business going well, Neeleman began considering service to other west coast cities. JetBlue's cross-country flights were well received because they were so far primarily offered by the major airlines that charged higher fares. The airport that interested Neeleman was Long Beach because of its close proximity to Los Angeles' large population, and also because it was not a busy airport like Los Angeles. After researching the market for a while,

Neeleman decided Long Beach was to be the next big move for JetBlue. His next strategic move again went against the grain of the industry. Neeleman decided he must acquire all slots at Long Beach regardless of whether he could use them or not. He feared that American's response would be too fierce if he left any room for it to compete at the same airport with sharply cut fares.

Neeleman hired Kristy Ardizzone to help obtain the slots; she knew the area and the people better than Neeleman, and could put JetBlue in the right position to reach its goal. Through a series of talks and negotiations, Neeleman and JetBlue somehow managed to do the impossible. It acquired all the slots at Long Beach airport, and service from New York began on August 29, 2001. With this newly added route, Neeleman once again found a huge number of customers who were anxious to have the opportunity to fly a quality discount airline from coast to coast between two of America's largest cities. Until now, the major airlines dominated long-distance flights, and were a major source of profit for the legacy carriers.

Numbers were looking good and everything was running smoothly for JetBlue when an unexpected event shook the world and the airline industry—9/11. After the terrorist attacks of September 11, 2001 in the United States, the airline industry was devastated, as passengers felt unsafe boarding a commercial airliner. However, in the wake of the swooning demand for air service, JetBlue again managed to do what no one else was capable of. By October 12, JetBlue was back to flying 85 percent of the passengers it had before 9/11, and appeared to be one of the few airlines that would survive the tragedy.[454] What's more, JetBlue managed to capitalize on the tragic event that caused customers to be concerned about flying safety. Neeleman decided to replace all cockpit doors with new bulletproof Kevlar doors and install cabin cameras, allowing pilots to monitor cabin activity. Given its small fleet of airplanes, JetBlue was able to make these changes quickly, and JetBlue was safer to fly than the major airlines. With these changes in place, JetBlue remained profitable throughout the fall and winter, despite an over-all decline in air travel.

While the major carriers experienced serious financial problems following 9/11, JetBlue did not lay off any of its employees and yet remained profitable. With all of its accomplishments, JetBlue decided to take the unique discount airline public on April 12, 2002. JetBlue's share price doubled in the first month following the initial public offering, and it was one of the hottest stocks in the market. The summer continued to benefit JetBlue as it nearly doubled the previous year's net income. The company had also been consistently profitable for five quarters, and its performance statistics (load factor and flight completion) were the best in the industry. All in all, things were looking spectacular for the young airline, but along with the glamor and success came much scrutiny from analysts and competitors.

IS JETBLUE HERE TO STAY?

As JetBlue continued to enjoy its success, Neeleman knew he must not become complacent. He also knew that JetBlue was a competitive target for the major airlines. By August 2002, JetBlue's flights were more than 90 percent full with a 100 percent flight completion rate, and its highly satisfied customer base continued to grow.[455] JetBlue was voted the country's number one domestic airline for 2002 by *Condé Nast Traveler*. Even with the stunning performance and acclaim, Neeleman continued to be questioned about the airline's stability and staying power. Specifically, Neeleman was asked if JetBlue was going to follow the direction of the failed start-up, People Express. Neeleman remained steadfast in expressing that JetBlue differed from People Express in terms of capitalization, management, and financial results. Neeleman commented, "The most money People Express ever made in a year was $20 million; we're doing that almost in a quarter."[456] He added that, unlike People Express, JetBlue operated under a strong management team to handle its rapid expansion. In contrast to JetBlue, the atmosphere at People Express was chaotic.[457] Neeleman professed not to worry about JetBlue's permanence, and made moves to continue his success as competition heated up.

In September 2002, Neeleman struck a deal to buy LiveTV, the company providing in-air satellite TV service to JetBlue. Neeleman knew that JetBlue's in-flight entertainment was the envy of his competitors and he wanted to keep access to this entertainment out of competitors' hands. While this business move helped him curb competition on the entertainment side, the major airlines were devising a strategy to challenge JetBlue. As 2002 drew to a close, US Airways and United Airlines both declared bankruptcy, while American was expecting losses to top $1 billion; meanwhile, JetBlue posted a 16 percent profit margin for the fiscal year 2002. By the end of 2002, JetBlue was the envy of the money-losing major airlines.

In an effort to compete with the luxury discount airliner, Delta announced its new low-cost carrier, "Song", in early 2003. In response to Delta's competitive move, Neeleman decided that JetBlue would start flying from Delta's home airport in Atlanta to Long Beach as a bit of home turf, "in-your-face rivalry."[458] JetBlue began service from Atlanta to California in May 2003, only to stop the service eight months later since the discount airline AirTran was already in a turf war with Delta in Atlanta. Neeleman further remarked that Atlanta was not a strategic city for JetBlue, and it planned to enter more strategic and less risky markets.[459] Like Delta, United announced its new airline, dubbed Ted, as a new low-cost discount airline to compete in the market. However, Ted had little impact on JetBlue's successful operations. Similarly, Song had a limited impact on JetBlue, although

Neeleman eventually decided that it was a good idea to pull out of Atlanta.

The rest of 2003 would yield several other successes and interesting moves for JetBlue which helped it become one of the best performing airlines. In February, JetBlue beat the long-time champion discount airline SW in cost-per-available-seat mile (CASM). JetBlue cost a little more than 6 cents a mile in comparison to SW's cost of 7.3 cents, while the major airlines' cost per available seat mile were generally in the 9–10 cent range. Even so, Neeleman pointed out to his employees that competitors such as Delta and American were actually offering fares to Florida and other cities for less than JetBlue. Because of the great people working to maintain the JetBlue experience, its fan base continued to grow and more flyers were choosing JetBlue over the competition.

In June 2003, in keeping with his tradition of shaking up the industry, Neeleman announced that JetBlue had placed an order for 100 Embraer 190 aircraft. This move strayed from the SW one-plane model. The Embraer 190s were considerably smaller airplanes than the ones JetBlue currently flew. Neeleman's plan was to use the smaller aircraft to serve the untapped market of smaller communities. He indicated that JetBlue had studied the mid-size domestic market for a year before making the business move in what he called a "real sweet spot" of the industry.[460] JetBlue used the smaller airplane to cherry pick routes not served by other discount airlines, including areas near surrounding large cities such as Chicago, Atlanta, and New York. The hot question in the industry remains—will this new strategy work? Unfortunately, it is hard to answer this question since the first Embraer Jets will not be delivered until early 2006. Some analysts believe that Neeleman may again have made an innovative business move.

Throughout 2003, JetBlue maintained an outstanding operational and financial performance record that quietened some skeptics. During its third year of operation, JetBlue sales climbed to almost $1 billion, a distinction no other airline has even come close to achieving. In addition, the annual Airline Quality Rating praised JetBlue's stellar operating statistics: no passengers were denied boarding, 0.31 per 100,000 passengers' complaints, and 3.21 mishandled bags per 1,000 bags, all well below the industry averages.[461] JetBlue ended 2003 with a 17 percent profit margin and some of the best operational performance numbers in the industry.[462]

JetBlue had 55 aircrafts providing 220 flights a day at the beginning of 2004—and was hungry for more. Neeleman planned to expand his market share in the New York area and made an unusual request for spots at the hectic LaGuardia airport, the airport he once criticized for being too congested to operate effectively. With flights scheduled to begin September 17, 2004, Neeleman explained his surprising move by simply commenting that the people of Manhattan were requesting JetBlue's presence at LaGuardia. He further added that he hoped to get a toe in the door at LaGuardia in case either of the two major carriers, Delta and US Airways, who were both facing financial difficulty, stumbled and opened the door for JetBlue to expand rapidly at LaGuardia.[463]

In early 2004, JetBlue began an effort to acquire the run-down semi-abandoned Terminal Five at JFK. Preservationists in the area lobbied against the idea of tearing down the historic Terminal Five. In a compromising move, Neeleman suggested undertaking a two-part expansion consisting of a complete renovation of the existing terminal, as well as the construction of a new section at Terminal Five. After linking the two sections of the terminal and adding the normal JetBlue touches, Neeleman foresees the new terminal providing 26 new gates capable of handling an additional 250 departures a day.[464] The new $875 million terminal marks the largest expansion in JetBlue's history. It will be funded primarily by the Port Authority with JetBlue contributing $50 to $100 million.[465] An airline industry analyst stated: "Its timing couldn't be better. The profitable discounter is expanding while its competitors are at their weakest."[466] However, only time will tell as to whether or not Neeleman's expansion of the JFK terminal and the purchase of the smaller Embraer 190s will prove lucrative. So far, his track record with unusual entrepreneurial moves has done well.

The remainder of 2004 proved challenging for JetBlue as it was hampered by heightened competitive pressure and an unusually rough hurricane season. Nonetheless, JetBlue continued to win business victories over other airlines and expanded its number of destinations. Free ticket promotions by American and other aggressive moves by competitors managed to cut into JetBlue's profit margin. But Neeleman contends that with JetBlue's low-cost structure, its results and fares are sustainable.[467] Meanwhile, JetBlue was ranked the overall number one domestic airline by the 2004 Airline Quality Rating study. JetBlue also announced new flights from JFK to San Diego, Denver, San Juan, and Puerto Rico.[468] The airline is considering starting service to 10 Midwest cities including Milwaukee, Chicago, and Minneapolis. It is also increasing the number of daily flights to the Dominican Republic, to meet the opportunity of serving New York's fastest growing Dominican population.[469] Neeleman also announced that more direct flights from Buffalo to cities like Boston, Chicago, and Atlanta could be forthcoming. Not long after this announcement, American withdrew its nonstop flights from JFK to Long Beach and Phoenix, marking another victory for JetBlue in the long-haul market.

The last two quarters of 2004 proved to be especially challenging to JetBlue and the entire airline industry.

Hurricane season was in full bloom in Florida and hurt JetBlue's Florida traffic. Four Florida hurricanes and the associated skyrocketing fuel prices resulted in a 71 percent drop in profits in the third quarter.[470] Even with an estimated $8–$10 million loss due to the Florida hurricanes and soaring fuel costs during 2004, JetBlue produced better results than most other airlines. Despite the troubling third and fourth quarters, JetBlue still managed to show a profit margin of 8.9 percent for 2004 and a 26.8 percent increase in revenue. JetBlue also flew 99.4 percent of its scheduled flights with 81.6 percent on-time performance, and a load factor of 83.2 percent.[471] JetBlue navigated through some tough times in 2004 and was able to continue its streak of never having an unprofitable quarter until the last quarter of 2005. Profitability was up and down in 2006 but the airline seemed to be solidly in the black by the end of 2006 after a series of cost-cutting measures, including the sale of older planes and deferring the delivery of new ones.

Figure 9.1: JetBlue Quarterly Net Income, 2000–2005

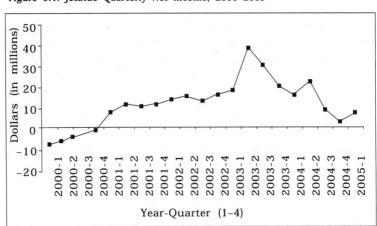

Source: Figures courtesy of Compustat at Wharton and JetBlue press releases.

JETBLUE'S CUSTOMER SERVICE: WHERE ABOVE AND BEYOND IS THE CALL OF DUTY

As discussed in the earlier sections, JetBlue keeps costs low because its pilots and crewmembers work together to provide the best possible service. Neeleman flies once a week on JetBlue flights and works alongside flight attendants as a regular crewmember. In the midst of serving snacks and getting rid of trash, Neeleman secures feedback about Jet Blue's service and ways in which it might be improved. At many companies, it would be rare to hear of the CEO acting in such a manner—making personal contact with both crew and passengers. JetBlue crewmembers have found Neeleman's hands-on approach truly inspiring and powerful. As a result they share the company's passion and commitment to excellence.[472]

JetBlue's commitment to providing low fares and good customer service, delivered by a highly respected and dedicated workforce, has earned it a place at the forefront of the industry.[473] Also critical to its success are its low costs due to the use of some leading-edge technology, the economy of its Airbus fleet, and flying airplanes more hours per day than the competition. A further factor which contributes to JetBlue's large and expanding customer base is its satellite TV at every seat.[474] Neeleman agrees that JetBlue has attained a loyal following because of the whole JetBlue experience—not simply as a result of in-seat entertainment and low fares.[475] Neeleman has commented several times that his biggest concern about the future of JetBlue is not the rapid expansion or competition, but rather the fear of mediocrity. He intends to continue to inspire and motivate JetBlue's people to share in his passion for superior quality customer service.

What lies ahead for JetBlue is the big question. Will the airline continue to set precedents and become a legend, or will problems develop and cripple what some refer to as an extraordinary airline? Factors such as rapid expansion, its new fleet of small feeder airlines, predatory pricing by other airlines, and excessive airline capacity which causes fares to fall, can create serious difficulties for JetBlue.

Neeleman admits that maintenance expenses are at an all-time low, and as time progresses, these expenses will grow. Fuel prices remain uncertain, and if they continue to rise, JetBlue's profits could be affected. The airline plans to quadruple in size by the year 2007. It took SW 27 years to grow to the size that JetBlue plans to achieve in only 11 years.[476] However, as Neeleman has proven time and again, new opportunities come from taking new risks. In addition to serving smaller markets with smaller-capacity planes on order, he also plans more international flights to Canada, Mexico, and the Caribbean in the coming years.

JetBlue's staying power also depends on whether the Federal government and airplane manufacturers and suppliers continue to subsidize the high cost major airlines that have lost tens of billions of dollars in 2001–2004. Or, will the free market and competition reign supreme and allow JetBlue's model simply to replace some of the services provided by the major airlines?[477]

Regardless of the long-term outcome, Neeleman has certainly made his presence felt in the airline industry, and for now, JetBlue looks like a model that should expand and grow. At the beginning of 2005, JetBlue flew to 32 destinations in 12 states with 71 aircrafts. By 2011, JetBlue aims to operate 290 airplanes providing service to 50–60 cities with 30,000 employees.[478] With this predicted and planned expansion, Neeleman knows that a key to JetBlue's future success is to ensure the commitment to excellence is not diluted in any way.[479] Neeleman continues to believe that striving for improvement in service is the only way for his dream airline to survive. Neeleman recently stated: "We're not perfect ... we know we'll never be perfect. But we're working really hard to try to be better and better every day, to be the best service company."[480] JetBlue has succeeded to this point by providing exceptional service, and Neeleman is "betting his airline that good service, delivered by passionate employees, will give JetBlue a lasting edge."[481]

Chapter Ten

Ryanair Leads the Growth of Discounters in Europe

IF RYANAIR'S management were to say just one thing about the future of the airline industry, it would be that the no-frills Irish airline would one day be the world's largest. Chief Executive Michael O'Leary has already formulated an advertising campaign for that day featuring a passenger proudly stating: "I'm flying Ryanair—the world's favorite airline."[482] The company website already boasts that it will be the largest European airline within a few years. By the end of 2010, O'Leary expects that it will carry 50 million passengers a year.[483]

RYANAIR'S BIRTH

One of Ryanair's founders was Tony Ryan, an Irishman whose family has a rich history in aviation. Ryan founded Guinness Peat Aviation (GPA) while working for Aer Lingus, the main airline operating in Ireland. GPA's business was to arrange leases between airlines with a surplus of aircraft to meet the demands of airlines with aircraft shortages. Aer Lingus owned a considerable shareholding in this company. Through GPA, Ryan became one of Ireland's wealthiest entrepreneurs, and the financial security gained from GPA paved the way for Ryan to pursue other business interests.

Ryan's entrepreneurial spirit and experience in the aviation business evoked in him a desire to start his own passenger airline business. His idea was to provide charter service between Ireland and the UK for business and leisure trips. Eventually, his strategy evolved into running a low-cost, no-frills operation. Despite two failed attempts (engineered by Aer Lingus), Ryan finally succeeded in launching Ryanair.[484]

Ryan Christy, a long-time friend of Ryan's who worked on the sales team at GPA, also wanted to start an airline. His focus was on a route between Waterford, Ireland and London-Gatwick. The two met together in a pub to discuss a joint-business venture. As luck would have it, Liam Lonergan, founder of Club Travel, was also in the process of seeking a license to fly between Dublin and Luton Airport as a new gateway to London. He needed a financial backer and turned to Ryan. The three men pooled their ideas and named the new carrier Ryanair.[485]

Ryanair began operating on November 28, 1985, with a 15-person capacity Bandeirante turbo-prop plane flying from Southeast Ireland to London-Gatwick[486] (Ryan Christy's chosen route from his hometown of Waterford). At that time, Aer Lingus and the British flag carrier, British Airways, dominated the route from Dublin to London. In fact, the two airlines had a profit-sharing agreement so neither carrier was compelled to lower its ticket prices. Aer Lingus was less than thrilled with Ryan's decision to launch a direct competitor to its airline and attempted to thwart the action, especially considering his role as a board member at GPA, which had ties with the major airline. Ryan established the company as a trust for his three sons—Cathal, Declan, and Shane—who would be the main shareholders. Since Ryan was not directly involved in the operations of the new airline, there was little the GPA board could do.[487]

Ryan knew he would need a good management team to launch the new airline successfully. He had a gift for spotting talented leaders, and he recruited some of his top management team members from Aer Lingus. In addition to salary, each member of Ryanair staff was granted 500 shares in the new airline. The compensation plan was designed to ensure that each employee was committed to creating a successful organization. Starting a new airline was no picnic, and Ryan knew he would need to offer incentives for the crew to work the long hours required to get the airline going. Commenting on the hours the early staff worked, former employee Charlie Clifton said he often "arrived home after working a flight only to be met by a taxi waiting outside to bring him back to the airport."[488]

In May 1986, when Ryanair added the Dublin-London (Luton) route and acquired two more planes, things began to pick up for the airline. It flew 82,000 customers on its two routes the first year. At the time, 800,000 passengers were flying this route while most people opted to take the nine-hour ferry ride because it was more affordable. The flight costs were rather exorbitant at around £200 (approximately US$350) and greatly limited the opportunities for Dubliners to fly home to visit family during the year. When Ryanair launched the Dublin-Luton route, it undercut the two flag carriers' rates by more than 50 percent. Aer Lingus immediately retaliated using predatory pricing to offer a £95 flight to compete with Ryanair's £99. Thus began a brutal price war between the two carriers. Ryanair responded by reducing it fare to £94.99. Aer Lingus was determined to deal decisively with the new kid on the block and allowed reservations staff to change fares constantly, in order to compete. One individual remarked that the reservations department at Aer Lingus was like "a twenty-four-hour dealing room" with prices changing hourly.[489]

Ryanair did not just face obstacles from other airlines when it began operations. The Dublin airport was less than accommodating. Aer Rianta, the state-run airport authority, owned Dublin airport and did not go out of its way to make the new airline comfortable. Ryanair had a hard time obtaining check-in desks and threatened to use orange crates as check-in counters if the airport would not provide them. Eventually the airport authority met Ryanair's request, but did so reluctantly because it did not want to irritate Aer Lingus, its premier customer.[490]

On March 1, 1988, Ryanair began offering daily service to Manchester, one of Aer Lingus's most coveted routes. Aer Lingus retaliated by slashing its fares, adding three more daily flights to Manchester, and heavily recruiting sales representatives in the area. Ryanair faced serious financial problems and was provided additional funding when Ryan purchased another airline, London European Airways. The airline was purchased so that passengers could be carried to other European destinations from Britain. At that time, airlines were regulated and were not permitted to fly from one country to another. This meant that Ryanair could not fly from Britain to Belgium, and so forth. London European Airways already operated routes from Luton to Amsterdam and Brussels, and had authorization from the UK Department of Transport to fly additional routes from Luton to Paris and Frankfurt. The Ryan family hoped the new airline would generate enough cash to finance Ryanair. However, it proved to be an even greater cash drain. It was at this time that Ryan hired a new personal assistant, Michael O'Leary.[491]

The Man Behind Ryanair's Success

O'Leary became Chief Executive of Ryanair in 1993 and has been included in *Forbes Magazine* as one of the world's top 25 businessmen[492]. He began his career as a tax accountant with KPMG, working with a partner who provided wealth management advice to affluent clients. One of these clients was Ryan himself. During an audit, Ryan met O'Leary and was impressed. Later, when Ryan was in need of a personal assistant at GPA, he remembered O'Leary and offered him the job. O'Leary had grown restless with his job at KPMG and agreed to work for Ryan as his personal assistant. His salary was based on profits that he generated for Ryan's ventures.[493]

In light of the financial difficulty Ryanair was facing, Ryan installed O'Leary as a director at Ryanair to keep an eye on the financial situation. A new CEO, P.J. McGoldrick, was hired to rein in the firm's financial extravagance and use his experience and expertise to help the airline run more efficiently and profitably. McGoldrick implemented a business class service slightly better than what was provided by Aer Lingus.[494] At the time, Ryanair also had a frequent-flyer program.[495] O'Leary recalls the state of the airline when he was hired to help McGoldrick with the restructuring:

> Unfortunately, we made the traditional airline mistakes: over expanded into a broad network of unsustainable routes, an unmanageable fleet of eight aircraft in which there were four aircraft types, feeling a compulsive need to serve food and freebies to every single passenger in every single market going everywhere, with the result that we finished up going nowhere other than back to the Ryans for massive dollops of financial support.[496]

During McGoldrick's leadership, Ryanair started a flight to Stansted airport in London, a brand new airport that had yet to attract much business. Aer Lingus already flew from Stansted and when Ryanair started flying from that airport, it chose to deal swiftly and decisively with the new airline. Aer Lingus raged a fierce retaliatory price war that brutally impacted Ryanair's financial situation which was already problematic due to employee spending. Because of Ryan's financial backing, employees were under the impression with regard to costs, prudence was not an issue. At this point, the airline was facing financial difficulties and costing the Ryan family millions of dollars.

Ryanair was trying to compete in service with Aer Lingus and British Airways by offering discount fares. They were trying to be everything to everyone. In order to be successful, it was going to require a dramatic turnaround and focus on creating a niche for itself in the industry. At this point, however, O'Leary was determined that the only safe financial option for the Ryan family was the liquidation of Ryanair as it was losing millions, and O'Leary felt that further financial losses were inevitable.[497]

Ryan did not want to give up. He approached the Minister of Transport, Seamus Brennan, and asked for exclusive flight rights to Stansted. He believed that if the airline could operate successfully on that route, then Ryanair could survive. Luckily, the Minister believed that Ireland should have a "two airlines" policy, meaning Aer Lingus should not be able to monopolize the Irish airline industry and unfairly drive out its would-be competitors. He conceded the Stansted route to Ryanair. Brennan "ordered Aer Lingus off the Stansted route and confined it to flying into Gatwick and Heathrow while Ryanair could fly to Stansted and Luton."[498] It was Stansted Airport where Ryanair would negotiate its famous deals at a fraction of the price that airports charged other airlines. The airline learned that flying to secondary airports was going to be one of its top cost-cutting strategies. Because the demand is not as high to fly to these airports, the airports were more than willing to strike a deal encouraging airlines to fly there and increase airport traffic and revenues.

Ryan instructed O'Leary to focus on cutting costs wherever he could. Despite O'Leary's insistence that the airline be shut down, Ryan encouraged O'Leary by stating that he would provide financial incentives if O'Leary turned the airline around. O'Leary negotiated a deal that would give him 10 percent if the airline had a £2 million profit and 25 percent of any amount exceeding £2 million. O'Leary stood to make millions if he could turn the airline around.

O'Leary's first major overhaul included sharply cutting the number of employees. In addition, he reduced their salaries, which were already less than that of their counterparts at Aer Lingus. Today, however, the airline's website claims that Ryanair employees are the highest paid, on average, in the industry.[499] O'Leary stood by his opinion that the small, struggling airline could not be run like the state carrier and that job cuts and salary reductions were necessary to keep the airline in business.[500] He also refused to refund customers who were paying low fares and who, in his opinion, had no business complaining about delayed flights or lost baggage.

O'Leary's financial stake in the business led him to help out wherever needed. It was not unusual to see him behind the check-in counter or in any other capacity where additional help might be needed to keep the airline running. Once, during a baggage-handler's strike, he and other executives personally loaded the baggage onto planes.[501] O'Leary ran the company as if it were his own, with his personal fortune at stake. His forceful personality also led to the abrupt departure of many senior managers.

Around the time of the Gulf War in early 1991, the world airline industry took one of its hardest blows ever. Only three of the world's largest airlines were profitable that year. Many of the flag carriers received state aid to stay afloat during the turbulent economics of that time. At the end of 1991, McGoldrick left Ryanair after announcing his belief that the airline was on the "threshold of a 'dramatic turnaround' and that despite the trauma endured by Ryanair, staff morale was very high."[502] Indeed, Ryanair was in need of a turnaround and soon O'Leary was going to change the airline's destiny.

"THE ROAD TO DAMASCUS"

At Ryan's insistence, O'Leary headed off to Dallas, Texas, to observe Kelleher's operations at SW. O'Leary credits his visit to SW as the impetus for turning around Ryanair's performance. When asked how important Kelleher is with regard to the airline industry, O'Leary responds,

> How important's Herb Kelleher? Herb Kelleher's like God. He's the original genius. Herb Kelleher would have been the Thomas Edison of low-fare air travel. This is the guy who created it, this is the guy who first dreamt of charging people ten dollars for two- and three-hour flights in the United States, and he's the one who revolutionized the industry. He's the Sam Walton of the airline industry.[503]

O'Leary's background as an accountant enabled him to focus on abundant cost-management opportunities at SW. First, there were no assigned seats. Customers choose their seats as they board the plane, allowing for faster turnaround time between flights. Colleen Barrett, the current President of SW, notes that

> We have examined assigned seating periodically, and all of our studies show that it takes more time than our current system. That is an extremely important consideration because, if we had to extend our ground times by as little as ten minutes for assignments, we would have to buy 31 more 737s at a cost of $36 million.[504]

Second, SW flew only Boeing 737s instead of a variety of airplanes as was common with the major US airlines. Adhering to one model keeps maintenance costs to a minimum, with fewer spare parts to be inventoried. Also, because employees do not need to become familiar with several types of airplanes, the company can reduce training time and costs.

A third cost-saving characteristic of SW was that it flew from smaller airports. This resulted in lower airport landing fees and quicker turnaround time, giving airplanes more time spent in the air. Turnaround time proved to be the most important lesson learned. On his "road to Damascus", O'Leary observed the 25-minute turnaround time, which accounted for significant savings for SW. O'Leary realized that faster turnaround time between flights would allow more flights per day to be scheduled.

In 1991, with the information he collected in Texas, O'Leary and his new management team—including the new CEO, Conor Hayes—were able to change Ryanair's destiny. O'Leary realized that if the price was right, customers would be willing to forego frills, especially on short point-to-point routes. Within four years, routes were cut from 18 to nine, and the Boeing 737-200 was made the standard company aircraft. Ryanair acquired 11 of these planes from other airlines. Fares were cut to the bare minimum, and on-board giveaways were eliminated. Average yield decreased almost 50 percent while traffic rose 300 percent resulting in increased profitability.[505]

Following the restructuring, *Fortune Magazine* concluded that Ryanair was more efficient than SW in terms of "Cost Per Available Seat Mile" flown. SWs CPASM was 7 cents while Ryanair's was 6.8 cents. Other statistics indicated that Ryanair was more efficient in terms of passengers per employee (SW: 2,443; Ryanair: 3,077) and employees per aircraft (SW: 81; Ryanair: 50).[506] More recently, Ryanair has eliminated seat-back pockets, reclining seats, personal air vents and window shades to save even more money.[507] However, in a recent move, Ryanair recently acquired in-flight entertainment, similar to JetBlue, but charges for its use to boost ancillary revenues.[508]

Ryanair, however, did not emulate SW's traits of focusing on employees (often rated in *Fortune Magazine's* "Top 100 Companies to Work For") or its customer service philosophy. In fact, O'Leary is famous for telling his customers where to "get off" if they complain about cancelled flights, and barring them from boarding a plane without a passport. Ryanair adhered to the rule that a passport was the only acceptable form of identification. People in the company half-jokingly insist that O'Leary would not even allow his own grandmother on a Ryanair flight if she did not have the proper identification.

Ryanair is given the most grief with regard to its no-refund policy. O'Leary even reneged on a publicity deal granting free flights for life to Ryanair's one-millionth customer. However, a court reversed this decision, citing O'Leary's overly hostile treatment of the customer. *Financial Times* reporter Simon Bowley notes that, "O'Leary's investors must have loved the fact that their money was entrusted to such a miser."[509] Ryanair's success lies in the fact that if there are any areas in which to save costs, O'Leary is going to do it.

In addition, O'Leary has no use for unions. In fact, he has waged fierce battles to keep Ryanair's baggage-handling crew and pilots from unionizing. Most recently, its pilots have been in talks with the British Airline Pilots Association (BALPA). Warwick Brady, the Director of Flight Operations at Stansted, sums up the attitude of Ryanair's management about unions in a recent memo:

> We have no objection to any Ryanair pilot joining Balpa, the Taliban, the Monster Raving Loonies or indeed the Moonies. Each individual is perfectly free to join whatever organization he/she chooses. Balpa, in return for your membership, will charge you one percent of your total salary, a sum that will amount to £1,000—yes £1,000—each year. If you want to waste £1,000 we recommend fast women, slow horses, or even greyhound racing; at least you'll have a few minutes of fun, which is more than you'll have with Balpa.[510]

O'Leary has long maintained that his employees are well compensated without needing union negotiations. Flight attendants can earn extra income by selling in-flight entertainment, meals, and drinks.

When Ryanair acquired the airline Buzz from Dutch carrier KLM in 2003, it cut 500 of the 600 jobs and refused to accept the union-backed contracts of the employees he transferred to Ryanair. Former Buzz employees work some of the longest hours in the business now that they are employed at Ryanair. A Ryanair pilot flies around 80 to 90 hours a month while the legal maximum is 100 hours. British Airways pilots fly about half as many hours as their counterparts at Ryanair. However, Ryanair's pilot compensation is close to the highest in the industry, earning one-third more than British Airways pilots. Employees at Ryanair also have stock options, and this additional perk further encourages employees to work hard. Ryanair is able to fly more than 24 million passengers each year with only 2,000 employees, while Lufthansa flies twice as many passengers with 30,000 employees.[511] Ryanair's high employee productivity is yet another factor contributing to its low costs.

RYANAIR TAKES OFF

With a new cost-cutting strategy in place, Ryanair management increased the pressure on Aer Lingus and British Airways. Ryanair began offering low fare "seat sales" on its flights. Aer Lingus started copying this tactic, in some cases matching Ryanair's fares. This led Ryanair employees to be concerned that the flight information they had to file with the Department of Transport was being leaked to the competition. The seat-sales tactic managed to scare British Airways off its flights between the UK and Ireland since it did not want to "waste its valuable Heathrow slots on ridiculous fares."[512] Aer Lingus was facing financial difficulty because it had not expanded its capacity when beginning the price war with Ryanair. By 1992, Ryanair's new strategy finally seemed to be working. The airline carried 2.5 million passengers and reported a profit of £850,000—a significantly conservative amount that could have been as high as £3.5 million. The accountants at Ryanair created higher-than-necessary cash maintenance reserve expenses. The impact of this accounting method was to make the company look less profitable than it actually was. Ryanair wanted to continue claiming that Aer Rianta's costs were exorbitant; also, Ryan had accumulated huge debts after GPA collapsed and creditors would have been closely monitoring its income from Ryanair.[513]

O'Leary became Chief Executive Officer after Hayes announced his departure at the end of 1993. He went into a cost-cutting frenzy, creating a policy that cover sheets not be used when sending a fax, and that pilots should buy their own pens and uniforms, and take notepads from hotels.[514] The new CEO negotiated unheard-of deals with the airports to which it flew by promising to bring more passengers to the smaller airports with its lower fares. In turn, the airports could make more money by selling the airline more services and by gaining economies of scale.

Ryanair management began looking at new routes to fly. Even in this area, O'Leary was extremely cost-conscious. He boasts that "some airlines enter a new route and aim to make a profit in three years. We will not enter a route if we cannot break even in three hours and grow the market by at least 100 percent."[515] Ryanair and rival discount airline, easyJet, have profited from adhering to a model of only entering markets where lowering the price sharply increases demand. This model is so effective that Stelios Haji-Ioannou, the founder of easyJet, is applying it to other business lines, such as easyHotel, easyBus, easyCruise, and possibly even easyTelecom and easyPizza. He remarks, "There's no point in say, offering a cut-rate burial service. The demand for funerals isn't going to go up regardless of the price."[516]

O'Leary next focused on airport charges. He discovered that if he flew to secondary airports he could negotiate much cheaper fees at a fraction of the charge he incurred at the major airports. Some airports even let Ryanair to fly in with no charges because the airline would bring in more passengers. The small airports knew they could make their money from parking fees and duty-free sales that the higher passenger volumes would generate. In a highly publicized dispute with Aer Rianta, the state-owned airport authority in Dublin, O'Leary claimed that, "It is now vital we are competitive with the deals we are getting with airports around Europe. Of the 27 airports we use, 23 will absorb the cost of lost duty-free revenue. Aer Rianta's charges are the highest we pay anywhere."[517] O'Leary thought the fees Ryanair paid at Dublin airport was outrageous, especially considering the fact that Ryanair's home country was charging him the most.

Ryanair's management made deals with airports promising a certain volume of passengers each year, or pay the difference. In return, the airports would give Ryanair a huge discount on fees per passenger. Some airports even allowed Ryanair to land with no fees. O'Leary was able to negotiate deals so that the airports would pay Ryanair to come to them. In return Ryanair would bring in large numbers of passengers that not only benefited the airport, but also the local economy. The highly publicized deal that Ryanair received from Brussels South Charleroi Airport and the government of the surrounding Walloon Region was later ruled a state subsidy, and the European Commission required Ryanair to pay back four million euros. This ruling is going through the appeals process.

Some argue that the airline has gone too far with its cost-cutting strategy particularly with Ryanair's refusal to pay for the use of wheelchairs by disabled passengers. The airport authorities own the wheelchairs and charge for their use, and most airlines readily absorb this fee. Ryanair, however, refuses to do so, citing the airport as the responsible party. Disability action and equality groups are outraged by this policy, and newspapers have even published special columns dedicated to Ryanair complaints. Another example of Ryanair's refusal to bear additional costs shows its inflexibility. When the airline caterer, Gate Gourmet, began charging for ice previously supplied free with beverage purchases, Ryanair refused to pay and instead served beverages without it. Not only did this irritate customers who pay for the drinks—only to get them warm, but also the flight attendants, whose commissions are based on their in-flight sales. It was embarrassing for the attendants to have to tell frequent flyers that the airline was "out of ice today" on a recurring basis. However, when the Gate Gourmet realized that Ryanair was not giving in despite all the complaints, Gate Gourmet conceded and resumed supplying ice.[518]

Ryanair flies to many secondary airports located several miles outside of major cities, some as far as or more than 100 km away. Since these airports have lower landing fees and permit faster landings and take-offs, enabling it to fly more hours per day, the discount airline benefits. However, to build demand, Ryanair advertises its flights based on the name of the closest large city. Ryanair found itself in trouble with the advertising ethics boards regarding its claims to fly to cities such as Frankfurt and Paris. Frankfurt-Hahn airport is actually 110 km from Frankfurt, and the Paris-Bauvais airport is 56 km from Paris, approximately a one-hour drive. One reporter described the Paris-Beauvais airport as "a corrugated metal warehouse with no toilet seats in the bathrooms." She goes on to describe the atmosphere inside the terminal as "so informal that a group of French political science students felt free to unpack a soccer ball and start a lively scrimmage in front of the check-in counters—accidentally striking one passenger with the ball."[519]

Ryanair has also been penalized for its other advertising campaigns. One censure involved Ryanair's ad featuring the Pope claiming the "fourth secret of Fatima" due to the low fares Ryanair offered there. Another ad claimed British Airways is an airline of "Expensive bastards," providing a list comparing Ryanair and British Airways rates. The result was additional censure from the Advertising Standards Authority.[520] Despite the good or bad publicity the airline receives, it maintains the position that there is no such thing as bad publicity. Most advertising themes are generated by Ryanair's employees. Sinead Finn, Ryanair's Director of Sales and Marketing, proclaims, "I don't see any value in paying for outside agencies when we have 1,800 employees with an average age of only 28. At the moment I have a bank of 250 different advertising ideas."[521] Tim Jeans, former Sales and Marketing Director at Ryanair, adds that the advertising is made to look "cheap and unpretentious" to attract more of the general public to fly. He further notes that, "Ryanair promises nothing and thus manages to exceed the expectations of most of its passengers."[522]

Another cost that Ryanair first cut and then eliminated was travel agent commissions and fees. Travel agencies had long profited by booking flights for the airlines and receiving a 9 percent commission. Ryanair decided to trim this commission to 7.5 percent, incurring the wrath of many travel agents who then decided to boycott booking Ryanair flights.[523] However, that response backfired since its customers sought out the travel agents who continued to book cheap Ryanair's flights. Later, Ryanair realized that, like SW, it could completely eliminate most travel agent costs by enabling customers to book flights themselves through a website. Ryanair.com was created in 2000, and by 2002, the airline was receiving 94 percent of its bookings online. The website secures nearly 500 million page-views each month, and was named the most popular airline on the Web in 2003 by Google.[524] Airline staff members constantly monitor the online bookings so that when demand is down they can slash prices, and when demand is strong, they can raise fares.[525]

The website also boosts profits by providing ancillary revenues (Figure 10.1). Through Ryanair's website, customers can book hotel rooms, rental cars, buy travel insurance, and sign up for a Ryanair credit card. In the fiscal year 2004, Ryanair's ancillary revenue figures increased 35 percent, reflecting strong growth in non-flight scheduled

Figure 10.1: Ryanair Six-year Ancillary Revenue Growth

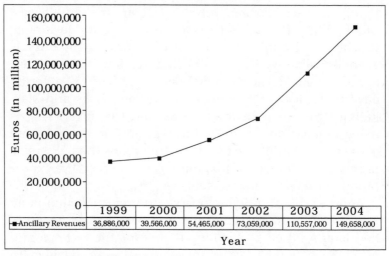

	1999	2000	2001	2002	2003	2004
Ancillary Revenues	36,886,000	39,566,000	54,465,000	73,059,000	110,557,000	149,658,000

Year

Source: Ryanair Annual Reports.

revenue. Ancillary revenues also include any meals or drinks bought on flights and excess baggage charged. Flight attendants are encouraged to sell food and drinks on board flights with their commission compensation directly tied to their sales. In the opinion of some passengers, such incentives create pushy flight attendants. Ryanair has eliminated its catering costs while serving free drinks onboard flights from new companies wanting to advertise their beverages and stimulate demand.[526]

Excess baggage charges can be steep, and the weight limit is quite low in comparison with other airlines. Ryanair has also used SW's idea of generating revenues by having its planes fly billboards painted with Kilkenny beer, Jaguar cars and the *Sun* newspaper advertisements, among others. These sponsorship deals are akin to having an additional passenger aboard each flight.[527]

Ryanair boasts the best punctuality rates on its website, updating the figures monthly. An entire page on the website is devoted to a comparison of Ryanair's punctuality ratings against easyJet's. The website states, easyJet (is) just another high-fare almost always-late airline. It is hopeless when it comes to efficiency and on-time performance, and its fares are 70 percent more expensive than Ryanair. Ryanair is committed to telling the public the truth—there is only one low-fare, on-time airline and that's Ryanair, not easyJet.[528]

Due to Ryanair's targeted 25-minute turnaround, on-time or even early flights are the norm. Because of low traffic congestion in the secondary airports, the airline is able to take off as soon as all passengers have boarded. *Wall Street Journal* reporter, Jane Spencer, noted that,

> Despite the unusual airport, Ryanair delivered on efficiency. Our flight to Spain, listed as almost two hours long, managed to arrive in Spain a startling 55 minutes early. As soon as all scheduled passengers arrived, the plane simply took off.[529]

Ryanair uses only one type of aircraft to reduce training time for its pilots and staff and also spare parts inventory. O'Leary lovingly refers to his fleet of Boeing 737s as his Toyota Corollas.[530] When Ryanair placed a huge order in 1998 for 45 next-generation 737-800 series aircraft, Boeing, the world's largest aircraft manufacturer, was a little nervous about conducting a multi-billion dollar business deal with a relatively unknown airline. Boeing developed a computer simulation to test for flaws that might damage the airline's ability to pay down the road, such as drops in demand and changes in exchange rates and aviation fuel prices. "We could not find a quarter when they were not profitable. The lowest we could do was a breakeven. It is probably the most robust model we have encountered," according to Eric Hild, Boeing's Director of Sales for UK and Ireland.[531]

Ryanair's success has put quite a damper on the profits of other airlines in Europe. In fact, the once all-powerful Air France, Lufthansa, and British Airways now have lower market capitalization than Ryanair. During 2002,

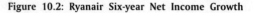

Figure 10.2: Ryanair Six-year Net Income Growth

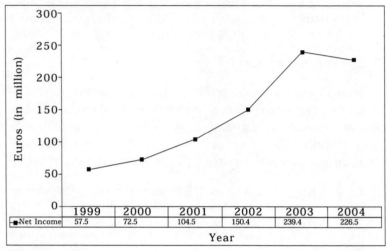

	1999	2000	2001	2002	2003	2004
■ Net Income	57.5	72.5	104.5	150.4	239.4	226.5

Year

Source: Ryanair Annual Reports.

while almost every airline in the world recorded huge losses after the terrorist attacks in the United States, Ryanair reported an incredible 59 percent increase in profits (Figure 10.2), thriving in the face of the events surrounding 2002.

Ryanair almost forced Aer Lingus into bankruptcy in 2001, and since then, the flag carrier has restructured its business, modeling itself after none other than Ryanair. Alitalia, the Italian flag carrier, has come close to bankruptcy while other major players have disappeared. But Ryanair posts passenger and revenue records each year. O'Leary commented about his rival British Airways,

> They have waterfalls in the headquarters out at Heathrow, they swan around sipping cappuccinos, thinking they are masters of the universe. But British Airways is stuck on the horns of a dilemma. Its costs are high, so it charges high prices, while we are going at it like gangbusters.[532]

THE ROAD AHEAD

Ryanair flew 34.8 million passengers in its fiscal year 2006 and operated in 17 bases across Europe, with the most recent additions being Madrid and Marseilies.[533] At the end of 2006, Ryanair was flying more than 425 routes to 130 destinations, and had 103 planes in its fleet. The airline was expecting to carry 42.5 million passengers in 2007. In 2002, Ryanair made headlines when it announced a long-term partnership with Boeing. It placed an order to acquire 150 new Boeing 737-800 series aircrafts between 2002 and 2010. And in 2003, Ryanair placed an order for an additional 100 aircrafts to facilitate its rapid European growth plans.[534]

Ryanair flies 189 routes to over 87 destinations and it flew 74 aircrafts at the end of 2004. Its fleet of airplanes includes fifty-five 189-seat Boeing 737-800s, thirteen 130-seat Boeing 737-200s, and six 148-seat Boeing 737-300s.

Ryanair boasts that it is Europe's second largest international scheduled carrier behind Lufthansa and just ahead of British Airways with Air France not far behind.[535] In October 2004, for the first time ever, the airline flew more passengers across Europe than British Airways. With the arrival of the remainder of the Boeing fleet, Ryanair will have the capacity to fly over 50 million passengers in a few years and it plans to be the largest airline outside the United States by 2008. If Ryanair continues as it has been doing, it should be able to reach this goal. However, it could be detrimental to Ryanair's growth plans if the airline is no longer allowed to obtain favorable landing agreements with smaller airports. However, as one of its advertisements claims, for the time being, Ryanair is "taking off!"

Chapter Eleven

Big Response to First Discount Airlines in Asia

LOW-FARE AIRLINES have operated in Asia only since the beginning of the 21st century. The first discount airline in Asia was Air Asia, based in Malaysia. It began offering deeply discounted fares in early 2002. Word rapidly spread about Air Asia's strong demand and so Air Deccan was formed in India, with operations beginning in August 2003. It became clear that there was large demand from the general public for low-cost basic airline service. Both Air Asia and Air Deccan adopted several of the techniques used by SW in the United States and Ryanair in Europe.

AIR ASIA AND ITS SUBSIDIARIES

Malaysia, in Southeast Asia, is a country of 23 million people, with regular flyers accounting for just 3 percent of the population. Malaysia Airlines had been the sole domestic and international carrier in Malaysia until the industry was deregulated in the second half of the 1990s. The first new airline to be formed following deregulation was Air Asia. It began operating on November 15, 1996 with two Boeing 737-300s. On major domestic routes, Air Asia competed with Malaysia Airlines, but was unable to attract enough customers to operate profitably. Air Asia also obtained rights for international service to four cities, but soon discontinued service to two of them. As a consequence of its continuing loses, Air Asia was sold to a local company, Tune Air, on December 8, 2001. The new owner agreed to assume 50 percent of its net liabilities, which amounted to $54 million.[536]

Tune Air decided to continue to use the name Air Asia, but changed the nature of its operations from a full-service high-price airline to a no-frills low-price airline. Tony Fernandes, Chief Executive Officer of the new discount airline, extensively studied the operations of SW in the United States and Ryanair in Europe. He indicated that many of the characteristics of Air Asia would be based on the nature of these two highly successful discount airlines. He noted that the four most profitable airlines in the world were discount airlines. Given his obsession for cost reductions, Fernandes actually reduced Air Asia's cost per mile to less than the costs at SW and Ryanair.[537]

Some airline analysts doubted if the first discount airline in Asia could survive, when the long-established Malaysia Airlines had lost a large amount of money in recent years flying domestic routes. Fernandes's response was that a period of recession was a good time to start a low-cost airline because around the world cost-conscious consumers and companies increasingly fly discount airlines, and book fewer flights on traditional airlines. Air Asia planned to charge 50 percent less than Malaysia Airlines, and believed this would generate a strong demand for it. Air Asia executives believed that with low fares, the discount airline could attract many first-time flyers. Conor McCarthy, co-founder of Air Asia said, "We are looking at growing that market, and attracting people off the motorways and railways and onto aircraft." Furthermore, Malaysia recently signed an open-sky agreement with Thailand, making it possible to serve the larger regional market in the future.[538]

To launch the new discount airline, Air Asia announced a two-month special introductory offer for January and February 2002. The response was overwhelming, causing Air Asia to add 16 telephone lines and 20 computer terminals at its call center. Fernandes then stated, "by next weekend we will be dealing with 300 travel agents compared to 25 now." His goal was to develop strong demand and to be profitable by the end of the first year of operations.[539] Malaysia's Transportation Minister Ling Sik said Air Asia's low fares would boost domestic tourism with more people flying, which would be good for the country. He further stated that the new airline "would be good for Malaysia Airlines as it will provide competition and may prompt the national airline to drop some unprofitable routes and eventually concentrate on international routes."[540]

How Air Asia Can Undercut Malaysia Air by 50 Percent

During 2002, the new owners of Air Asia planned to expand its fleet of airplanes from two to six Boeing 737-300 aircrafts, each with a capacity of 148 seats, and to increase the number of cities served from five to ten. It took steps to create the first low-cost, discount airline in Asia. These included:

- Adoption of a non-union culture
- No frequent-flyer program
- Using one type of aircraft to save maintenance and training costs
- Switching on the air conditioning only before the flight takes off
- Using secondary airports rather than primary airports to save on landing and parking fees
- Using a staircase rather than an aerobridge
- Leasing aircraft at an attractive rate.[541]

EIGHT MORE WAYS AIR ASIA REDUCED ITS COSTS

Payment Method

Initially, Air Asia charged eight different fares for a typical flight. The earlier a person booked a flight, the cheaper the fare. Even last-minute tickets cost less than the fares of Malaysia Airlines. Customers could pay for their tickets by using one of the major credit cards—Visa, Master Charge, American Express, or Diners—but cash or checks were not accepted. There was a discount for booking flights over the Internet.

Tickets

In contrast to most airlines, Air Asia developed a "ticketless" system to help minimize its costs. People buying tickets were issued a booking number, although that was not required for checking in. To board an airline, all passengers had to do was show their identification card; a passport was required for tourists.

No Frills

The discounter served no complimentary meals or drinks, and customers wanting these items had to pay for them.

Check-in

Passengers could check in no sooner than two hours before a flight, and no later than 45 minutes before a flight was scheduled to take off.

Boarding

Passengers were required to board flights no later than 30 minutes before departure. Those who arrived later than that were not allowed to board the flight, had to forfeit their seats, and received no refunds or transfers.

Seating

Seating was on a "first-come basis", allowing passengers to choose whatever available seat they wanted.

Paperless Cockpit

Pilots were issued laptops on which they prepared for flights and accessed flight manuals. It was estimated that this contributed to savings of 4,800 man-hours during the first year of operations.[542]

Extending the Life of Airplanes Tires

Fernandes continued to be "fanatical about finding ways to lower costs" in order to offer deeply discounted fares, support rapid growth, and make a profit. His chief engineer told him one day that the life of tires on landing gears cost $6,000 for each six-wheel Boeing 737. He went on to say that the tires would last considerably longer if pilots made a "shallower approach to landing." Bypassing the chain of command, Fernandes immediately ordered Air Asia pilots to adopt this mode of landing. As a result, tires lasted 180 landings in comparison to 70 landings before the change.[543]

THREATS TO THE SURVIVAL OF AIR ASIA

In August 2002, just eight months after Air Asia started flying, Malaysia Air—the dominant full-service and high-cost carrier—reduced its domestic fares by 50 percent and matched the low fares of Air Asia's discount airline. Malaysia Airlines was already losing millions on its domestic flights, in large part due to flying large-capacity, wide-bodied jets on its domestic routes. These bigger aircrafts were purchased for their longer and profitable international flights. According to Fernandes, Malaysia Air's reduction of its domestic prices by 50 percent represented unfair competition, as it was already losing money on these flights. He said that if Malaysia Airlines' price cuts continued, his discount airline would be driven out of business within four months. He further said "We welcome competition, but it has to be fair and on a level playing field...."[544]

Fernandes sent a note to Malaysia's Transportation Minister protesting Malaysia Airlines' sharp price cuts on Air Asia routes. He argued that the significant price reductions, in face of already large losses on its domestic routes, represented "unfair competition." He further noted that the Malaysian government was underwriting the plan to drive Air Asia out of business by assuming the losses of Malaysia Airlines. He went on to say that Air Asia "is a seven-month old baby and we operate with only five aircraft, yet we have made a profit .... If we close down, it won't do any good to the aviation industry."[545]

Ling Silk, Malaysian Transportation Minister, announced that his administrators would meet with both airlines to ensure that that Malaysia Airlines' sharp fare reductions constituted "fair and healthy competition." He said, "Lower fares would benefit consumers, but they must also be financially viable to the airline in the long run." Malaysia Airlines' 50 percent fare reductions resulted in a 40 percent drop in Air Asia's bookings within a few days. The major airline's fare reduction came as a surprise since it had requested a 51 percent increase in domestic fares on the previous year as it was losing $200,000 every month. At the time of the fare war, Air Asia operated just five Boeing 737-800s while Malaysia Airlines operated 39 737-400s. Fernandes stated it was clear that the high-cost, high-service Malaysia Airlines was intent on pushing the young discounter out of business so that it could again raise its fares. The hearings revealed that in other parts of the world, start-up discount airlines were put out of business by larger and better-financed airlines using temporary price cuts like those of Malaysia Airlines.[546]

Shortly after Malaysian Airlines' sharp fare reduction, Fernandes appeared uninvited to one of its exclusive cocktail parties. Before a crowd of people he confronted the guest of honor—Malaysia's Transportation Minister. He charged that the state-owned airline was attempting to crush its small start-up competitor and drive it out of business. He pleaded with the minister to stop Malaysia Airlines' unfair price reductions. Soon afterwards, the Minister of Transportation ordered the airline to stop the selective price cuts targeted at Air Asia.[547]

In contrast to what had happened in the United States, the Malaysian Aviation Administration ruled against Malaysian Airlines' predatory behavior which forced it to restore prices to their prior levels. In the United States, the Supreme Court had failed to stop predatory pricing by American against small start-up discount carriers. Once the small discount airlines were driven out of business, American major airlines raised their prices to the levels they were before temporarily lowering them. As discussed in the earlier chapters, predatory pricing has been used extensively in the United States by the high-cost major airlines to thwart the growth of discount airlines, and maintain high prices in many markets.

AIR ASIA'S LOW-COST SERVICE BECOMES A BIG HIT

After Malaysian Airlines failed to use predatory pricing to drive the discounter out of business, Air Asia continued on a path of rapid growth. From July to December 2002, Air Asia sold 80 percent of its seats, at times even reaching 100 percent, and it was highly profitable. During 2002, Air Asia earned $8 million on sales of $66 million— incredible results for any new airline. In addition, from the beginning of 2002 to mid-2003, Air Asia increased its fleet from two to eight airplanes and the number of passengers it carried climbed from 16,000 to 150,000 per month.[548] Rapid expansion continued as a key aspect of Air Asia's strategy. In June 2003, it placed an order with Boeing for 10 additional aircraft over the next year, increasing its fleet size to 18 aircrafts.[549]

By the end of 2003, nearly two years after its launch, Air Asia was flying to 17 cities in Malaysia. According to Fernandes, "I think that it is now a well-established product. If you go out into the Malaysian market, people have a good idea of what the no-frill, low-fares model is." Conor McCarthy, an adviser to Fernandes, said,

> What we really wanted ... was a company that worked on the basis of the average man on the street being able to afford our air fares, and people who would not have considered flying, or would not fly as often as they do now.[550]

Air Asia's success led to the establishment of a number of new discount airlines in Malaysia and in nearby countries that emulated its discount strategy.

Air Asia Starts International Expansion

After two years of shaking up Malaysia's airline industry, Fernandes began making plans to expand Air Asia internationally. He said in late 2003 that, "We've got lots of balls in the air right now and really exciting things are happening."[551] Fernandes indicated that there was a large opportunity for growth by expanding north to Thailand and South to Indonesia. Furthermore, while Malaysia had a population of 24 million people, Thailand had a population of 62 million people and Indonesia had 212 million people in 2003. He said there was considerable opportunity to provide discount airline service to these adjacent countries. Air Asia would stimulate air travel among a population that previously could not afford to travel by air, or people who lived in areas not served by other airlines.[552] The international expansion plan would help Air Asia cement its position as the largest low-cost carrier in all of Asia.

Flying to Thailand

In February 2004, Air Asia created a new airline in Thailand with plans to fly to six cities with four aircrafts by the end of the year. Air Asia held a 49 percent share in the new discount airline, while the Shin Corporation, owned by the family of Thailand's prime minister, had a 50 percent stake in Thai Air Asia. Fernandes said, "Shin Corporation was chosen because of its financial strength, and synergy in information technology and telecommunications," which would support the airline's Internet and mobile-phone bookings. Air Asia would run the new airline to be called Thai Air Asia. The chief executive officer of Shin Corporation said,

> Last year, only 10 percent of Thailand's population traveled by air. Based on these numbers, we have concluded that our budget airline has huge market potential and we are confident that it will return a profit in the first year.

The carrier projected a demand of one million tickets during 2004 with prices 40–50 percent below the established airlines.[553]

Thai Air Asia grew steadily in the first year and a half from early February 2004 through August 2005. By mid-2005, it operated a fleet of six Boeing 737-300s flying to 11 cities in Thailand and to four international destinations.[554] Thai Air Asia was active in trying to boost tourism to the four southern provinces struck by the December 2004 tsunami. The Tourism Authority of Thailand chose the new discount airline to lead a conference to discuss ways to increase air traffic within Thailand and to overseas locations. The country's large and established Thai Airways International helped Air Asia to expand and shared four international routes it had monopolized. This decision was based on the fact that its discount fares would stimulate international air traffic by the general public, which otherwise could not afford to fly to Thailand.[555]

Expansion into Indonesia

The Indonesian government decided to license seven new airlines in 1999 to provide commercial service. One of these was PT AWAir International Airline. However, PT AWAir ceased operations on March 8, 2002 with management citing tough competition. Air Asia entered into an agreement to purchase a 49 percent share in PT AWAir in March 2005. The acquisition was not expected to have any material impact on Air Asia's consolidated earnings through June 2005. In its prospectus, Air Asia Indonesia said that it planned to adopt a low-cost model. It would be similar to Thai Air Asia in that it would be 49 percent owned by Air Asia. Fernandes said that "It will be remodeled after the Malaysian carrier," and that "AWAir can only serve to strengthen domestic travel in Indonesia."

SUCCESS RECORD AND PLANS FOR THE FUTURE

By the second half of 2005, Air Asia and its two subsidiary airlines were serving more than 100 domestic and international routes with a fleet of 30 Boeing 737-300s (148 seats each). Over its first three and a half years of operations, Air Asia carried 11 million passengers and was the largest discount airline in Asia. During the second half of 2004, it earned $14.62 million, while many airlines were reporting staggering losses.[556]

The new low-cost carriers in Southeast Asia anticipated major consolidation, due to higher fuel prices. Fernandes said that Air Asia was open to acquiring other airlines, but "it depends on what they have to offer." By mid-2005, Air Asia had already been approached to take over a smaller low-cost airline, but Fernandes felt the price was too high and declined. Given that close to a half dozen discounters flocked to Southeast Asia in 2004 and 2005, there was no question about the eventual consolidation among the new airlines. The issue is exactly when this will take place. With soaring jet fuel prices, major consolidation of the discount airlines in Southeast Asia is expected to happen very soon.[557]

The discount airline continuesd to enjoy strong demand, and Air Asia and its subsidiaries placed an order for 40 Airbus 320s in January 2005, with an option for 40 additional airplanes. Air Asia was then operating a fleet of 30 Boeing 737-300s with its network covering 17 domestic destinations and 10 regional routes. In March, the order was increased from 40 to 60 Airbus planes, one delivered each month starting in December 2005 and continuing through 2010.[558]

Air Asia's huge achievement led it to be one of the recipients of the Market Leadership Awards in April 2005. Lifting the achievement award statue in the air, Fernandes stated,

> Our staff has done an amazing job. We persevered through words I never heard before: SARS, tsunami, bird flu, and oil prices of $60. But through all that we have continued to make money, which primarily is due to our cost, which at present is 2.1 cents per ASK. That's audited and true and Michael O'Leary [of Ryanair] cannot say that he's lowest any more.... I dedicate this award to our staff.[559]

There is no question about there being a huge untapped market in Asia for discount air service which more of the general public can afford, and that the market is going to grow. Overall air travel grew by 20 percent in Southeast Asia during 2004. But there are also some challenging differences that discount airlines experience in Southeast Asia. There is a range of rules in the Southeast Asia region that are not confronted by discount airlines in Europe and the United States. According to Andrew Pyne, a former Cathay Pacific Airway executive, "In Asia, the environment is still highly regulated, very restricted. So without a clear understanding of these regulations, you would never get beyond first base." Furthermore, Asian governments have been reluctant to build lower cost, budget-based airports that provide cheaper landing and take-off fees and provide faster turnaround time.[560]

Air Deccan in India

Captain G.R. Gopinath, the founder of Air Deccan of India, stated that his *eureka* moment occurred during a trip to the United States. While passing through Phoenix he was amazed to find that the "airport handled about 100,000 passengers per day." He said that, "It suddenly shook me when I did the numbers. It came to 30-odd million passengers a year." That was roughly twice the number that flew each year in all of India. He went on to say that India had a growing middle-class population, roughly the size of Europe, which he felt was ripe for services of a first low-cost carrier. Skeptics told him that the concept of a low-cost carrier would never work in India for several reasons, including the fact that most of the people did not have Internet access, which Air Deccan planned to use to reduce booking costs. After launching the first and extremely successful low-cost carrier in India, he said, "Thank God I never went to a consultant."[561]

Air Deccan was launched as the first no-frills airline in India in August 2003. It was to provide air service to secondary cities in the southern part of India with six turboprop airplanes having a capacity of 48 passengers. The new discounter was modeled after SW, with point-to-point service. Air Deccan adopted a "lean-and-mean" approach to staffing levels and "aims at maintaining a low aircraft-to-employee ratio" to help hold costs down and keep ticket prices low. According to Gopinath, "there are just 400 flights a day now throughout India, a country of a billion people." Air Deccan planned to start operating 70 flights a day in the near future, which would make the new discounter a significant player in the domestic airline market. Gopinath's target market was the 4.7 billion people who ride India's extensive railroad system each year.[562]

Following the successful launch of the new discount airline, the airline's director of operations stated that

Air Deccan's vision is to 'empower every Indian to fly', and we are doing so not only by offering low airfares, but also providing air connectivity to unconnected cities. With our expansion, we have realized that the challenges ahead of us are tough and it requires our focused effort to visualize and actualize the dream.... We are concentrating on expanding our network in India by increasing frequencies to the existing destinations and opening ... newer destinations.[563]

Air Deccan planned to charge 30 percent less than the standard airfare of the established full-service airlines. To keep its costs low, there was only one passenger-serving per airplane; passengers paid for drinks and food, and tickets were booked online. Gopinath also planned fast turnaround times for landing and take-offs so that his aircraft would fly more hours per day than existing airlines. Gopinath was no novice to the airline industry. He ran Deccan Aviation, India's largest private charter company. India's growing domestic market provided a significant opportunity since many of its regional airports could only be served by Air Deccan. Passenger turboprop airplanes do not require long runways, as do jet aircraft. Clearly, Gopinath was providing ground-breaking service with his fleet of six, 48-seater turboprop airplanes to unserved cities in India.[564]

There were several operating advantages to flying Bombardier turboprop airplanes that were important to Air Deccan's strategy of charging lower prices than its major competitors. The cost savings associated with its turboprop aircraft included:

- 14 percent lower crew costs
- 18 percent lower capital costs
- 20 percent lower airframe weight-related costs
- 26 percent lower airframe maintenance costs
- 28 percent lower fuel consumption
- 83 percent lower engine maintenance costs.[565]

One of the first cities to benefit from the startup of Air Deccan was Hubli, a city of low-rise office buildings, shuttered textile mills, and brownish-colored apartments located in the red-dirt hills of Karnataka. People who wanted to travel to the state capital of Bangalore, 250 miles to the southeast, had to travel by bus or train, a journey of seven to 10 hours. Now they could fly to Bangalore in about an hour by purchasing a ticket two weeks in advance for $40 each way. This was about the price of a berth on an air-conditioned train. Or if they booked their flight 45 days in advance, the cost would be reduced to a mere $11.[566]

According to the senior administrator for Hubli, "without air connectivity, a city has a ceiling. It cannot grow further and it will stagnate." He went on to state that since the air service began, firms have started considering Hubli as a location for outsourcing and software development, as well as other uses. But air service is still in its infancy in Hubli. At times, cows and people wander on to the runway, and the passenger lounge is not much larger than a living room. Furthermore, delays on account of weather are common since the airport does not have landing instruments and there is only audio communication between the ground and the airplanes.[567]

Acceptance and Rapid Expansion

In August 2005, Gopinath was interviewed by *Businessline*, almost 18 months after the initial flight of the first discount airline in India. He reported that the discount airline had experienced a great response and that the airline was carrying 1,000 passengers a day, and that its market share had rapidly climbed to 8 percent in India. He went on to say that by February 2006, Air Deccan would be flying 100 flights per day and, by March, it would have flown one million passengers. He added that the number of employees had increased in 18 months to 1,000. Gopinath explained that, we learned as we went along, and kept fine-tuning the operation and that has been important to our success. A key to our success is low cost and low price and a high level of capacity utilization.

Air Deccan's revenue increased by 5 percent by charging for drinks and snacks, and selling advertising on the outside and inside of its airplanes.[568]

When it began operating in August 2003, Air Deccan tried to gain the attention of Airbus and Boeing, but it was ignored since there was no precedent in India for offering discount airline service. Instead, it settled on buying turbojets from France's ATR and concentrated on providing discount air service to smaller communities that had little or no air service. From one standpoint this may well have been a blessing since there was a huge pent-up demand for discount air services to mid-sized and major cities throughout India. Air Deccan provided an alternative for commuters of taking either an hour-long flight or spending 6–8 hours traveling to destinations by train or bus. By March 2005, Air Deccan was considered a huge success, selling 90 percent of its seats on 106 flights to 32 destinations.[569]

Air Deccan continued to expand its service to smaller cities in other parts of India, placing an order for 30 French turboprop airplanes in February 2005. Gopinath said that the new 42-passenger turboprops would help the discounter provide service to more small towns. As part of the deal, it would also acquire six used aircrafts. Delivery of the aircrafts would be spread over a five-year period with six to eight aircrafts being delivered each year.[570] Furthermore, given the discounter's rapid growth over its first 18 months of operations, Air Deccan was able to gain the attention of the major airline manufacturers—Airbus and Boeing. In April 2005, Air Deccan placed an order for 30 Airbus A320s worth $1.9 billion before discounts. Airbus also assigned three individuals with expertize in logistics, pilot training, and engineering support to work with Air Deccan as it gradually added larger aircrafts to its operation. The A320s were purchased to operate on routes between larger cities where they would compete with India's two established airlines and a host of new airlines. Air Deccan's plan was to launch service on metropolitan routes by July 2005, beginning with a flight to Delhi. The A320 carries 180 people in its all-economy class layout.[571]

Kapil Kau, head of Asia Pacific Aviation Consulting firm, said, "Air Deccan's success has changed everyone's mindset." He further noted that the air travel market was growing at an annual rate of 25 percent leading to the two major aircraft manufacturers to exert considerable effort to win new customers. Indian airlines are expected to purchase as many as 300 airplanes from 2005 through 2010. According to Richard Aboulafia, the Teal Group aerospace consultancy in Fairfax, Virginia, "India is the hottest growth market on the planet."[572]

Starting with four flights per day in August 2003, Air Deccan expanded at a torrid pace to 120 flights a day covering 36 destinations by July 2005. Its fleet consisted of 19 airplanes including 14 ATR turboprops and five A320 Airbus planes. With a fleet of 30 aircrafts planned by the end of 2005, Air Deccan became the second-largest carrier in India in a short two-year period of time. The discounter was expected to continue growing, adding one new Airbus 320 a month to its fleet over the next 60 months.[573]

CHALLENGES ON THE HORIZON

Some airline specialists question whether Air Deccan's future growth will occur as easily as in the past. Beginning late 2005, the discounter started flying on more major routes as it received one larger-capacity Airbus each month for 50 months. On major routes it would experience new competition from India's established airlines. Air

Deccan did not have this competition when flying its turboprop jets which provided service from smaller communities to large cities. The existing carriers could match Air Deccan's low fares when it began providing service between major cities. This could keep the discounter from selling enough seats to operate profitably on the major routes. This was not a far-fetched thought; the major airlines used this strategy to drive all of the new discount airlines out of business or into bankruptcy in the United States over the first 10 years of airline deregulation from 1978 to 1988. Furthermore, selective price cuts by the major airlines have prevented many start-up discount airlines from succeeding since then.[574]

There are further challenges confronting the successful expansion of Air Deccan as it increases service to major cities with its larger-capacity Airbus 320s. Five new discount airlines have, or will soon start to operate. Another problem facing Air Deccan and other new discount airlines is that conditions are different in India from those in Europe and the United States. They are not as conducive to expanding discount air service in India. Clearly, the low-cost carriers can reduce costs of in-flight services by not providing free in-flight food and having more seats per aircraft. But they cannot hedge fuel prices like SW has done to hold its costs down. In addition, the low penetration of the Internet in India means that the discounters will need to rely more heavily on booking agents who charge considerable fees. Another difference is that most of the larger cities in India have just one airport. They do not have lower-cost secondary airports that discounters use in the United States and Europe which save on landing fees and reduce turnaround times, permitting them to fly more hours per day. These differences could inhibit deep discounting of fares by Air Deccan in India.[575] For these reasons, only time will tell how successful the discount model will be in providing service between major cities in India.

Air Deccan made the decision to find a strong and experienced airline manager to fill the position of chief operating officer to respond to the challenging times ahead. Air Deccan considered a list of candidates from SW, easyJet, Ryanair, and Lufthansa. The airline finally decided to hire a senior official from Ryanair, the largest discount airline in Europe. Air Deccan's new manager, Warick Brady, began his challenging management position in September 2005. According to managing director Gopinath, he was selected "keeping in mind the massive growth and induction of aircraft that was planned...."[576] Clearly, the challenge would be huge to deploy the large number of new airplanes at a profit. Rapid expansion has contributed to the downfall of several one-time successful start-up discount airlines, so continuing to deploy planes at a profit was clearly a major challenge.

ASIAN OUTLOOK

The discount airline industry has grown steadily in the United States since airline deregulation in 1978. At present, it is estimated that close to 30 percent of US travelers choose to fly discount airlines instead of the more expensive and long-established major airlines. During the 1990s, European low-cost discount airlines grew rapidly. Market penetration of European discount airlines is expected to increase and maintain market share as large as that of discount airlines in the United States. As discussed earlier in this chapter, discount airlines first penetrated Asia beginning in 2002, and have grown steadily since then. The first discount airline was Air Asia, which operated in Southeast Asia (Malaysia, Indonesia, and Thailand). Air Asia demonstrated that there was a large pent-up demand by the general public and business travelers for discount air service from smaller cities to larger ones.

Given the strong response to Air Asia's operations in Southeast Asia, the tide of discount airlines spread to India. Air Deccan became the first discount carrier operating in India, also experiencing strong demand. More recently, discount airlines have initiated service in China. These airlines are expanding throughout Asia with more of the general public able to fly to distant cities, instead of having to travel by bus or train. The benefits to the general public and business travelers are considerable and the growth of discount airlines is helping to stimulate economic growth in Asia.

More recently, the young Asian discounters have placed sizable orders for larger capacity aircraft to be delivered from late 2005 through 2010. The once-small discount airlines are starting to provide service not just from small cities to larger ones, but also between larger cities. Increasingly they will provide a threat to the established airlines in Asia, and destructive price wars could be in the making. Furthermore, some of the major airlines in Asia are starting their own discount airlines, recognizing the existing and large pent-up demand. As a result of rapid increase of air travel in Asia (estimated to be 20 percent or more a year in several large countries), both Boeing and Airbus have targeted Asia which has a rapidly expanding demand for new airplanes.

Chapter Twelve

The Rise and Fall of the Major Airlines from 1995 to 2004

EARLIER CHAPTERS have discussed how the major airlines created their fortress-hub networks following deregulation. Leveraging their monopolistic market position, the second half of the 1980s proved to be fairly good years for the large legacy airlines after they destroyed the low-price start-up airlines. However, from 1990 to 1994, poor economic times and battles among the major airlines turned out to be disastrous. During this time period, the major airlines lost $12.64 billion more than what the airline industry had earned up to this point.[577] However, with the Internet and electronic-commerce boom, the economy grew rapidly over the remainder of the decade. The major airlines prospered from 1995 to 2000, making record profits.

There was a countervailing force developing at the same time that the major airlines were prospering. Low-cost and low-price carriers steadily grew their small base during this period. When the economy moved into recession in 2001 and growth slowed, the discount airlines grew rapidly and cut more deeply into the market share of the major airlines. The downturn was the worst in the history of the majors, and they incurred record losses. This chapter concludes with the perspective that the commercial airline industry is forever changed, and that the

number of major airlines needs to be reduced significantly.

1995–2000: The Boom Years

Having just experienced years of record losses, 1995
represented a true turning point for the major airlines.
All the top six legacy carriers had finally turned the corner
and were operating in the black once again. Fueled by the
new Internet and electronic-commerce boom, the major
airlines were rolling in cash and, in 1997 these major
airlines earned $4.8 billion. The industry outlook was so
positive that analysts were suggesting that these were
pivotal years for individual airlines and that continued
growth for years to come was almost certain.[578] Unfortunately, during these boom times, the majors became
overly fat and happy. Misguided business decisions were
common in the late 1990s, as everyone seemed to believe
in this idea of continued growth. As a result, many of the
problems the major carriers are struggling within the new
millennium were instigated during the boom at the end
of the previous millennium.

Before delving into the problematic issues of the boom
years, it is important to understand that the airline
industry as a whole has never been viewed in a favorable
light by many investors. Even in mid-1998, right after the
most profitable year ever for airlines, skeptics on Wall
Street were unconvinced. At that time, the S&P 500 was
trading at 23 times earnings per share while airline
stocks were only valued at 10 times earnings.[579] Glenn
Engel of Goldman Sachs & Co. explained it this way: "The
airline business has never made money over the course
of the business cycle. Until people know what it will do in
a downturn, investors will have the same attitude toward
airline stocks."[580] In most cases, the low valuations and
continuing outcry from experts should have been enough
to warrant caution for managers of the legacy airlines.

One anonymous industry analyst went as far as to say, "this industry has been viewed as something close to a gambling casino; [investors] see it as a labor intensive business being run by ego-driven managers. The market believes it's a lousily managed business."[581]

From the airlines' perspective, everything was just fine as the late 1990s provided plenty of profitability to cover the management's costly decisions. It was during this time that the major carriers fully exploited their monopolistic control over certain markets. The fortress hubs and connecting spoke system flown by regional carriers helped the legacy airlines maintain this imbalance of power. Business fares were significantly increased to improve airline revenue. This strategy worked so well that the cost side of the equation was allowed to increase substantially. The major airlines granted highly favorable contracts to labor unions, expanded capacity, and increased the number of aircrafts they operated. At the same time, most of the major carriers lost sight of the customer service aspect of the business. This led to consumer alienation and, in general, the flying public began to feel they were being taken advantage of at every turn. To make matters worse, this was also when the low-cost providers were able to make major inroads.

As discussed in earlier chapters, the major airlines relied heavily on the use of a hub-and-spoke model in order to use larger aircrafts and gain efficiencies. They also used predatory pricing to drive out most competitors that tried to enter their high-price fortress hubs. The system included using regional airlines to ferry in passengers to the legacies' hub, and then fly them on the legacy carriers to another of their hub markets. In November 1997, *Money* magazine reported, "If a major airline has the route from one city to another more or less to itself, you can expect it to charge exorbitant prices."[582] During the boom years, the major airlines felt that many of their fortress hubs were impenetrable. Or, if a low-cost provider did begin operating out of a particular hub, the major airlines believed the low-cost provider would simply not be able to survive in competition with the major carrier. The legacy carriers were making too much money during this time to worry about the growth of the low-price carriers.

To keep their income growing, the major carriers raised prices wherever possible and used complex revenue-management systems. In reviewing the 1997 performance of airlines, Jeff Long, an airline industry analyst at New York-based J.P. Morgan Securities, commented, "Heightened fares and improved yield management further enhanced airline financial performance."[583] During the boom years, revenue management and the computer systems that ran the algorithms, played a major role in covering up the runaway growth in airline costs. While pilots were routinely given pay increases, the number of working days was simultaneously decreased. Even as the boom was coming to an end in the summer of 2000, United promised its pilots industry-leading wages.[584]

The legacy carriers promoted long-haul traffic, and purchased larger aircraft primarily designed to carry a large number of passengers. Some analysts feared that the major airlines' rapid capacity growth would become an issue. In the summer of 1998, the *Washington Post* reported that airline capacity had been growing steadily for several years. This growth was cause for concern in Brian Harris's opinion, an airline analyst with Salomon Smith Barney. Industry experts worried that overcapacity could lead to pricing wars between the carriers.[585]

In their scramble for growth, the legacy carriers seemed to have forgotten about one very important aspect of the business—the customer. Time and time again, the major airlines were berated for their inability to keep up with passenger luggage or take care of passengers when flights were overbooked or delayed. As reported in the 1997 *Airline Quality Rating Report* (AQRR): "Passengers are increasingly upset with the treatment they receive from airlines despite apparent gains in overall quality."[586] Headley and Bowen, authors of the AQRR, also found that consumer dissatisfaction had reached an all-time high in 1997. According to BACK Information Services, an aviation-consulting firm, the major airlines were spending less on food. In 1996, the major airlines spent $3.02 per passenger, down 25 percent from $4.02 in 1989.[587] After Congress threatened to enact "a passenger bill of rights," the major airlines promised to begin improving overall service. Nonetheless, Headley and Bowens' AQRR reported that service deteriorated in almost every category in 1999.[588] The report concluded that if airlines did not clean up their act, consumer loyalties would vanish and passengers would "become driven by price and schedule" alone. This prediction proved correct, and for 2004, three discount airlines were ranked as providers of the best overall service. In ranked order, the leaders were JetBlue, AirTran and SW—all discount carriers with a customer-focused staff.

The low-cost airlines understood that the general public, and even many business travelers, were becoming more interested in lower fares. As can be seen in Figure 12.1, the profitability of the discount airlines grew steadily from 1995 to 2000. The discount airlines were also profitable from 2001 to 2004 while the major airlines were losing billions of dollars. By the time the millennium rolled around, it was clear that the low-cost airlines were here to stay, and there was nothing the major carriers could do but begin a defensive battle.

In June 1999, *Aviation Week* reported:

U.S. major airlines ... are caught in a financial squeeze play. Revenues are stalled out while labor and fuel costs are rising. New aircraft are joining the fleet, boosting seat capacity at a rate 4 percent greater than last year, while traffic demand has been sluggish. And in spite of several fare increases this year, the yield—the average price paid for a ticket—is still sloping downward due to heavy discounting.[589]

Figure 12.1: Historical Net Income of the Top 5 Discount Airlines

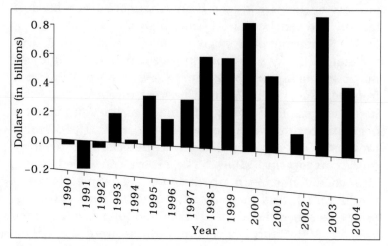

Source: CompuStat—North America Database, The Wharton School.

The problem was that the major airlines had let costs grow out of control, and the result was that the discount airlines were siphoning off more and more of their business.

2000–2002: THE BUST AND THE REAL REASON BEHIND IT

All the problems besieging the legacy carriers over the last five years could easily be blamed on the terrorist attacks of September 11, 2001. It is beyond the scope of this manuscript to describe fully the severity of both the physical and economic destruction on that one day. Though this single event was devastating to the airline industry as a whole, it should never be viewed as the major cause of the airlines' problems.

This statement would appear odd if you just looked at year-to-year profitability of the top-six legacy airlines, as presented in Figure 12.2.

The figure shows that the large airlines appeared to be doing just fine through the year 2000, and then were

Figure 12.2: Historical Net Income of the Top 6 Legacy Carriers

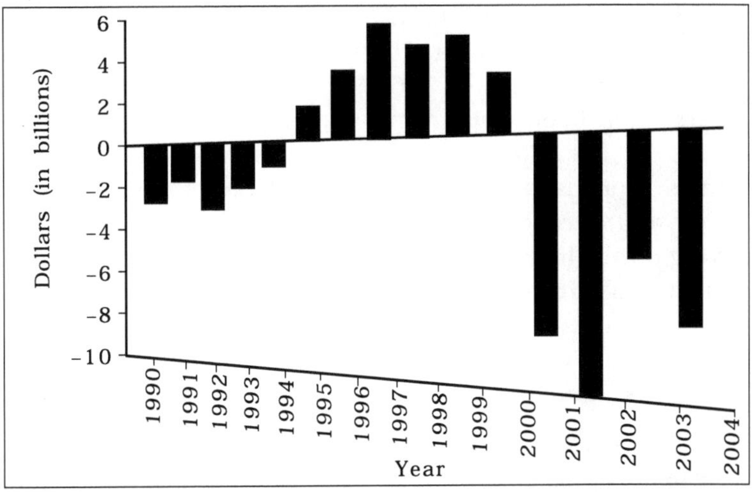

Source: CompuStat—North America Database, The Wharton School.

suddenly hit with huge losses in 2001 and 2002. This seemingly demonstrates that all the troubles began in 2001, but deeper research tells a different story.

The real downturn for the major airlines began in the second quarter of 2000, as the economy slowed after the bursting of the "Internet Bubble" that had driven the economy for several years. Without a robust economy to drive airline traffic higher, the flaws of the legacy airline operations began to be revealed. As reported by the *New York Times*, during "the boom of the 1990s, the airlines made plenty of money. To the annoyance of passengers, they not only limited discounts but kept capacity relatively tight."[590] These boom times also let costs get way out of hand for the major airlines, and by mid-2001, analysts began issuing warnings as the airlines were reporting worse and worse results with each passing quarter. In discussing the first quarter results of 2001, the *Aviation Daily* reported in June that, "rising costs were again the story during the period as airlines also faced higher wages that will continue to climb in the current year [2001]."[591]

UBS Warburg, a financial firm, was outspoken about the results it was seeing. In July 2001, Samuel Buttrick, one of Warburg's airline analysts, stated: "In the past two months [June and July, 2001], profit forecasts for 2001 and 2002 have been cut at the fastest rate in the last decade."[592] The big carriers already knew something was amiss months before the events of September 11 took place. UBS's report went on to mention that as the general flying public looks for cheaper airline tickets, it only made sense that the discount carriers would be viewed with much greater favor.[593] The report went so far as to suggest that the major airlines should be reconsidering their business model:

> It would be refreshing to see carriers take initiatives to both stimulate business demand and, more importantly, restore the value proposition of business travel—lost in recent years to higher fares and increased travel times. This would require a level of innovative product and pricing management that would seem to go beyond current capabilities. Meanwhile, it's hunker-down time.[594]

Even though the major carriers knew they were in trouble, they simply refused to let go of the old broken model that they held so dear. In the end, the legacy airlines did not seem to understand what "hunker-down time" really meant; this ignorance is what allowed the events of September 11 to blindside them so tragically.

Directly following the terrorist attacks, the major airlines were hit with crippling losses in market value. Continental and US Airways both saw declines of around 50 percent, while American, United, Delta, and Northwest were all down 37–45 percent. Not surprising however, SW, with its strong balance sheet and focused low-cost operational model, only lost 24 percent of its market value.[595] Furthermore, unlike the full-fare airlines, the smaller carriers were quickly able to gain concessions from their employees, including those who were unionized, to work through this difficult time:

At AirTran, unionized pilots voted overwhelmingly to accept temporary pay cuts and to work reduced flying schedules to pitch in and help the low-fare carrier based in Orlando, Florida. AirTran said the move is expected to save about 22 percent in pilot-related costs.[596]

The long and short of the matter is this: investors realized just how vulnerable and ill-managed the larger carriers had truly become, which in turn caused the detrimental effects of September 11 to multiply many times over for the major airlines.

After the terrorist attacks, many low-cost providers and regional carriers were able to rebound much more quickly than the lethargic major carriers. This fact was becoming apparent within a month of the attacks when Morgan Stanley analyst, Kevin Murphy, commented, "Smaller is better in this environment for a whole host of reasons."[597] Because the regional carriers were by nature smaller operators, much like the low-cost providers, they were able to deal with the massive downturn with greater ease. The *Washington Post* reported in October 2001: "Regional carriers enjoy lower costs because their jets use less fuel, their pilots are paid much less than those who fly the commercial jets, and they typically use no beverage service and fewer flight attendants."[598] These facts represent an operating model much like that of the low-cost providers.

A good example of one of the regional carriers is Atlantic Coast Airlines, which was able to remain nimble when having to deal with the decline in business. At the end of October 2001, Atlantic Coast had

reduced costs by offering voluntary pay cuts for executives, discontinuing various bonus programs for all employees, and freezing merit-pay increases and non-operational positions. The company also offered 30-day unpaid leave and reduced hours on a voluntary basis and at the discretion of each department.[599]

This example shows the types of concessions that smaller airlines were able to obtain—something that the major carriers struggled with over time. United was one of the airlines struggling to foster support from its employees; during this time, Merrill Lynch and Co. airline analyst, Michael Linenberg, said, "United continues to reel from its industry-leading pilot contract, which raised the airline's labor costs this year."[600]

In general, the low-cost providers were able to bounce back much faster than the older major carriers; this fact is reinforced by their ability to maintain staffing levels or quickly rehire employees who were laid off. An industry report released in the first two months of 2002 reported that several airlines such as SW, Frontier, and AirTran, were not laying off any mechanics. The Teamsters working at AirTran had agreed to significant concessions in order to retain the jobs of all 530 mechanics employed there. The report went on to say: "JetBlue had made no staff reductions in any department and continues to grow, expecting to operate 102 daily flights in the beginning of 2002, up from 84 per day in early September [2001]".[601] So, while the big guys were fighting with their unions over labor contracts, the smaller carriers resolved pay issues quickly and began operating normally again; furthermore, some even expanded, as was the case with JetBlue.

Over the first half of 2002, one attitude was prevalent throughout the industry—the major carriers could simply not survive operating in the same way. In June of 2004, Mo Garfinkle, an industry consultant from Washington D.C., commented that, "he felt the industry's hub-and-spoke system, by which passengers are funneled from less lucrative markets through major airports, is broken".[602] The shifting of market share from the major carriers to the low-cost airlines certainly backed this sentiment. In May 2002, "domestic travel fell 10 percent among major airlines compared to last year, while discount carriers jumped 11 percent".[603] Even some executives of major carriers no longer saw the "hub-and-spoke system" of the major airlines as profitable. Leo Mullin, CEO of Delta at the time, stated, "there is no longer a truly efficient and effective flow of traffic through hubs".[604] Michael E. Levine, a former senior airline executive who later became an instructor at Yale Law School, summed up this concept well. Levine noted:

> The numbers for the big network airlines don't work, none of them work, everyone during the boom years made commitments that just don't stand up in the current condition, and never will again.[605]

The small low-cost carriers were able to adjust to the decline in demand following September 11 quickly, and began to grow rapidly again as they stole market share away from the majors. On the other hand, the six major airlines fell deeper and deeper into debt, registering record losses of almost $10 billion in 2002. From this point onward, the major carriers implemented numerous strategies, with varying degrees of success, in an attempt to return to profitability.

2002–04: Majors Attempt to Fix the Hub-and-Spoke Model

Following the attacks of September 11, 2001, the major airlines began planning new strategies. Much of the commercial airline industry had become commoditized. The availability of Internet booking allowed customers to bypass the old travel agents and check for the best price at the best time. Meanwhile, the major airlines were bumping into low-cost providers everywhere they turned, resulting in all-out warfare. At the same time, the low-cost providers began to increase their levels of service as they gained market share. These factors led Phil Roberts, Vice-President and Managing Partner of Unisys R2A, an airline consulting company in California, to later say, "eventually the whole industry will operate on a low-cost basis, making it possible to blend bargain fares with reasonable levels of service".[606]

In order to fit into this new industry paradigm, many of the legacy carriers immediately started making changes. Don Carty, American's CEO, was one who was ready and willing to make any necessary changes. In July 2002, Carty forcefully stated: "We need to be more productive, we need to be more effective as an organization, and we need to be more responsive. We need to learn a lot of lessons from some of the new airline models".[607] Carty saw the looming financial troubles, and was ready to shift the fundamental practices of the airline to try and turn things around.

Unlike Carty, some in the industry simply felt this was a decline created by the bad recession beginning in 2001, and if they could just weather the storm, things would soon return to normal. A report issued in 2002 by the Association of Corporate Travel Executives provided some insight on this subject:

> Historically, airlines have been reluctant to pursue reform for a few reasons. First, some airline executives seem to believe that when the economy strengthens, business travelers will come back in full force, and there will be a return to the pricing power of the late 1990s.[608]

The report echoed the same fact that there is a

> perception among some labor leaders that there is no need to move toward a more rational labor model. Like some airline executives, they believe a rebound in business travel is nearly 100 percent tied to the economy.[609]

The real story is that passenger's acceptance of the discount carriers was increasing. A survey in 2002 indicated that the number of people flying low-cost carriers increased 73 percent in 2001 from 2000, and a similar number planned to start flying low-cost carriers in 2002.[610] Even with all the statistics, some major airline executives refused to listen. For example, Gordon Bethune, chairman and CEO of Continental, said in a conference call with reporters: "What we need is an economy that works and some competitors with IQs over 40."[611]

Even for the carriers who were willing to make changes, having to deal with increased competition from the low-cost carriers was not an easy task. In 1991, only 15 percent of the legacy-carrier routes were also being flown by low-cost providers. And, in early 2003, almost 55 percent of these hub routes faced competition from discount airlines.[612] Gary Chase, an analyst with Lehman Brothers, stated: "The network airlines remain between a rock and a hard place with respect to low-fare competition". He added that "network airlines have no attractive options relative to low-fare airlines, and that the gaping cost disadvantages of major airlines prevent them from taking a truly competitive stance".[613] Worse still for the legacy carriers, the experts did not see that a general increase in commercial flying would be of any help. For example, Smith Barney travel analyst Michael Rietbrock stated,

> a rebound in business travel won't necessarily translate into a financial recovery for the major-hub airlines with 37 percent of companies planning to increase use of cheaper, advance-purchase fares instead of pricier last-minute, fully refundable ones.[614]

With the legacy carriers unable to increase the top-line revenue as they had in prior years, many of them began huge campaigns to cut costs. One of the primary areas targeted for savings was labor costs. To accomplish this task, a number of methods were employed. These included reduced wages, more flexible work rules, and trimmed benefits. Many overly generous union contracts created during the boom years slowed this effort. It was quite difficult for many of the legacy airlines to reduce these costs as union leaders stood their ground and initially refused to renegotiate their contracts. In contrast, many of the low-cost carriers, such as SW, did not face a real problem because their pay rates were already lower and work rules were flexible. These flexible work rules allowed employees to do more work for the same pay—easily recognizable when pilots are seen helping passengers board the plane.[615]

Another way for the major carriers to reduce costs and to become more competitive was through fleet simplification. However, many of the large airlines operate a dozen or more types of aircraft. Pilots must be trained and certified to fly each aircraft, which adds to major airline costs. Furthermore, many of the major airlines operate older aircraft that require large inventories of spare parts and more costly maintenance. In contrast, SW flies only one type, and JetBlue two types, of aircraft. *Aviation Week* made the statement, "aircraft fleet simplification ... (is) the answer".[616] This trade journal went on to report that airlines should easily be able to operate with three or fewer types of aircraft. An article written in late 2004 was critical about how stubborn the legacy carriers were: "An even better indication that legacy-airline managements are floundering is that some are changing the style of employees' uniforms while others are repainting their aircraft as if these acts alone would solve their problems".[617] Cutting costs was then, and still is today, a key aspect for the survival of the major carriers, and drastic changes are necessary to achieve this goal. If everything else with a major airline is not running right, then the problems still remain; as summed up by airline analyst Samuel Buttrick of UBS Warburg: "lower costs don't fix broken revenue models".[618]

As a whole, the legacy carriers have made a valiant effort at reducing costs. This attempt can be seen from Figure 12.3; a report by the GAO shows the overall effectiveness the major carriers have had in lowering their expenses. In contrast, the low-cost providers have actually experienced an increase in their overall cost structure, as shown in Figure 12.4, with the majority of these costs coming from an increase in labor wages associated with the expansion of their operations.

It is expected that as the low-cost providers get older, plane maintenance, pilot seniority, and pilot wages will all increase. Most industry experts agree that pilot wages and seniority spikes will increase the cost of operations for the discount airlines in the end, but to what extent is still uncertain. The story that neither of these graphs is able to portray is that in order for the legacy carriers to cut costs drastically, they also have had to reduce the number of flights they offer, or even pull out of certain

Figure 12.3: Change in Legacy Airline Costs, October 1, 2001 to December 31, 2003

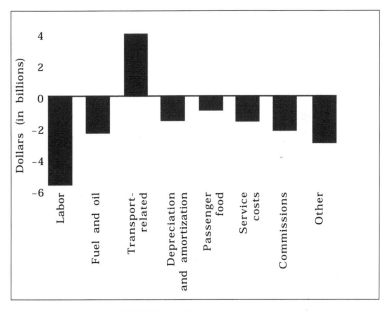

Source: GAO analysis of DOT from 41 data.
Notes: Other includes fees, taxes, and other charges; filling costs, membership dues, and losses.

Figure 12.4: Change in Low-cost Airline Costs, October 1, 2001 to December 31, 2003

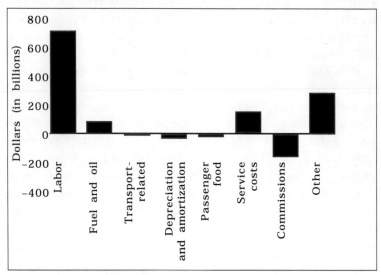

Source: GAO analysis of DOT from 41 data.
Notes: Other includes fees, taxes, and other charges; filling costs, membership dues, and losses.

markets altogether. In contrast, the low-cost providers are still growing; hence, the increase in cost structure is well justified. Figure 12.5 provides a better understanding of this point as it compares the unit cost, or cost-per-available-seat mile, for the major airlines versus the low-cost carriers. From this figure it is clear that the discount airlines have increased their efficiency by actually decreasing the cost-per-seat mile. On the other hand, even though the major carriers have been successful in cutting costs over the last few years, they have done so by reducing the number of available flights. As a result, this has left the legacy airlines with a higher overall cost structure. The figure further shows that the gap between legacy and discount carriers is widening over time.

If the major airlines could get costs under control again, it logically follows that they would then be in a better

Figure 12.5: Unit Cost Differential, 1998–2003

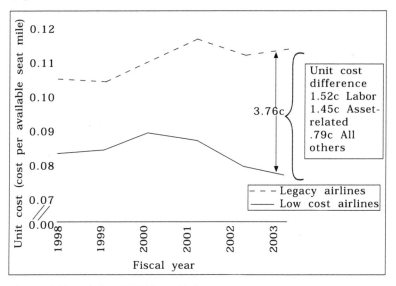

Source: GAO analysis of DOT from 41 data.

position to begin offering lower prices and competing with the low-cost providers. In retrospect, over the last few years, it did not really matter if the costs had been brought into line or not; the major carriers have been forced to start slashing prices in order to keep people flying their airline. Alan Bender, Professor of airline economics at Embry-Riddle Aeronautical University said, "the U.S. legacy airlines are not showing obvious signs of implementing a low-price strategy; rather they are reacting to low-cost carriers' fares and repricing lower simply because they have to."[619] Bender also claimed that the legacy carriers are still holding on to significantly higher fares in some markets, even though competition with low-cost providers exists in these markets. The major airlines are on the defensive when forced to butt heads with the low-cost providers, and costs must certainly come down to allow the full-fare airlines an opportunity to offer more competitive prices.

Another issue facing the legacy carriers is the problem of over-capacity. As is true with any industry, when capacity overstretches demand, there tends to be a shakeout where some companies go under while others merge or partner in some kind of relationship. In the airline industry, true consolidation among differing airlines does not happen because several government agencies tend to reject such mergers on the ground of anti-competitive practices. Instead of actually merging with one another, the major airlines have sidestepped this regulation by following a practice called code sharing. Code sharing enables airlines to sell seats on each others' planes, which allows the sharing airlines to offer more routes and flight times with little or even no additional cost. One example of code sharing can be seen with United and US Airways, which tried to merge in 2001 but were rejected for anti-trust reasons. Therefore, in mid-2002, the two airlines entered into a code-sharing agreement in order to gain the efficiencies of a larger network of flights.[620]

The government also regulates code sharing, and attaining approval from all the right people can be quite challenging. In 2002, Continental, Delta, and Northwest proposed a three-way domestic code-sharing agreement that prompted both the DOT and the Department of Justice to establish requirements the airlines would have to meet before receiving approval for the deal.[621] The situation was only made worse when the two regulatory bodies did not agree on what these requirements should be. In this case, the issues were finally resolved, and in early 2003, the Justice Department approved the alliance, "provided they agree not to coordinate fares and don't combine competing non-stop flights".[622] Of course, these are some of the major reasons the airlines were seeking the code-sharing agreement in the first place. Therefore, the issue remains that the industry suffers from the problem of over-capacity, and sooner or later the legacy carriers must be allowed to merge outright or truly consolidate their efforts through the use of fully integrated code sharing.

Another way the legacy airlines have tried to regain their dominance in the industry is through an increased focus on customer service. Originally, low-cost providers such as SW treated people like cattle, shuffling them onto the aircraft and providing little-to-nothing extra perks on board. As a result, the full-fare airlines could justify the huge premiums they charged in the belief that consumers would want to pay more and get a few perks along the way. But as time passed, many of the low-cost providers began offering special perks as well, including better food service, and, in the case of JetBlue, free satellite TV built into the seat backs for each passenger to enjoy. This challenge has again forced the hand of the legacy carriers, and some of them are pushing to increase customer satisfaction to compete with the low-cost carriers. United recognized this need in May 2003, and created a new position of Executive Vice-President in charge of Customer Relations. John Tague, former President and CEO of ATA, was chosen for this position and charged with the simple task of finding ways to make their customers happy.[623] These customer-service efforts could, over time, draw more passengers to United, but in the short run, the airline may end up totally bankrupt waiting around for the flying public to come back to them.

The most recent "quick fix" for the legacy carriers has been efforts by some airlines to develop a new way to increase the frequency of flights through the hub airports, a concept informally known as the "rolling hub". Typically at a hub airport, many short-haul flights land near about the same time so that passengers can be put on another connecting outbound flight to another hub. This causes the hub airports to have extremely busy times followed by hours of down time where the employees are paid simply to sit around and wait for the next rush. Worse still, the airlines have to pay for planes to sit on the ground while waiting for all the connecting spoke flights to arrive at their hub airports. In late 2002, American saw this as a great opportunity to regain some efficiency and began what they called a de-peaked schedule, aimed at spreading out their flight departures.[624] George Hamlin, Senior Vice-President at Global Aviation Associates Ltd. of Washington, later commented, "before this, American was paying people [and for aircraft] to sit still, and now they are paying them to move".[625] SW has always claimed that the only way to make money is to keep planes flying, and now with the rolling hub or de-peaked schedule idea, it appears that the legacy carriers have decided "if you can't beat them—you might as well join them."

Delta has been the latest major carrier to try out the rolling-hub concept with the implementation of a plan called "Operation Clockwork". To make up for lost time, Delta has pushed the new plan as a "big-bang theory" of changing their operating model. Delta CEO Gerald Grinstein commented: "The changes would alter more then 51 percent of the carrier's network, which would result in the largest single-day schedule transformation in Delta's history."[626] Just as the new plan was being put in place, Lee Macenczak, Senior Vice-President and Chief Customer Services Officer, stated:

> [Operation Clockwork] gives us better utilization of our staffing and gates, and a better experience for the customer because we won't have these huge rushes of people arriving at the same time. It's a permanent cultural change for Delta.[627]

To help further with keeping everything moving, Delta is also instigating a "departure-zero" rule: "Instead of waiting five or more minutes for late passengers, planes will have to shut their doors five minutes before departure time".[628] This rule aims to create nearly $100 million in cost reductions and newly generated revenues. The final piece is to force the Atlanta hub to operate a nearly continuous schedule by decreasing the time between flights by half.[629] With uncertain times ahead and bankruptcy still looming, this may represent Delta's last chance to return to profitability.

The legacy carriers began to incur staggering losses in 2000, and with high energy prices and growing competition from discount airlines, these losses will continue through 2006 and into the future. There are a few people in the airline industry who say they have been here before and things will turn around again. However, times are different now. Even with the major airlines cutting costs, passengers are not prepared to pay the premium fares the six legacy airlines charge. Major executives from Delta and Northwest have recently stated that in a few years there could be just two or three major airlines in operation. The key to moving forward is allowing the airlines more freedom to merge and/or code share, thereby permitting the well-overdue shakeout to happen. It makes no economic sense for the Federal government to try to bail out bankrupt airlines with taxpayers' money—it is a costly dead-end street.

When the airline industry was deregulated in 1978, people expected there would be a large number of discount airlines entering high-price markets, driving prices down. Twenty-five years later, that is just what is happening to the airline industry. The flying public (business and leisure travelers) has numerous opportunities to fly discount airlines and save large sums of money. The bottom line is: it is good for travelers and good for the economy. We expect that the evolution of the airline industry could turn out to be much like what occurred in the department store business. Four decades ago, the discount stores came into existence and have rapidly grown by providing the general public lower prices for the merchandise they need. Today, most people would say that the growth of general merchandise discount stores has been good for the country, and people who want the more costly goods and services of the department stores can still meet their needs. Department store chains such as Neiman Marcus, Saks Fifth Avenue, Macy's, and Bloomingdale's still exist for customers who want to purchase more costly merchandise via service-oriented clerks.

The Federal government must move aside and stop trying to rescue the failing major airlines. A competitive marketplace requires easy entry into, and exit from, the industry. If "entry and exit" into the market is allowed to work, the competitive nature of the airline industry will work strongly in the public's interest.

Chapter Thirteen

Growth of Discount Airlines

THE MARKET share of direct flights operated by discount airlines grew from 10 percent in 1990 to nearly 30 percent in 2004. As a consequence, the flying public has saved tens of billions of dollars in lower fares offered by the discount airlines. Many forecasters believe that the market share of the discount airlines will continue to grow, given the lower fares and superior service many of them provide. Three of the largest discount airlines were ranked highest in the quality of customer service in 2004. In contrast, there is the broad expectation that the market share of the major airlines will continue to contract, and that there will be a large consolidation among them.

Professors Jagdish Sheth and Raj Sisodia's work published in the book named *Rule of Three*, suggests that there could be just three major airlines in the future, instead of six at present. Furthermore, some major airline executives have stated that the number of these airlines needs to be reduced from six to three (or even two) in order to restore their financial stability. Unfortunately, the Federal government is bailing out major bankrupt airlines, and keeping too many high-cost and high-price major airlines in business. Bailing out the bankrupt United and US Airways is bad for the airline industry, and in turn, bad for the public which is forced to pay the huge pension costs these airlines carry.

The airlines may even request that the Pension Benefit Guarantee Fund Corporation (PBGF) take over their pension liabilities. In essence, this would mean growing Federal debt and more financial burden on the public. What is going on in the airline industry does not make market sense. But it can perhaps be explained by the political clout of airplane manufacturer Boeing, and the companies that finance it.

When the airline industry was deregulated, there was widespread belief that lower-cost discount airlines would thrive by charging lower fares. Many economists expected that the discount airlines would take away large market shares from the high-cost legacy airlines. Unfortunately, after a short period of growth following deregulation in 1978, the discount airlines' market share declined. This decline took place during the second half of the 1980s, as all the new discount airlines declared bankruptcy, and all but one went out of business. However, in the 1990s, discount airlines began to grow again due to the Clinton Administration's action to increase competition from discount airlines. Policies were implemented that led to the formation of several new discount airlines in the mid-to-late 1990s, and since 2001 their market share accelerated as business travelers, along with the general public, sought lower fares. Discount airlines began serving more cities that had so far been the exclusive domain of the major airlines.

THE RISE OF THE DISCOUNT AIRLINES

Since the early 1990s, several new discount airlines have emerged, modeled in part, after SW's successful operations. Given their lower cost structure, the discount airlines offered basic air service at considerable savings in comparison to the prices charged by the six major

airlines. Three of the most successful new discount airlines (as we discussed earlier) were AirTran, Frontier, and
JetBlue.

The low fares of the discount airlines became particularly attractive since the beginning of the recession in
2001 and the negative impact of the terrorist attacks of
September 11, 2001, on the US economy. Hence, the low-
airfare discount airlines grew in popularity, and since
2002, two new discount airlines have come into existence. America West changed from being a full-service to
a discount airline in 2002. In 2004, a regional airline that
had formerly provided feeder service for two major airlines
became an east coast discount airline called Independence Air. Furthermore, US Airways has proposed con-
verting its operation to a discount airline, now that it has
merged with America West. Unfortunately, the rapid growth
of new discount airlines could be more than what the
market can absorb. Thus, over the next few years, there
could be a shakeout among the weaker discount airlines,
as well as a consolidation of the major airlines.

AMERICAN WEST BECOMES A DISCOUNT AIRLINE

America West is the oldest US airline that began operations following deregulation in 1978. Over the years, it
expanded by rapidly adding new aircraft to its fleet and is
now the eighth largest airline in the country. Its two
primary markets are Phoenix and Las Vegas, and from
these cities it flies to major airports in the SW—including
Los Angeles, Orange County, and San Diego. America
West received a $429 million loan from the US Air Trans-
portation Stabilization Board in 2002, after obtaining $50
million in concessions from its lenders and employees.
Douglas Parker, the Chief Executive Officer of America
West, explains that the airline made major changes in
2003, and lowered its costs, thereby becoming profitable
once again. In the process of lowering its costs, many

pilots and flight crew were discharged and 250 management positions were eliminated.[630]

America West also changed from operating a traditional hub-and-spoke system to a less costly and more efficient point-to-point system. In the process, it lowered its cost-per-seat mile flown, bringing it close to the level of SW and JetBlue—two of the lowest-cost airlines in the industry. In addition to reducing costs, America West changed its pricing strategy to make it similar to that of the discount airlines. It reduced fares for tickets purchased seven days in advance to 50–75 percent less than the major airlines' fares. The result was a large increase in business travelers, which actually improved its overall yield. Parker stated that

> Rather than getting low-yielding fares from leisure travelers and some very high yields from some last-minute business travelers, we were able to sell tickets in the middle of the price spectrum, which improved overall yields.

America West also started flying longer routes, which further contributed to the reduction of its average cost-per-seat mile flown.[631] As a result of these changes, America West turned in a profit during the last three quarters of 2003 while the major airlines were incurring substantial losses.[632]

ATLANTIC COAST AIRLINE BECOMES A NEW DISCOUNT AIRLINE

For a number of years, Atlantic Coast Airline had been a feeder airline for United and Delta, flying passengers from small cities in the East to one of the two airlines' hub airports. In early 2004, the feeder airline announced that when its contracts with these two major airlines expire, it would become a new discount airline called Independence Air. Discount airlines were expanding into the Northeast where previously there had been little competition from the low-cost airlines. Management of the feeder airline believed there was a good opportunity to provide lower fares to the flying public. Independence Air hired a consulting firm based in Washington, D.C. to evaluate its change-over plan. It received a 53-page report, *Next Generation Low-Cost Carriers*, which discussed a number of factors associated with the success of low-cost carriers. The report concluded that Independence Air had a "better-than-average" chance of succeeding if the airline held down its costs, carefully selected its routes, and consistently evaluated route profitability.[633]

Independence Air's first flight as a discount airline was on June 16, 2004. Over the latter part of 2004, it started providing discount service to 35 cities from Dulles International Airport in Washington, D.C. with a fleet of 87 Bombardier regional jets. Initially, the plan was to fly to destinations in the Northeast and mid-Atlantic region during 2004. In September, Independence Air took delivery of its first 132-seat A319s jet (out of a total of 27), and began flying longer routes to the Midwest and West.

Independence Air had determined that it required a load factor of 70 percent to break even. One of the problems the new airline immediately experienced was that the major airlines often matched its prices and cut their fares by as much as 90 percent. In December 2004, Independence Air's load factor was 53.2 percent, and in January 2005, it fell further to 45.7 percent. This is the same predatory-pricing problem that dozens of other new discount airlines have faced since deregulation in 1978. As the major airlines would temporarily meet their prices, small discount airlines were unable to attract enough business to operate profitably, and were forced to cease their operations.[634] This is the fate that also befell Independence Air. When it announced on its cease operations on January 2, 2006 that it would cease flights on January 5, the upstart airline had dwindled down to three flights a day and 2,700 employees. The airline blamed 'continued financial challenges' for the decision. "While we were clear in reminding everyone that this was a possibility, we remained optimistic that there would be a way to avoid reaching this juncture," said CEO Kerry Skeen. "To date there has not been a firm offer put forward that meets the financial criteria necessary to continue operation as is."[635]

A MAJOR MAKES PLANS TO BECOME A DISCOUNTER

US Airways is the smallest of the six legacy airlines, and its business is concentrated in the densely populated northeastern part of the country, where 30 percent of airline travel originates. However, unlike most of the other major airlines, US Airways primarily flies relatively short routes between its three hub markets located in Philadelphia, Pittsburgh and Charlotte—and then from its hub markets on to other cities. As a result, it has the highest cost-per-seat mile flown among the major airlines. In the 1990s, US Airways began to face increased competition from SW. The largest discount airline had expanded from the SW to the West coast, on to the North Central part of the United States, and finally to the Northeast—the home base of US Airways. At the same time, AirTran also began to provide service from Atlanta to US Airways' markets in the Northeast. In early 2004, Stephen Wolf, US Airways' chairman, told a congressional subcommittee that "The Arlington-based carrier is facing a perilous future" since it is neither a national carrier like United and American nor a discounter like SW.[636]

US Airways approached several major airlines about the possibility of a merger to form a stronger major airline. American had been permitted to merge with bankrupt TWA. Similarly, United and US Airways (both now in Chapter 11 bankruptcy) proposed a merger in 2000. They felt this proposition was reasonable, since routes of the two airlines did not overlap to any significant degree, and they could generate significant operating savings. However, the US Department of Justice vetoed the merger on the grounds that it would create too much market power. US Airways had no option but to pursue another course of action it had been considering. If it could obtain further wage concessions from its unions, it would become a discount airline. Facing the alternative of the liquidation, the airline's unions agreed to further wage cuts.[637]

In 2004, US Airways held discussions with America West about the possibility of a merger. America West had successfully transformed from a major airline to a low-cost discount airline in 2002 after obtaining a government loan, and US Airways also wanted to become a discount airline. Negotiations intensified in 2005, and on May 19, 2005, the two airlines officially announced their plans to merge. After receiving clearance from U.S. bankruptcy court and America West shareholders, the merger was officially consummated on September 27, 2005. The new airline adopted the US Airways name and the US Airways color scheme for all planes. It also coordinated the two flight schedules and began more cross-country flights, which are often more profitable than the shorter routes. W. Douglas Parker of American West became CEO. At the time, he said that the combined airline would be in "a position of strength and future growth that neither of us could have achieved on our own". US Airways Chief Executive Officer Bruce Parker became Vice Chairman, and said the joint airline would "bring more choices for our customers".[638]

The proposed merger definitely has its pros and cons. There were airline analysts who believed that there are clearly too many airlines and that to create a viable industry, the airlines must consolidate. The US Airways and America West merger has been called "Project Barbell". America West's operation is concentrated in the SW, with its two major markets in Las Vegas and Phoenix. By contrast, US Airways' major hub airports are located in the Northeast and include Charlotte, Pittsburgh, and Philadelphia. Merger of the two airlines permits the new discount airline to fly more cross-country flights.[639]

However, some analysts question the logic of the merger. Philip A. Baggaley, an airline analyst with Standard and Poor's rating service, asked even though the merger would create a larger airline, "how can it compete with SW?" America West's primary competitor is already SW. If US Airways and America West merge, it would bring the new airline into more direct competition with the healthiest airline in the United States. Michael Allen, of Back Aviation Solutions, stated that "There's limited proof that airline mergers actually work." William Warlick of Fitch Rating Services agreed, and added, "They are messy by their very nature."[640]

SUMMARY

The barriers that the major airlines used to thwart the growth of discount airlines have crumbled over the last 10 years. Unless the Federal government continues to support bankrupt major airlines, the discount airlines will continue to grow, taking their market share from 30 percent of direct flights at the beginning of 2005 to 50 percent by 2010. SW is expected to remain the most profitable airline in the United States by offering "basic airline service at low prices". Other discounters, such as JetBlue, offer both lower fares and upgraded service with leather seats and seat-back television. The public response to JetBlue is likely to remain strong given its economical long-distance flights and good service. Discounters such as AirTran offer both coach-and first-class seating, and have a fleet of new airplanes with leather seats. AirTran is also more economical to fly and maintain. However, smaller discounters like AirTran and Frontier face a financial risk as more traditional airlines attempt to become discounters and low-cost carriers start competing with one another for market share.

According to executives of Delta and Northwest, consolidation of the major airlines is necessary. Major airlines should be permitted to combine and significantly reduce the number of airplanes they fly, in order to become profitable once again. However, "turning around the major airlines is by no means a sure thing." The cost to the public is huge, as major airlines in bankruptcy drop their pension cost on the Pension Benefit Guarantee Corporation. Clearly, there are no easy answers.

One thing is certain though: the longer the problem of the majors is allowed to fester, the worse the situation is going to be for the US economy. There are too many high-cost airlines, and the Federal government should stop subsidizing their operations. The situation is very serious—it requires the attention of the best brains in the industry along with a clear-thinking Congress and President. Unfortunately, the Federal government is allowing United and US Airways to dump its pension cost on the U.S. Pension Guarantee Fund so they could emerge from bankruptcy. This means the public picked up tens of billions of dollars of pension payments for these two airlines.

Making matters still worse, Delta declared bankruptcy in September 2005. If Delta succeeds in dumping a large portion of its pension funds on the government and US citizens, the three remaining major airlines (American, Northwest, and Continental) will want to do the same. The question can be fairly raised as to "why firms that declare bankruptcy and cannot cover their costs" are not forced to liquidate as has been the standard practice. The Federal government bail-outs of United and US Airways are only going to worsen the situation for the other major airlines.

There is a small chance that the Federal government will not rescue Delta and other major airlines as it did with United and US Airways. *The Wall Street Journal* published an editorial by David Wessel called "Airlines May Have to Fly Without Lifeline" on June 2, 2005. The author claims that the Bush administration's diagnosis of the airline industry is that "The industry is plagued by overcapacity. Big airlines are losing money because costs are so high they can't compete. The sooner some high-cost airlines die, the better." He indicated that the Bush Administration has quietly adopted the position of "let the market do it" and decide who succeeds and who fails. If, in fact, the free market is allowed to work, then the number of major airlines will decline, and the market share of the discounters will expand rapidly, given the large savings they can provide the flying public.[641]

Chapter Fourteen

Recommendations for Successful Airline Deregulation

SO WHAT have we learned after decades of airline deregulation in the US and Europe, and more recently from India and other Asian countries? Is there a right way to deregulate? Is it possible to glean recommendations for the best way to implement the deregulation process? Here are some recommendations for policy makers, new entrants, incumbents, and suppliers that will provide a smooth transition, ultimately result in an ordered field of competition and provide benefit for air transportation consumers.

RECOMMENDATIONS FOR POLICY MAKERS

The experiences of USA and India have clearly shown that a rapid, or "big bang", approach to deregulation is not a good model to follow. For the incumbent airlines, it is not reasonable to expect that overnight there will be a 180 degree switch from being a competition-sheltered organization with protected routes, regulated pricing, and lack of meaningful competition to being a savvy marketing strategy and customer oriented organization that deftly fights off swarms of low-cost start-up airlines.

It is not that protected carriers need sympathy or a guaranteed spot as a competitor; this is a matter of providing an opportunity to adjust from an industry structure that was mandated by the government to a new regulatory vision. Additionally, this helps to minimize the interruptions and uncertainty for airline industry consumers.

It also takes into account the difficulty in exiting from investments in capital and labor that are an inherent part of being a major carrier, regardless of the regulatory environment. The airline industry is both capital and labor intensive, especially for common carriers. An incumbent carrier may realize it has to reduce capital and labor costs to compete against new low-cost and nimble entrants who can have lower cost structures and fewer obligations. But it usually cannot make the adjustments quickly because of huge employee obligations such as pensions and health insurance for retirees, or contractual agreements with unions that are a legacy of their regulated past. They also have an enormous amount of physical infrastructure that is embedded and cannot be quickly liquidated, such as investments that have been made in airport expansions and improvements. The incumbents have a license or rights to fly and the sale of these is not easy because they have to go through a government approval process.

Exiting the business is not so much a market-driven process as a regulatory process. So, given that there are high capital and labor obligations and exit is very hard, any kind of rapid deregulation will come as a shock. Regardless of the industry, if you are highly regulated, and the rest of the industry is highly deregulated, you are in an untenable position.

If the market is opened too quickly, it will most likely result in major difficulties for the incumbent, which is usually the national carrier. The ensuing chaos and possibility of collapse of the incumbent creates undue hardships and can even result in a political backlash against deregulation. There are numerous issues that must be addressed in the transition and many of them cannot be resolved overnight. For example, if the regulated carrier's employees are government employees, what do you do with their pension plans? The problems created by a rush to deregulate can be seen in India, whose "open skies" policy has resulted in airport strikes and industry turmoil. The country's domestic market was first opened to untethered competition which created a lot of nightmares for the incumbent national carrier, Indian Airlines. And now the international carrier, Air India, is facing a similar situation as that segment is open to full market forces.

To create a "soft landing" that will allow incumbents time to reorient their organizations to face a new world of competition, to make for a less disruptive process for the flying public, it is important that regulators develop a strategy for a staged deregulation that gives incumbents a measured timetable for the transition. This is not intended to guarantee incumbents a continued role as the dominant carriers, or to even ensure they will survive once full-blown competition is in place; it is just a way to give them an orderly opportunity to prepare for the inevitable. It is a better alternative to the turmoil of an all-or-none strategy of deregulation.

Staged Deregulation

There are a number of steps in a staged deregulation that will pave the way for a smooth transition from strong government oversight to a market-oriented approach.

Privatize National Carriers and Reorganize Them into Corporations

If the incumbent is a government-owned carrier, the first step is to go through a process of privatization, even if it is initially a public–private partnership. This will move the carrier from a government bureau mindset driven by national policies, rules, and regulations to a competitive enterprise mindset where decisions are driven more and more by the markets, and less and less by capacity and capital expenditures. Because it is a regulated monopoly, what you must do is change the nature of the regulated monopoly first so it does not collapse when you open up for full-blown market competition. In the US, this is what has been done with electric utilities and the telephone business, and the failure rate has been a lot less in those industries.

In the UK, the airline privatization process took this route. The British made sure that the regulated carrier, British Airways (BA), was introduced to the market-driven approach in stages. Passenger satisfaction ratings became an important benchmark for success and as a result the attitude of BA employees shifted into a new competitive mindset.

Set a High Standard for Entry by New Carriers

Starting an airline is a very expensive proposition, especially if you are yearning to be a common carrier or are planning to be in the industry for the long haul. Because of the massive investment involved, it is better to set the bar high for entry to ensure that new competitors will do more than create a temporary disruption in industry stability. These carriers must be able to document and validate that they have the financial resources and commitment to scale with significant operational competence. This is how it was done in the US cellular phone industry, a similarly capital intensive sector. When the government decided to expand the cellular phone market and auction off licenses for frequencies, only two or three companies or consortiums were allowed to purchase in each band.

This is the philosophy that has been adopted by the Chinese government as well when they decided to allow two alternatives to the national airline, China Airlines. The other two behave like private corporations but they have enough financial backing to survive for a period of time that will allow them to develop their market position and hone their competitive instincts. India did it the opposite way. The government flung open the doors to unbridled competition and there was a flood of new entrants. Most of them lacked the financial resources and business savvy to compete and few survived. A second wave of eager start-ups is now taking place and there will certainly be another tumultuous shakeout. Instead of going through successive waves of expansion and contraction, a more orderly process would be served by setting the bar high for entry, whether the new entrants are government or privately backed.

Create Oligopolistic Competition

Most governments dislike cartels and oligopolistic competition because of price collusion and capacity collusion. But the "Rule of Three" theory advocates that in the long run, no matter how many companies the industry starts with, there is always a shakeout and only three companies become full volume-driven competitors. Research on service industries that have only three competitors shows they have lower prices, better innovation and more market coverage. This does not mean you cannot have other airlines in the industry. There is still a need for niche carriers to serve smaller segments of customers and geographies.[642]

The Rule of Three played out in the American airline deregulation. Of the 70 airlines that existed before deregulation, after the shakeout only Delta, American, and United remained as integrated carriers. The Chinese, however, are taking a different approach. If you know that ultimately the outcome will be to have only a handful of competitors, it seems better to not go through the trouble of loss of capital and jobs, and keep three as the blueprint for the industry. This oligopolistic structure will create greater stability and achieve the same result of a few strongly competitive players.

Develop a Shared, Industry-wide IT Platform

In the US, airlines have historically viewed their computerized reservation system (CRS) as a competitive advantage. If you were a travel agent and had a Sabre system, the first screen was of American Airlines listings, the company that happened to own Sabre. This type of captive CRS gives undue competitive advantage and should not be allowed. There should only be one platform and it should be a separate, stand-alone entity, similar to Visa or MasterCard for banks. This system should be set up as a separate company so that airlines and consumers are treated equitably.

If you do not go through a staged deregulatory process as outlined above, incumbents are likely to feel trapped in a no-win situation and engage in irrational behavior, such as predatory pricing, gate control, or hub control. Or they could resort to using political and regulatory maneuvers to reshape regulation in their favor. They may even take competitors to court to slow down their ability to compete. And despite all of these irrational maneuvers, they will still end up destroying themselves.

RECOMMENDATIONS FOR NEW ENTRANTS

Enter Only When You Can Expand the Market

The key message for new entrants is to enter only when you are confident you will increase the total number of passengers in the market. When you bring in additional aircraft you are expanding the capacity on a route or routes. However, if your advertising and promotional efforts are only resulting in competition for the same number of seats that were served by the incumbent, instead of increasing the overall number of passengers, the end result will be a lose-lose proposition: lower margins for the incumbent and the eventual end of your operations.

It is tempting to target a few highly profitable routes as the basis for a competitive pricing strategy. You may capture some of the market in the short term, but the incumbent will be able to lower prices and be better able to weather a short-term drop in profitability because they have other routes that contribute to the bottom line. Your long-term chances for survival are not good in this scenario.

One way to expand the market is to look for segments of the population that are traveling by means other than air transportation. This could be people who go from point A to point B in their own or rental cars, or take a train. Travelers debate even the merits of price, convenience, and traveling time of airlines versus other modes of transportation for distances of about 250–300 miles. If you come into one of these markets with a price that tips the balance in favor of air travel, you can tap into a new pool of fliers, and not have to compete for the same seats that are currently being served by an incumbent.

You may also find an opportunity to create an entirely new market. This is why PSA succeeded in California. For many people, to travel from San Diego to LA, or LA to San Francisco, it made sense to give up the 3–4 hour driving time and wear-and-tear on their vehicles, or in the case of bus or train passengers an even longer travel time, for the convenience of a short, reasonably priced plane ride. SW Airlines had a similar experience in Texas by exclusively flying the Dallas, Houston, and San Antonio routes.

Enter Markets Where There is an Excess of Infrastructure

Look for markets that not only have an excess demand but also an excess of infrastructure, as evidenced by empty gates or even shuttered airports. It is not enough to have one gate and two aircrafts when you enter a market; you need to have 10 gates or more. This allows you to come into the market with the scale of passenger capacity and shared cost structure necessary to build a profitable operation. This is also a strategy that creates less friction with incumbent airlines.

Excess capacity can occur for a variety of reasons. One could be that a new airport has been built or an existing one is expanding. But building or expanding airports is a very lengthy process that can often stretch on for decades, and by the time it is completed any excess capacity may have already been absorbed.

Therefore, it is much easier to identify airports that already have excess capacity, and locate operations there. This was the case with Chicago's Midway Airport, which at one time was the world's busiest airport. After airlines began to favor the longer runways at cross-town O'Hare International Airport in the 1950s and 1960s, business dropped dramatically at Midway. Eventually, the airport underwent a major renovation program and the excess capacity became home to low-cost carriers such as Midway Airlines and SW Airlines. Similar transitions took place at Houston's Hobby Airport and Love Field in Dallas.

The most common reason for excess capacity is when an airline reduces or ceases operations in a particular market, or goes out of business. This is especially impactful when an airport has been serving as a hub for the airline's operations. One of the many examples of this occurred when Piedmont Airlines, which used Dayton Airport as a major hub, was absorbed by USAir. Flights from Dayton were dramatically reduced as a result. Although the airport has recovered somewhat because of new flights from other airlines, it still has considerable excess capacity, and would be a good launching point for a start-up airline.

Coexist with the Incumbents

In the beginning, you should develop a strategy for coexisting with the incumbents, especially if they are government-owned enterprises. If you jump in and attack them broadly across their customer base, they will certainly retaliate with full force and resort to using their considerable political power and political connections. It is possible that with the stroke of a pen you could be destroyed. It is better to look at expanding the market (as we talked about earlier) by appealing to segments the incumbent has not focused on (e.g., families that drive to vacation destinations), or going after a subset of the incumbent's market (e.g., low-end business commuters). This way the incumbent does not feel as threatened by your presence and will have less reason to take drastic retaliatory actions.

Make Sure You Have a Banker in Your Pocket

Just like telecommunications and steel, the airline industry is capital intensive. This is what we call a "deepwater phenomenon," where the deep water is the enormous amount of capital you need to sustain your survival and growth. Therefore, access to financial resources is key for long-term viability. Most new airlines are started by entrepreneurs who generally do not have huge amounts of personal capital so it is important to have a "banker in the pocket" who can secure the large amounts of financial capital necessary to start operations, smooth out the ups and downs of initial market competition, and provide the means for financing additional aircraft and operations as you expand.

Enter When There is Excess Aircraft and Labor Pool

The airline industry has been particularly prone to economic shocks, such as those caused by the oil crisis of the 1970s and the attacks of September 11, 2001. During these times the incumbent airlines generally put a halt to new aircraft purchases. However, because of the high fixed costs of aircraft production, major vendors such as Boeing, McDonnell-Douglas, and Lockheed have a difficult time adjusting their production downward. In these times, it is possible to buy new planes at a much lower cost and a good opportunity for a low-cost airline to purchase or lease inventory. The same is true for labor pool. When the industry as a whole is in recession there is generally a large workforce of available, and less expensive man-power. An excess of labor can also occur after the end of a war, when military pilots and mechanics are likely to make a transition to civilian life.

Don't Try to Compete on Price Alone

Having an aggressive pricing structure is necessary to be competitive, but it is not a sufficient condition for success by itself. Low costs will not be sustainable because unless you happen to be in a period where there is an excess pool of skilled labor, your costs will rise along with your success as you compete for a relatively fixed pool of specialized employees. Mechanics and pilots are two positions that must be certified and licensed and, especially in the case of pilots, it takes time to generate them internally. One of the biggest challenges for India's airlines at the mo-ment is finding enough pilots to fly the mushrooming number of routes. To deal with this, Indian airlines have begun importing pilots from other countries.

A second reason to not compete on price alone is because the competition will usually match a low price. So in addition to low price, you must have a differentiating strategy such as exemplary customer service. Most suc-cessful new entrants have had low price and high cus-tomer satisfaction, two areas that are usually negatively correlated. Strategic models, such as Michael Porter's Five Forces of Competition, tell us that you can either be a low-cost or a differentiator. In this case, the model does not apply.

SW, AirTran, Ryanair, easyJet, and JetBlue have been successful at this. They generally differentiate through the following characteristics:

- punctuality;
- friendliness;

- a modern fleet;
- a better IT platform; and
- a better customer experience in general.

Leverage Your Economies of Scale in Procurement

If you are a successful new entrant, you must leverage your economies of scale in procurement. Indeed, it is better to buy than to do it in-house. As a customer, you have better clout over your suppliers than as an employer over employees and unions. With your economies of scale you can negotiate better contracts with Coca-Cola, paper goods manufacturers, food companies, Boeing, Airbus, and other suppliers.

RECOMMENDATIONS FOR INCUMBENTS

Transform Yourself before Deregulation

You must transform yourself as a company during the deregulation process. The staged deregulation process discussed earlier allows for an orderly transition from a protected carrier to a competition oriented one. This will not guarantee your success but it does at least provide a more level playing field. Otherwise, if you try to jump into the competitive market without the necessary changes in operations and attitude, you are setting yourself up for a David and Goliath scenario, and you will be the losing giant. Neither Pan Am nor Eastern Airlines were prepared for their entry into deregulation and both died as a result. In Europe, many of the national carriers, such as Sabena, Iberia, KLM, and Swissair had the same problem. There were some who did take the steps to be prepared, for example, SAS and BA.

Do Not Cross Subsidize

You should wean yourself from cross subsidies as much as possible before deregulation. When you plot an established airline's revenues by routes, you will find that many of them are not making money. These routes usually have underutilized capacity or the price is too low to cover the per passenger cost of flying. In effect, these routes are being subsidized by profitable routes that have higher price points and more capacity utilization. Usually the subsidies are between international and domestic flights because international prices are still fixed. Another common cross subsidy is between business customers and tourists.

One reason airline industry incumbents strongly believe in cross subsidization is because they use incremental costing. In other words, the costs of flying from point A to point B are largely fixed once the plane takes off, so the incremental cost of serving demand is close to nothing. So what they do is at a certain point the price drops to add more customers and sometimes the best prices are an hour or two before the flight.

Be Careful of Price Wars

When a new entrant enters the market, they will most likely use low price as a key element of their competitive strategy. An incumbent must examine the situation carefully before jumping into a counterattack and if it appears that meeting the lower fare will not significantly affect the overall revenues. However, if a lower fare does not result in more paying customers, the incumbent stands to lose because it will end up with an unprofitable route. Without an expanded market, the niche player will be under pressure to either quickly take a large share of the market or raise its fares.

Be Careful of Antitrust Pricing

Another dangerous temptation for incumbents is to use retaliatory pricing as a defense against a new entrant. Even in cases where meeting the competitor's price makes sense because there will be an expanded market to absorb the lessened per passenger revenue, incumbents must be careful to not be perceived as practicing a selective pricing strategy designed to shut down the new competition. This type of antitrust activity has been used successfully in the past but regulators are now more prone to step in if an obvious attempt is made to gain unfair competitive advantage.

Separate High Profit Routes from Low Profit Routes

Segment the market as an incumbent so that price sensitive customers are separated from non-price sensitive customers, and highly profitable routes are separated from low profitable routes. As the incumbent, you have the scale to segment the market and you offer three levels of service: good, better, best service levels.

Do not Build Hub and Spoke Operations

Hub-and-spoke operations are inherently inefficient, especially when compared to the point-to-point service of SW and JetBlue. The problem is that demand is much more consistent on a point-to-point basis and more variable for a hub-and-spoke network. Operating a set of route means you have to commit substantial upfront fixed costs, and the more variable the demand, the greater the potential for loss of profit. In addition, since a hub-and-spoke network requires airplanes of various sizes you can not benefit from streamlining maintenance.

The hub-and-spoke model is also less customer friendly. When a large number of routes come together at the same location, you often have an overcrowded airport. And if one aircraft does not arrive on time it can disrupt travel for a series of the following flights. If this happens at the end of the day, passengers can become stranded overnight.

With a point-to-point system, preferably non-stop, your schedule is based on origin to destination. You also schedule flights based on frequency of demand: the more the traffic the greater the frequency. You cannot do this with a hub-and-spoke systems because when all flights come together there is a huge peak load. If a hub is hit by bad weather, everything falls apart because all your eggs are in one basket.

The only place the hub-and-spoke systems may be viable is for international flights where your domestic customers will be very few. Singapore and Dubai airports do only international flights with no domestic flights. This was not by design; it is just that they have nowhere to fly domestically.

RECOMMENDATIONS FOR SUPPLIERS

Transporting passengers is the most downstream activity in the airline industry. This is also the final point in the pricing structure. When the industry was highly regulated this was not a problem because pricing was fixed based on the basis of costs that were passed down through the supply chain and the airline's own operations. Pricing was based on cost plus profit. But now market forces are in play, and market forces use competitive pricing as a mechanism for removing inefficiencies in the cost structure. As a result, it is now a price minus cost industry where maximum efficiency must be achieved in internal and external cost centers.

This has implications not only for airlines who must minimize their costs in order to be price competitive with each other and with transportation substitutes such as automobiles and trains. It is important that suppliers realize that helping airlines and the airline industry to increase the efficiency of the supply chain and grow their revenue stream is in their own interest.

The computer industry is an example of what can happen when suppliers forget their customers must also make money. More than 80 percent of the cost of getting a computer to a customer goes to upstream suppliers, and the majority of that goes to two companies: Microsoft and Intel. The company with the final branding or distribution, whether it's Hewlett-Packard (HP), Gateway, Best Buy or Circuit City, must wring their internal costs out of the remainder. It has become increasingly less likely that a profit remains after that. Even Dell, which has become successful by developing a highly sophisticated manufacture-on-demand system, is making money. This model is not sustainable and will result in the demise or defection of Microsoft's and Intel's customers. This is the case now with Intel, which is struggling with competitors such as Advanced Micro Devices (AMD). Microsoft is also looking at major discontent from its customers and serious attempts to break away from the Microsoft family of software applications.

There are three broad categories of items that are provided by suppliers to the airline industry:

- Capital goods (e.g., aircraft, vehicle, tow vehicles, trucks, baggage tractors, boarding stairs, aircraft parts)
- Infrastructure: either physical infrastructure (e.g., airport authorities) or soft infrastructure (e.g., IT industry)
- Operating costs (e.g., fuel, maintenance, uniforms, food and beverage)

Here are some recommendations for how suppliers can contribute to their airline customers' success.

Do not be an Arms Merchant

Do not load up sales on an airline because you may end up picking up the cost of Chapter 11 protection. In that case, you will get less than you are owed, or nothing at all. In the long run, overselling creates a situation where the customers are burdened with non-revenue producing assets. This is especially dangerous in a capital intensive industry such as air transportation.

Provide More Revenue Generating Products and Services

Identify new products and services that airlines can use to broaden their sources of revenue, especially high-margin items. These new revenue streams will translate into additional profit for the airlines, and for the supplier. Airlines already use sales of alcoholic beverages and in-flight shopping to supplement revenue from ticket sales. There are many other areas where airlines could expand their offerings (and in some cases have), including gaming, broadband access, gourmet beverages and food items, and expanded shopping. Suppliers must think in terms of how their products can be customized or reinvented to increase these types of airborne revenues.

Streamline the Supply Chain so it Will be More Efficient

The current airline industry is still mostly a legacy of the regulated monopoly era where airlines themselves own everything. Suppliers can help airlines take out this vertical integration by providing services that can be shared. This could include the sharing of gates, equipment, maintenance, aircraft, and IT systems. This will allow the airlines to focus on their core business of flying people from one destination to another. The electronics industry has taken this approach by outsourcing production through contract manufacturing and focusing their efforts on the design, marketing, and distribution of the final product. By developing third-party solutions, the supplier industry can create a more efficient supply chain.

Help Airlines Grow the Overall Air Transportation Business

Suppliers should look for ways to promote the airline industry as the preferred means of travel and to encourage passengers to fly more. This could be a side effect of an ad campaign that promotes a supplier's product, as Boeing did with the introduction of the Sonic Cruiser, or it could be a more specific campaign by an association or ad hoc group of suppliers to promote the industry. Regardless of the way in which the suppliers help expand the overall business, it is important to keep that mindset because it benefits both the airlines and the suppliers. This is the attitude Procter & Gamble (P&G) has taken with its largest customer, Wal-Mart. P&G has bought out companies, such as Clairol and Wella, that had products that were distributed through drug stores or department stores. P&G then introduced these recognizable brands into the Wal-Mart distribution system. Airline industry suppliers must think the same way.

RECOMMENDATIONS FOR EMPLOYEE UNIONS

The traditional airline industry approach to wages and benefits was sustainable when there was a guarantee that revenues would cover cost of living increases, generous health care programs, and a host of other employee benefits. Now that the industry is subject to market forces on the prices it can charge, there is no way airlines can support the longstanding union expectations about wages and benefits. This is especially difficult because the airline industry is not just deregulating, it is also globalizing. In other words, governments are allowing "open skies" where the industry is subject not just to domestic competition but also to international competition. Because of this, employee unions must realize they are an integral part of the reduction of the industry's cost structure. When there is a huge wage disparity between nations, certain country's airlines will have inherent advantages—just as we have seen in manufacturing and in the IT industry. So there has to be some kind of cost parity between airlines. This does not necessarily mean that employees in higher wage countries will take the full brunt of the cost equalization, but it is a major incentive for employee unions to think outside the box in order to reduce the industry's overall costs.

Form "Cooperatives" to Take on Industry Functions

A given function could be spun out of airlines and owned and operated by the employees or unions themselves to serve not one airline but a group of airlines. Some of the obvious examples are maintenance and pilots. There is already some outsourcing of maintenance by airlines, but there remains an opportunity to do it on a much larger scale and remove a lot of duplication of costs. Pilots could do the same thing. There are few compelling reasons why pilots have to belong to one airline. This will result in more flexibility of labor flow for pilots and airlines. They become contractors instead of employees, much like a large percentage of the workers in the IT industry are. Unions should proactively seek out these kinds of opportunities to create employee-based companies.

Notes

1. Paul S. Dempsey and Andrew R. Goetz. *Airline Deregu-lation and Laissez-Faire Mythology*. Westport CT:Quorum Books, 1992, p. 59.
2. Ibid., p. 162.
3. Ibid., p. 167.
4. Ibid., p. 169.
5. Ibid.
6. Ibid., pp. 173–74.
7. Ibid., p. 174
8. Ibid., p. 179.
9. Ibid., p. 175.
10. Jonathan B. Wilson. "The Lessons of Airline Deregu-lation and the Challenge of Foreign Ownership of U.S. Carriers," *The George Washington Journal of International Law and Economics*, Vol. 24, No. 1, 1990, pp. 116–24.
11. Ibid., p. 117.
12. Ibid., p. 120.
13. Ibid., p. 122–23.
14. Ibid., p. 124.
15. Bill Wilkins. "Airline Deregulation: Neoclassical Theory as Public Policy," *Journal of Economic Issues*, Vol. XVII, No. 2, June, 1984, p. 419.
16. Ibid., p. 420.
17. Ibid., p. 421.
18. Ibid.
19. Ibid., p. 422–23.
20. Anthony Brown, *The Politics of Airline Deregulation*, Knox-ville: The University of Tennessee Press, 1987.

21. Ibid., p.103.
22. Ibid., p. 106.
23. Ibid.
24. Ibid.
25. Ibid.
26. Ibid., p. 108.
27. Ibid., p. 116.
28. Ibid.
29. Ibid., p. 117–18.
30. Ibid., p. 133.
31. Ibid., p. 118.
32. Ibid., p. 122–23.
33. "Sky's the Limit: Despite Lower Fares, West Coast Airlines Are Flying High," *Barron's National Business and Financial Weekly*, June 16, 1996, p. 5.
34. Jackie and Kevin Freiburg, *Nuts!*. New York: Broadway Books, 1996.
35. Kevin Trinkle, http://www.psa-history.org/articles/hist.html, accessed on April 14, 2005.
36. SW company website.
37. "Sky's the Limit", *Barron's*.
38. Freiburg, *Nuts!*.
39. J. Heskett, "Southwest Airlines" case study (abridged update), Harvard Business School Publishing; Harvard, MA, 1993, p. 2.
40. PSA website background information
41. Freiburg, *Nuts!* p. 39.
42. HBS case study, p. 2.
43. Freiburg, *Nuts!* pp. 17, 18.
44. "Sky's the Limit", *Barron's*.
45. Ibid.
46. Freiburg, *Nuts!* pp. 22, 23.
47. "Special Report: Turbulent skies", *The Economist*, July 10, 2004, Vol. 372, p. 68.
48. Roger Eglin and Berry Ritche, *Fly Me, I'm Freddie*. Rawson: Wade Publishers, 1980, p. 150.
49. Ibid., p. 145.
50. Ibid., p. 154.
51. Ibid., p. 205.
52. Ibid., p. 195.
53. Ibid., p. 73.
54. Ibid.
55. Ibid., pp. 73, 74.
56. Ibid., p. 75.

57. Howard Banks, *The Rise and Fall of Freddie Laker*, London: Faber and Faber Limited. 1982, p. 95.
58. Ibid., p. 78.
59. Ibid., p. 88.
60. Ibid., p. 9.
61. Jeffrey Robinson, "But Will It Fly," *Barron's*, April 18, 1983, p. 41.
62. Robert E. Dalla, "Settlement Reached in Laker Suit," *Los Angeles Times*, July 13, 1985, p. 1.
63. "Upstarts in the Sky: Here Comes a New Kind of Airline," *Business Week*, June 15, 1981, p. 78.
64. "People Express Leases Three Boeing Co. 747s", *Wall Street Journal*, Feb. 22, 1984, p. 1.
65. William M. Carley, "Rapid Ascent: People Express Flies Into Airline's Big Time In Just 3 Years Aloft—Its Newark, N.J. Hub Hums With 150 Takeoffs a Day, Tope in New York Area—Will Growing Pains Set In," *Wall Street Journal*, March 30, 1984, p. 1.
66. Ibid.
67. Ibid.
68. Ibid.
69. "People Express Traffic Rises", *Wall Street Journal*, April 5, 1984, p. 1.
70. Edwin A Finn Jr. and Roy J. Harris Jr., "Five Airlines Cut Cross-Country Fares, Sparking Fear of Price War In Industry," *Wall Street Journal*, June 11, 1984, p. 1.
71. William M. Carley, "People Express's Newark-Chicago Entry Underscores Shift in Strategy of Carrier," *Wall Street Journal*, August 9, 1984, p. 1.
72. Trish Hall, "People Express to Serve Detroit, Miami In Its Challenge to Major Carriers' Routes," *Wall Street Journal*, August 17, 1984, p. 1.
73. William M. Carley, "People Express Will Add Route To San Francisco—Flights From Newark, N.J., Are Readied To Challenge United, American, TWA," *Wall Street Journal*, September 10, 1984, p. 1.
74. "People Express to Add Service to Cleveland", *Wall Street Journal*, October 3, 1984, p. 1.
75. "People Express to Add Newark to Denver Route", *Wall Street Journal*, October 31, 1984, p. 1.
76 "People Express to Add Orlando Flights", *Wall Street Journal*, November 2, 1984, p. 1.
77. "People Express Plans New Service", *Wall Street Journal*, November 28, 1984, p. 1.

78. "People Express Traffic", *Wall Street Journal*, January 3, 1985, p. 1.
79. Laurie Cohen, "American Airlines Slashes Fares on Many Routes; Industry Stock Prices Slip as Rival Carriers Follow—New Discount Category, 70% Below Coach Rate, Has Many Restrictions," *Wall Street Journal*, June 18, 1985, p. 1.
80. Delia Flores and Harlan S. Byrne, "United Air Says It Will Retain Some Discounts—Decision Is Triggering Fears of Renewed Fare Wars; Airline Stock Prices Fall," *Wall Street Journal*, February 7, 1985, p. 1.
81. See note 35.
82. "People Express Posts $18.8 Million Deficit for the First Quarter", *Wall Street Journal*, April 24, 1985, p. 1.
83. Janet Guyon, "People Express Sets Service to 5 Cities, Including Hubs of Delta, American Air," *Wall Street Journal*, July 17, 1985, p. 1.
84. Jonathan Dahl, Matt Moffett, and Daniel Hertzberg, "People Express Obtains Pact to Buy Frontier Air's Parent for $24 a Share," *Wall Street Journal*, October 9, 1985, p. 1.
85. Robert E. Dallos, "People Express, Frontier Unit Slash Air Fares Subsidiary Will Become Discount, No-Frill Line," *Los Angeles Times*, February 11, 1986, p. 2.
86. "Frontier Airline Announces Price Cuts Up to 60 Percent", *Journal Record*, February 11, 1986.
87. William M. Carley, "People Express, in Major Strategy Shift, Will Seek to Attract Business Travelers," *Wall Street Journal*, April 29, 1986, p. 1.
88. William M. Carley, "Bumpy Flights: Many Travers Gripe About People Express, Citing Overbooking—Lost Bags Also Are Common; Chief Says Public Benefits From Carrier's Low Fares—Can It Lure Business Trade?", *Wall Street Journal*, May 19, 1986, p. 1.
89. "Alternatives 'Exhausted' Frontier File Chapter 11," *Journal Record*, Oklahoma City, Okla., August 29, 1986.
90. Robert E. Dallos, "People Express Fades into History as Merger is Okay'd"; *Los Angeles Times*, December 30, 1986, p. 1.
91. Brook Adams, "A Firmer Hand on the Airlines Without Turning the Clock Back, Deregulation Needs Revision," *Los Angeles Times*, December 19, 1988, p. 5.
92. Ibid.

93. Paulette Thomas, "Airline Amity: Rivals' Aid to Braniff In Leaving Dallas Hub Suggests New Coziness—Ten Years After Deregulation, Carriers Appear to Avoid Competitors' Flight Paths," *Wall Street Journal*, August 31, 1988, p. 1.
94. Martha M. Hamilton, "The Hubbing of America: Good or Bad?", *The Washington Post*, February 5, 1989, p. 1.
95. Robert E. Dallos, "Airline Travel Revolves on Hubs," *Los Angeles Times*, May 4, 1986, p. 1.
96. Harlan S. Byrne, "United Air's New Tactics Bring Success," *Wall Street Journal*, October 10, 1984, p. 1.
97. Ibid.
98. Scott Kilman, "Growing Giants: An Unexpected Result of Airline Decontrol Is Return to Monopolies—Big Carriers Are Dominating Nation's Hub Airports, Legislators Are Concerned—Higher Fares and Less Service," *Wall Street Journal*, July 20, 1987, p. 1.
99. Ibid.
100. See note 1.
101. Hobart Rowen, "Air Fares: Higher and Higher," *The Washington Post*, November 17, 1988, p. A5.
102. Ibid.
103. Martha M. Hamilton, "GAO Links Hub Dominance to Sharply Higher Air Fare," *The Washington Post*, June 8, 1989, p. E2.
104. Robert L. Rose, "Flight Maneuvers: Major U.S. Airlines Rapidly Gain Control Over Regional Lines—They Say Service Improves, But Critics See the Market Closing to New Entrants—Big Stick: Reservation Codes," *Wall Street Journal*, February 17, 1988, p. 1.
105. Ibid.
106. Ibid.
107. Ibid.
108. Ibid.
109. "TRB from Washington: Skyway Robbery," *The New Republic*, April 25, 1988, p. 4.
110. Ibid.
111. Danna K. Henderson, "Commission Cost Nosedive," *Air Transport World*, October 1996, pp. 104-6.
112. "Airline Competition: DOT's Implementation of Airline Regulatory Authority", United States General Accounting Office, June 1989, p. 17.
113. "Sabre Sad To Engage in 'Subtle Bias' Against Airlines," *Airline Financial News*, August 19, 2002, p. 1.

114. See note 18.
115. Ibid.
116. Steven Borenstein, "Hubs and High Fares: Dominance and Market Power in the U.S. Airline Industry," *The Rand Journal of Economics*, Autumn 1989, p. 344.
117. Kenneth M. Mead, "Airline Competition: Industry Competitive and Financial Problems", United States General Accounting Office, September 11, 1991, p. 1.
118. Ibid., p. 3.
119. "Airline Competition: Higher Fares and Less Competition Continue at Concentrated Airports," United States General Accounting Office, July 1993, Washington D.C., p. 2.
120. "Higher Fares and Less Competition Continue at Concentrated Airports," United States General Accounting Office, July 1997, Washington D.C., p. 2.
121. Ibid.
122. "Legacy Carrier Revenue Premiums Fourth Quarter 2002," Domestic Aviation Brief Number 20, Office of Aviation and International Affairs, Aviation Analysis, Washington D.C., p. 1.
123. Richard M. Weintraub, "Rivals Challenge American Airlines in a Texas Court," *The Washington Post*, July 10, 1993, p. F.1.
124. Ibid.
125. Ibid.
126. Bridget O'Brian, "Verdict Clears AMR on Illegal Pricing Charges—Carrier Didn't Try to Force Northwest, Continental To Fail, U.S. Jury Says", *Wall Street Journal*, August 11, 1993, p. A.3.
127. Peter S. Greenburg, "How Consumers Pay for Air Deregulation", *Los Angeles Times*; September 3, 1989, p. V112.
128. Paul Stephen Dempsey, "Predatory Practices By Northwest Airlines: The Monopolization of Minneapolis/St.Paul," Press Release http://www.suncountry.com/about/pressmono. htm, accessed on June 25, 2002, p. 12.
129. Ibid., p. 2.
130. Bruce Ingersoll and James P. Miller, "Forced by U.S., Northwest Quits Pressuring Rival—Moved by the White House Ends Years of Inaction On Air Industry Pricing", *Wall Street Journal*, March 29, 1993, p. A3.
131. Ibid.

132. Ibid.
133. Dempsey, Paul Stephen, n. 128.
134. Ibid., p. 24.
135. Ibid., pp. 24, 25.
136. "Review of Competitive Practices in Atlanta," AirTran Holdings Inc. Atlanta, GA: 2002. May 25, 1999, p. 3.
137. "Unfair Exclusionary Conduct in the Air Transportation Industry", US Department of Transportation Press Release, Washington D.C., April 7, 1998.
138. Ibid.
139. Ibid., p. 4.
140. Stephen Labaton with Laurence Zuckerman, "Airline Is Accused of Predatory Pricing," *The New York Times*, May 14, 1999, p. A.1.
141. Ibid.
142. Anna Wilde Mathews and Scott McCartney, "U.S. Sues American Air in Antitrust Case—No. 2 Carrier Faces Charges of Forcing Small Rivals Out of Its Hub in Dallas," *Wall Street Journal*, May 14, 1999, p. A.3.
143. Laurence Zuckerman and Stephen Labaton, "American Airlines Is the Winner in a U.S. Antitrust Case," *The New York Times*, April 28, 2001, p. C.1.
144. Ibid.
145. John R. Wilke and Scott McCartney, "American Airlines Secures Antitrust Win—Judge Dismisses U.S. Case, Says Competitive Moves Were Company's Right," *Wall Street Journal*, April 30, 2001, p. A.3.
146. Dan Carney, "Predatory Pricing: Cleared for Takeoff," *Business Week*, May 14, 2001, p. 50.
147. Mark Wigfield, "U.S. to Appeal AMR Court Decision," *Wall Street Journal*, June 27, 2001, p. A.4.
148. Garry Kissel, *Poor Sailor's Airline: A History of Pacific Southwest Airlines*, McLean, VA: Paladwr Press, 2002, p. 14.
149. "Sky's the Limit: Despite Lower Fares, West Coast Airlines Are Flying High," *Barron's*, June 16, 1966, p. 5.
150. www.catchoursmile.com, p. 4.
151. www.jetpasa.com/index/history, p. 3.
152. www.catchoursmile.com, p. 5.
153. Ibid., p. 6.
154. Ibid.
155. Ibid.
156. www.catchoursmile.com/Main2, p. 1.
157. Ibid., p. 1.

158. Ibid., p. 2.
159. Ibid., pp. 3, 4.
160. Ibid., pp. 4, 5.
161. www.catchoursmile.com/Main3, p. 1
162. Ibid.
163. Garry Kissel, *Poor Sailor's Airline*, p. 110.
164. Ibid., p. 111.
165. Ibid., pp. 55–78.
166. Ibid., p. 171.
167. Ibid.
168. Ibid., p. 147.
169. Ibid., pp. 159, 172.
170. Ibid., p. 172.
171. Ibid., pp. 172–73, 186.
172. The PSA History Page, www.cactuswings.com/psa/article/hist, pp. 5, 6.
173. www.catchoursmile.com/Main3, pp. 3, 7.
174. Garry Kissel, *Poor Sailor's Airline*, pp. 239, 240.
175. Ibid., p. 7.
176. Ibid.
177. Ibid., pp. 246, 250.
178. www.catchoursmile.com/Main3, pp. 3, 6.
179. www.jetpsa.com/history, The History Of PSA, pp. 5–7.
180. Ibid., p. 6.
181. www.catchoursmile.com/Main4, p. 2.
182. www.jetpsa.com/history, The History of PSA, p. 5.
183. www.catchoursmile.com/Main4, p. 2.
184. Ibid., p. 3.
185. Freiberg, *Nuts!*, pp. 14–15.
186. Katrina Brooker, "The Chairman of the Board Looks Back," *Fortune*, May 28, 2001, Vol. 143, p. 63.
187. Freiberg, *Nuts!*, pp. 15–16.
188. Katrina Brooker, "The Chairman of the Board Looks Back," p. 62.
189. Freiberg, *Nuts!*, pp. 16–21.
190. Ibid., p. 33.
191. Katrina Brooker, "The Chairman of the Board Looks Back," p. 65.
192. Ibid.
193. Freiberg, *Nuts!*, p. 38.
194. SW website, "Airlines Fact Sheet, Southwest Airlines Distinctions," Online, 08/30/2004, http://www.south west.com/about_swa/press/factsheet.html#Distinctions.

195. Freiberg, *Nuts!*, p. 107.
196. Ibid., p. 84.
197. Ibid., p. 81.
198. Katrina Brooker, "The Chairman of the Board Looks Back," p. 66.
199. SW website, "Airlines Fact Sheet, Southwest Airlines Distinctions," Online, 08/30/2004, http://www.south west.com/about_swa/press/factsheet.html#Distinctions.
200. SW website, "Airlines Fact Sheet, Cities Served by Southwest," Online, 08/30/2004, http://www.south-west.com/about_swa/press/factsheet.html#SWA%20 Cities.
201. SW website, "History, Yearly Outline," Online, 08/30/ 2004, http://www.southwest.com/about_swa/airborne. html.
202. Airchive.com website, "Timetables and Route Maps, Southwest/Muse Air," Online, 10/20/2004, http://www. airchive.com/site%20pages/timetables-southwest. html.
203. SW website, "History, yearly outline," Online, 08/30/ 2004. http://www.southwest.com/about_swa/airborne. html.
204. Thomas Troxell, "Short-Haul Traffic: It's Propelling Southwest Airlines to Long-Term Gains," *Barron's National Business and Financial Weekly*, May 24, 1982, p. 40.
205. Katrina Brooker, "The Chairman of the Board Looks Back," p. 65.
206. Thomas Troxell, "Short-Haul Traffic: It's Propelling Southwest Airlines to Long-Term Gains."
207. Katrina Brooker, "The Chairman of the Board Looks Back," p. 65.
208. "Why Herb Kelleher Gets So Much Respect from Labor," *Business Week*, September 24, 1984, pp. 112–13.
209. Airchive.com website, "Timetables and Route Maps, Southwest/Muse Air," Online, 10/20/2004, http:// www.airchive.com/site%20pages/timetables-southwest.html.
210. SW website, "History, yearly outline," Online, 08/30/ 2004, http://www.southwest.com/about_swa/airborne. html.
211. Katrina Brooker, "The Chairman of the Board Looks Back," p. 65.

212. The Handbook of Texas Online, "Muse Air," Online, 11/17/2004,http://www.tsha.utexas.edu/handbook/online/articles/view/MM/epm3.html.

213. Laurie Cohen, "Southwest Air Signs Definitive Accord to Buy Muse Air," *Wall Street Journal*, March 11, 1985, p. 1.

214. Francis Brown, "Southwest Air to Close Its Transtar Unit; Continental Expected to Gain From Move," *Wall Street Journal*, July 30, 1987, p. 1.

215. Katrina Brooker, "The Chairman of the Board Looks Back," p. 65.

216. Francis Brown, "Southwest Air to Close Its TranStar Unit, p. 1.

217. Airchive.com website, "Timetables and Route Maps, Southwest/Muse Air," Online, 10/20/2004, http://www.airchive.com/site%20pages/timetables-southwest. html.

218. SW website, "History, yearly outline," Online, 08/30/2004, http://www.southwest.com/about_swa/airborne. html.

219. Ibid.

220. Airchive.com website, "Timetables and Route Maps, Southwest/Muse Air," Online, 10/20/2004, http://www.airchive.com/site%20pages/timetables-southwest.html.

221. SW website, "History, Yearly Outline," Online, 08/30/2004, http://www.southwest.com/about_swa/airborne. html.

222. Freiberg, *Nuts!*, p. 87.

223. "Morris Air Services," Online, 12/20/2004, http://www. flyryan.com/history/MorrisAir.htm.

224. SW website, "History, Yearly Outline," Online, 08/30/2004, http://www.southwest.com/about_swa/airborne. html.

225. Freiberg, *Nuts!*, New York, pp. 136–37.

226. SW website, "History, yearly outline," Online, 08/30/2004, http://www.southwest.com/about_swa/airborne. html.

227. Ibid.

228. Airchive.com website, "Timetables and Route Maps, Southwest/Muse Air," Online, 10/20/2004, http://www. airchive.com/site%20pages/timetables-southwest. html.

229. SW website, "History, Yearly Outline," Online, 08/30/2004, http://www.southwest.com/about_swa/airborne.html.
230. Ibid.
231. Ibid.
232. SW website, "Airlines Fact Sheet," Online, 08/30/2004, http://www.southwest.com/about_swa/press/factsheet.html.
233. Standard & Poor's, " Southwest Airlines Stock Report," The McGraw-Hill Companies, August 28, 2004.
234. Elizabeth Sounder, "Airlines Stake in Oil Hedging Rise with Prices", *Wall Street Journal*, August 18, 2004, p. 1.
235. Micheline Maynard, "Out of the Blue, Southwest Airlines Chief Resigns," *The New York Times*, July 16, 2004, p. C2.
236. Melanie Trottman, "At Southwest, New CEO Sits In a Hot Seat," *Wall Street Journal*, July 19, 2004, p. B1.
237. Dawn Gilbertson, "Southwest fighting Dallas Rule," *The Arizona Republic*, March 16, 2005.
238. David Field, Aggressive Southwest, December 2004, Vol. 20, Issue 12, p.1.
239. Trebor Banstetter, *Knight Ridder Tribune Business News*, March 24, 2005, p. 1.
240. Wendy Zellner, "Dressed to Kill...Competitors," *Business Week*, February 21, 2005, p. 60.
241. Trebor Banstetter, "Southwest looks at fight against Dallas airport restrictions in long terms," *Knight Ridder Business News* (Washington), March 29, 2005, p. 1.
242. *The Wright Amendment Consumer Penalty*, The Campbell-Hill Aviation Group, Inc., June 7, 2005, p. 3.
243. Lou Whiteman, "Southwest: Monsters of the Midway," The Deal.com, December 17, 2004, p. 1.
244. Scott McCartney, "The Middle Seat: Southwest Airlines Set To Crack Hawaii Market; Code-Sharing With ATA Marks a Big Growth Move; New York, D.C. Join Network," *The Wall Street Journal*, January 4, 2005, p. D.5.
245. Ibid.
246. Martin J. Morgan, "Southwest, ATA airlines form alliance", *Knight Ridder Tribune Business News*, January 14, 2005, p. 1.
247. Mark Skertic, "ATA wants to prove it means business with strategy change," *Knight Ridder Tribune Business News*, March 13. 2005, p. 1.

248. Julie Johnson, "Southwest smells blood," *Crain's Chicago Business*, April 4, 2005, p. 1.

249. *Southwest Expands to Philadelphia—Third Quarter 2004*, Office of Aviation and International Affairs, Aviation Analysis, Domestic Aviation Competition Issue Brief Number 26, p. 4.

250. Adrian Schofield, "Latest Expansion Will Use Last of New Planes, Southwest Says," *Aviation Daily*, August 19, 2005, p. 2.

251. Scott McCarthy, "The Middle Seat: Travelers Benefit When Airline Hub Closes; As Gates Free Up, Discounter Move in and Fares Drop; Lesson From Pittsburgh," *Wall Street Journal*, November 1, 2005, p. 1.

252. Mark Belko, "Southwest flies into No. 3 spot, but airport traffic lags," *Knight Ridder Tribune Business News*, Washington, August 9, 2005, p. 1.

253. Trebor Banstetter, "Southwest tops airline survey; American 4th," *Knight Ridder Tribune Business News*, May 17, 2005, p. 1.

254. "People Express Outbids Texas Air Corp. for Frontier Airlines", *Journal Record*, October 9, 1985.

255. "Frontier Airlines Announces Price Cuts Up to 60 Percent", *Journal Record*, February 11, 1986.

256. Pamela Brownstein, "People Express a Solid Idea That Went Awry, Say Analysts," *Journal Record*, June 26, 1986.

257. "People Express to Shut Down Frontier Airlines", *Journal Record*, August 23, 1986.

258. "Alternatives 'Exhausted,' Frontier Files Chapter 11", *Journal Record*, August 29, 1986.

259. "Houston-Based Texas Air Corp. to Buy People Express Airline", *Journal Record*, September 16, 1986.

260. "Frontier's Fate Still in Holding Pattern/Rumor of Buyer Surfaces", *Journal Record*, August 27, 1986.

261. "Sleeping' Frontier Airlines Considers Flying the Big Sky", *The Billings Gazette*, December 9, 1983.

262. Joan M. Feldman, "'We understand United As Well As United Does'," *Air Transport World*, July 2001, Vol. 38, pp. 35–38.

263. Jim Ludwick, "Meat and Potatoes Service: Airline Hopes Missoula Fliers Take a Liking to its Simple Tastes," *Missoulian*, August 3, 1994, p. D1.

264. Robert Schwab, "Where Sam Addoms Goes, Respect Follows: Resurrecting Frontier," *ColoradoBiz*, October 2002, Vol. 29, p. 16.

265. Matthew Okerlund, "Airline Ready to Link GF, Denver," *Grand Forks Herald*, June 8, 1994, p. A1.

266. Jim Ludwick, "Meat and Potatoes Service: Airline Hopes Missoula Fliers Take a Liking to its Simple Tastes," *Missoulian*, August 3, 1994, p. D1.

267. Amy Bryer, "Frontier Celebrates 10 Years," *The Denver Business Journal*, June 25, 2004, Vol. 55, p. A15.

268. Greg Griffin, "Frontier Airlines' Savior Bids Farewell," *Knight Ridder Tribune Business News*, April 1, 2002, p. 1.

269. Jim Ludwick, "Meat and Potatoes Service: Airline Hopes Missoula Fliers Take a Liking to its Simple Tastes", *Missoulian*, August 3, 1994, p. D-1.

270. "Frontier Airlines Posts Profit", *Wall Street Journal*, June 18, 1996, p. A4.

271. Amy Bryer, "Frontier Celebrates 10 Years", *The Denver Business Journal*, June 25, 2004, Vol. 55, p. A.15.

272. Greg Griffin, "Frontier Airlines Savior Bids Farewell", *Knight Ridder Tribune Business News*, April 1, 2002, p. 1.

273. Robert W. Moorman, "The 'New' New Frontier," *Air Transport World*, August 1996, Vol. 33, p. 86.

274. Amy Bryer, "Pioneer Pauses for Look Back," *The Denver Business Journal*, August 20, 2004, Vol. 56, p. A5.

275. Alex Markels, "Frontier, Seeing a Chance in Denver, Elbows In," *The New York Times*, September 29, 2002, p. 3.

276. Laurence Zuckerman, "Airbus Is Said to Win Order From Frontier," *The New York Times*, October 14, 1999, p. C7.

277. Phyllis Jacobs Griekspoor, "Frontier Airlines Scores High on Jets' Upkeep, Safety," *Knight Ridder Tribune Business News*, January 21, 2002, p. 1.

278. Amy Beyer, "Pioneer Pauses for Look Back", *The Denver Business Journal*, August 20, 2004, Vol. 56, p. A5.

279. "Frontier's Chief is Retiring," *The New York Times*, April 1, 2002, p. C3.

280. Lynn Bronikowski, "Jeff Potter, Frontier Chief Reaches for the Sky," *ColoradoBiz*, August 2002, Vol. 29, p. 68.

281. "Frontier Air Accuses United of Predatory Practices", *Wall Street Journal*, January 17, 1997, p. B5.

282. "Justice Dept. Reviews Claims of Airlines' Price Squeeze", *Los Angeles Times*, February 12, 1997, p. 1.

283. Scott McCartney, "Airlines: Upstart's Tactics Allow It to Fly In Friendly Skies of Big Rival," *Wall Street Journal*, June 23,1999, p. B1.

284. Joan M. Feldman, "'We understand United As Well As United Does'," *Air Transport World*, July 2001, Vol. 38, pp. 35–38.

285. Alex Markels, "Frontier, Seeing a Chance in Denver, Elbows In," *The New York Times*, September 29, 2002, p. 3.

286. Todd Neff, "United Airlines Launches Discount Carrier 'Ted' at Denver," *Knight Ridder Tribune Business News*, February 13, 2004, p. 1.

287. Micheline Maynard, "Not Yet Airborn, and Ted Is in a Fare War," *The New York Times*, January 24, 2004, p. C2.

288. Eric Hubler, "Frontier Airlines Flies Denver Schoolchildren to Museum in Kansas City, Mo," *Knight Ridder Tribune Business News*, January 15, 2002, p. 1.

289. Keith L. Alexander, "Four Small Carriers Make Deadline to Request Loan Guarantees," *The Washington Post*, June 29, 2002, p. E1.

290. Elizabeth Albanese, "Denver-based Frontier Is First Airline to Repay Post-9/11 Federal Loan," *Bond Buyer*, December 23, 2003, Vol. 346, p. 28.

291. Greg Griffin, "Frontier Airlines Applies for Direct Flight from Denver to Mexican Resorts," *Knight Ridder Tribune Business News*, August 7, 2002, p. 1.

292. "Frontier Wins DOT Approval to Offer Denver-Cancun Service", *Aviation Daily*, September 24, 2002, Vol. 349, p. 6.

293. Greg Griffin, "Flights at Denver Airport Shift Focus to Leisure Travel," *Knight Ridder Tribune Business News*, August 22, 2002, p. 1.

294. Dick Woodbury, "Frontier Airline Finds Great Success with Expanded Mexican Service," *Knight Ridder Tribune Business News*, March 8, 2004, p. 1.

295. "Frontier to Sell Flights Operated By Mesa Under New Pact," *Commuter/Regional Airline News*, September 17, 2001, Vol. 19, p. 1.

296. Greg Griffin, "Frontier Airlines Needs New Partner for JetExpress Regional Service," *Knight Ridder Tribune Business News*, July 3, 2003, p. 1.

297. SL. "Frontier Posts $6 Million Loss, Changes Denver Fare Structure," *Aviation Daily*, February 6, 2003, Vol. 351, p. 3.

298. Greg Griffin, "Denver-based Frontier-Airlines Reports Net Loss, Sees 'No Relief' Ahead," *Knight Ridder Tribune Business News*, July 30, 2004, p. 1.

299. "Frontier Lowers Fares, Eases Rules on Many Flights", *Wall Street Journal*, February 6, 2003, p. D2.

300. Greg Griffin, "Denver-based Frontier-Airlines Reports Net Loss, Sees 'No Relief' Ahead," *Knight Ridder Tribune Business News*, July 30, 2004, p. 1.

301. Andy Vuong, "Red Ink Continues to Flow at Frontier Airlines," *Knight Ridder Tribune Business News*, May 18, 2003, p. 1.

302. "Frontier Rebounding With Lower Costs, Higher Traffic", *Airline Financial News*, July 21, 2003, Vol. 21, p. 1.

303. Adrian Schofield, "Analysts Praise Frontier Cost Cuts Depsite $2 Million Loss," *Aviation Daily*, November 1, 2004, Vol. 358, p. 1.

304. "A New Frontier", *Airline Business*, June 2003, Vol. 19, p. 68.

305. Louis Aguilar, "Frontier Makes Deep Cuts in Denver Airport Walk-Up Fares," *Knight Ridder Tribune Business News*, January 23, 2004, p. 1.

306. "Frontier Set to Use Los Angeles Airport in Strategy Switch", *Wall Street Journal*, December 19, 2003, p. 1.

307. Amy Bryer, "DIA gates Settlement Brings Peace to United, Frontier," *The Denver Business Journal*, December 26, 2003, Vol. 55, p. A35.

308. Steven Lott, "Frontier Plans to Sharply Scale Back LAX Focus City", *Aviation Daily*, June 29, 2004, Vol. 356, p. 2.

309. Greg Griffin, "Frontier Hires Ad Agency," *Knight Ridder Tribune Business News*, October 17, 2002, p. 1.

310. Barry Janoff, "What Do You Call a Funny Airplane? A One Liner," *Brandweek*, August 18–25, 2003, Vol. 44, p. 28.

311. Amy Bryer, "Frontier's Animal Ads Proving Popular, Attention Getters," *The Denver Business Journal*, March 12, 2004, Vol. 55, p. A3.

312. Greg Griffin, "'Whole New Animal' Ad Campaign Boosts Growth for Denver's Frontier Airlines," *Knight Ridder Tribune Business News*, October 16, 2003, p. 1.

313. "Frontier Airlines Trims Routes But Lifts Its Marketing", *Knight Ridder Tribune Business News*, November 23, 2004, p. 1.

314. Louis Aguilar, "Frontier Airlines Targets United's Elite Fliers with VIP Program," *Knight Ridder Tribune Business News*, February 27, 2004, p. 1.

315. Greg Griffin, "Frontier Airlines Redoes In-flight Entertainment as Part of Rebranding Effort," *Knight Ridder Tribune Business News*, July 18, 2004, p. 1.

316. Amy Bryer, "Frontier Celebrates 10 Years," *The Denver Business Journal*, June 25, 2004, Vol. 55, p. A15.

317. Rick Barrett, "Frontier Airlines to Initiate Daily Flights Between Milwaukee, Denver," *Knight Ridder Tribune Business News*, May 30, 2003, p. 1.

318. "One on one with ValuJet's Robert Priddy", *Commuter/ Regional Airline News*, May 15, 1995, p. 1.

319. Richard M Weintraub, "The Low-Fare Air War Lands at Dulles: ValuJet Begins Flights to Atlanta With Plans to Expand Service to 13 Cities Soon," *The Washington Post*, January 13, 1994, p. D10.

320. Robert W. Moorman, "Southwest without the frills," *Air Transport World*, September 1994, pp. 113–17.

321. James P. Woolsey, "ValuJet: So far, so good," *Air Transport World*, December 1995, pp. 67–69.

322. Rick Brooks, "Which is Better: Chaos In the Aisles or at the Gate?", *Wall Street Journal*, February 8, 1995, p. T3.

323. "ValuJet Airlines", *Going Public, the IPO Reporter*, June 6, 1994, p. 9.

324. "ValuJet to Begin Service in October", *Air Transport World*, September 1993, p. 132.

325. Stephen C. Fehr, "Fire on ValuJet Raises Questions on Containment; Probe Focuses on Spread of Engine Blaze," *The Washington Post*, June 10, 1995, p. C1.

326. Rick Brooks, "ValuJet Close to Agreement on New Hub," *Wall Street Journal*, November 2, 1994, p. F1.

327. "ValuJet Buys 58 New McDonnell Douglas Aircraft", *Airline Financial News*, 23 October 1995, p. 1.

328. Anthony Faiola, "ValuJet Resumes Service On a Wing and a Fare; Airline Seeks to Lure Back Bargain Seekers," *The Washington Post*, October 1, 1996, p. C1.

329. Faye Bowers, "Fact vs. Guesswork in ValuJet Tragedy," *Christian Science Monitor*, May 24, 1996, p. 1.

330. "ValuJet Launches the MD-95", *Air Transport World*, December 1995, p. 69.

331. Don Phillips, "ValuJet Cabin Fire Melted Aluminum; Cockpit Voice Recorder Found, May Offer Clues to Final Moments," *Washington Post*, May 27, 1996, p. A1.

332. James Gerstenzang, "ValuJet to Stop Flying Till it Fixes Deficiencies," *Los Angeles Times*, June 18, 1996, p. A1.

333. Martha Brannigan, "ValuJet Sees Flights Disrupted Until 4th Quarter," *Wall Street Journal*, May 23, 1996, p. A3.

334. "Fallout from the ValuJet Crash", *The Washington Post*, July 23, 1996, p. C6.

335. Matthew L. Wald, "F.A.A. Shuts Down ValuJet, Citing 'Serious Deficiencies'," *The New York Times*, June 18, 1996, p. A1.

336. Robert A. Rosenblatt, "ValuJet Stock Plunges 35%; Chief Says Airline will Overcome Tough Odds," *Los Angeles Times*, June 19, 1996, p. 1.

337. Anthony Faiola, "ValuJet Passes FAA Safety Inspection; After 58-Day Review, Airline Awaits DOT Clearance to Fly Again," *The Washington Post*, August 30, 1996, p. D1.

338. Matthew L. Wald, "Valujet, Grounded for Safety Problems, is Cleared to Fly Again," *The New York Times*, September 27, 1997, p. A24.

339. Toby Eckert, "Mikelsons said 'no' to ValuJet," *Indianapolis Business Journal*, July 21, 1997, p. A1.

340. "AirTran Plans Orlando Service", *Wall Street Journal*, August 23, 1994, p. B4.

341. Robert W. Moorman, "'Takes a Licking, Keeps on Ticking'," *Air Transport World*, February 1995, pp. 63–65.

342. "One-on-one with AirTran Airways' John Horn", *Commuter/Regional Airline News*, November 6, 1995, p. 1.

343. Susan Carey, "Travel: Tiny Airlines Offer Better Ways to the Sun," *Wall Street Journal*, March 17, 1995, p. B15.

344. Andrew Meadows, "AirTran Flies into Upstate Market," *Spartanburg Herald-Journal*, January 21, 1996, p. B6.

345. "Regional Notebook", *Air Transport World*, October 1995, pp. 126–28.

346. "Valujet to Acquire AirTran Airways for $61.8 Million", *The New York Times*, July 11, 1997, p. D3.

347. Katy Eckmann, "Same Fla. City, Different Shop for AirTran," *Adweek*, October 20, 1997, p. 4.

348. Anthony L. Velocci, Jr., "Aviation Week & Space Technology," *Market Focus*, January 19, 1998, p. 11.

349. Mike Beirne, "AirTran continues its comeback," *Adweek*, July 26, 1999, p. 4.

350. Martha Brannigan, "Air Pressure: Discount Carrier Lands Partners In Ill-Served Cities—Shrugging Off Industry Woes, AirTran Thrives on Deals That Guarantee

Revenue—Flying High Rollers to Biloxi," *Wall Street Journal*, July 16, 2002, p. A1.

351. Mary Jane Credeur, "AirTran chips away at Delta," *Atlanta Business Chronicle*, May 14, 2004, p. A1.

352. Michael Wall, "DOT places Delta and other carriers on its radar," *Atlanta Business Chronicle*, November 5, 1999, p. 5A.

353. Martha Brannigan, "AirTran Holdings Appoints Leonard As President, CEO," *Wall Street Journal*, January 7, 1999, p. 1.

354. "One-on-one with AirTran Airways' Joe Leonard", *Commuter/Regional Airline News*, March 19, 2001, p. 1.

355. Gary Cohn "Eastern Airlines' Leonard Is Viewed As Heir Apparent to Succeed Borman," *Wall Street Journal*, May 23, 1985, p. 1.

356. Charles Haddad, "Catch Him if You Can. Joe Leonard's Low Costs have AirTran Outflying Delta," *Business Week*, September 15, 2003, p. 93.

357. "AirTran Airways Picks Fornaro as President", *Wall Street Journal*, March 24, 1999, p. 1.

358. Don Phillips, "Jet's Crew Discussed Landing on Highway; AirTran DC-9 Instead Returned Safely to N.C. Airport After Smoke Filled Cockpit," *The Washington Post*, August 22, 2000, p. A5.

359. Martha Brannigan and Chad Terhune, "AirTran Criticizes NTSB Chief Over DC-9 Fire," *Wall Street Journal*, December 4, 2000, p. C6.

360. Rajiv Vyas, "4 years after crash, AirTran in a climb," *Atlanta Business Chronicle*, May 12, 2000, p. A1.

361. Joan M. Feldman, "Once more into the breach," *Air Transport World*, August 2000, pp. 31–33.

362. David Goetzl, "AirTran flies in the face of big-time carriers," *Advertising Age*, May 8, 2000, pp. 3–5.

363. John Schmeltzer, "Orlando, Fla.-Based AirTran to Lease Boeing Jets Intended for American," *Chicago Tribune*, October 24, 2002, p. 1.

364. Joan M. Feldman, "Tough Times Breed Opportunity," *Air Transport World*, June 2002, pp. 40–42.

365. "Discount airlines lead way in online ticket sales", *Journal Record*, September 25, 2000.

366. Ian Lamont, "Talk to me," *Network World*, June 4, 2001, pp. 64–65.

367. Chris McGinnis, "Air chaos may route some travelers to AirTran," *Atlanta Business Chronicle*, March 9, 2001, p. A8.

368. James F. Peltz, "AirTran Flying a Steady Course; Low-Fare Carrier Is Expected to Post Its Ninth Consecutive Quarterly Profit," *Los Angeles Times*, April 17, 2001, p. C1.

369. "Industry Briefs", *Airline Financial News*, June 5, 2000, p. 1.

370. "AirTran Unit August Traffic Rose", *Wall Street Journal*, September 5, 2002, A6.

371. Tom Belden, "AirTran's Popularity Surges; Airline Becomes Fastest-Growing in Philadelphia," *Philadelphia Inquirer*, September 14, 2003.

372. Trebor Banstetter, "AirTran Brings Its Low-Cost Strategy to American's Home Hub," *Fort Worth Star-Telegram*, October 3, 2003.

373. "AirTran Pilots Agree to Help Carrier", *Aviation Daily*, September 18, 2001, p. 4.

374. "Lowest of the low", *Airfinance Journal*, March 2003, p. 1.

375. James Ott, "A 'Blooming' Airline; 737-700s will Transform AirTran Just as 717 Did, But Don't You Dare Call it a 'Major'," *Aviation Week & Space Technology*, June 21, 2004, p. 49.

376. Rick Barrett, "Rising Jet-Fuel Prices Hurt Already Suffering Airlines," *Milwaukee Journal Sentinel*, March 12, 2003.

377. "The Orlando Sentinel, Fla., Business Insider Column", *Orlando Sentinel*, April 29, 2002.

378. Steven Lott, "JetBlue to Add XM Radio, Fox; AirTran Plans First IFE System," *Aviation Daily*, January 9, 2004, p. 6.

379. Joe Leonard, "U.S. Government Subsidizes Inefficiency In Airline Industry," *Aviation Week & Space Technology*, June 21, 2004, p. 86.

380. Mark Belko, "AirTran to Offer Nonstop Flights between Pittsburgh, Pa., Orlando, Fla," *Pittsburgh Post-Gazette*, October 17, 2002.

381. "AirTran Reports Quarterly Profit Thanks to Cost Control, Share Gains", *Aviation Daily*, January 29, 2003, p. 1.

382. Lin-Fisher, Betty. "AirTran Airways Adds Flight at Akron-Canton Regional Airport in Ohio." *Akron Beacon Journal*, February 8, 2002.

383. "New Services", *Airline Industry Information*, February 22, 2002.

384. Jason Gertzen, "AirTran to Start Service in Milwaukee," *Milwaukee Journal Sentinel*, March 28, 2002.

385. Greg Griffin, "AirTran to Add Atlanta-Denver Nonstop Flights," *Denver Post*, January 8, 2003.

386. Jerry Siebenmark, "Boeing or Airbus? AirTran to make 100-airplane order," *Wichita Business Journal*, March 21, 2003, p. 1.

387. J. Lynn Lunsford and Nicole Harris, "Leading the News: Boeing Tops Airbus for AirTran Deal; Growing Discount Carrier Is to Pay About $6 Billion For More Than 100 Planes," *Wall Street Journal*, July 1, 2003, p. A3.

388. "Four Gates to Open at Dallas/Fort Worth International Airport", *Dallas Morning News*, July 9, 2003.

389. Trebor Banstetter and Byron Okada, "Discount Carrier AirTran Unveils Major Expansion at Dallas Airport," *Fort Worth Star-Telegram*, September 5, 2003.

390. Trebor Banstetter, "Delta Air Lines to exit Fort Worth, Texas-area airport; AirTran to expand," *Fort Worth Star-Telegram*, October 5, 2004.

391. Trebor Banstetter, "American Airlines to Reduce Fares from Fort Worth, Texas, to Los Angeles Area," *Fort Worth Star-Telegram*, June 10, 2004.

392. David Bond, "Delta, America West, Airtran Report on 2001 and Look Ahead," *Aviation Week & Space Technology*, February 4, 2002, p. 46.

393. Rachel Sams, "AirTran Wants $1.5 Million Guaranteed Revenue from Tallahassee, Fla," *Tallahassee Democrat*, March 2, 2002.

394. Rachel Sams, "Tallahassee, Fla., Report Finds Travelers Flying on AirTran Airways," *Tallahassee Democrat*, April 10, 2002.

395. Rachel Sams, "Tallahassee, Fla., Officials Fly AirTran Half of the Time, Review Finds," *Tallahassee Democrat*, June 3, 2003.

396. Rocky Scott, "AirTran to Drop Service to Tallahassee, Fla., Citing Operational Losses," *Tallahassee Democrat*, July 22, 2004.

397. Peter Dujardin, "AirTran Airways Begins Service to New York, Florida from Newport News, Va," *Daily Press*, March 6, 2002.

398. Peter Dujardin, "AirTran Airways Expects to Continue Getting Subsidy from Newport News, Va," *Daily Press*, February 6, 2003.

399. Peter Dujardin, "AirTran Adds Third Nonstop Flight from Newport News, Va., to New York," *Daily Press*, April 26, 2003.

400. Molly McMillin, "AirTran Airways Will Be in Wichita, Kan., Beginning May 8," *Wichita Eagle*, March 1, 2002.

401. Phyllis Jacobs Griekspoor, "AirTran Airways Has Been Successful in Helping Lower Airfare Cost," *Wichita Eagle*, June 13, 2002.

402. Dan Voorhis, "Wichita, Dan., Makes Payment to AirTran Airways," *Wichita Eagle*, July 3, 2002.

403. Dan Voorhis, "Discount-Carrier AirTran Runs Out of Wichita, Dan., Funds," *Wichita Eagle*, September 14, 2002.

404. "AirTran to End Direct Service between Wichita, Kan., and Chicago in February," *Wichita Eagle*, December 21, 2002.

405. Jerry Siebenmark, "Air service summit will look for ways to keep low-fare carriers in Wichita," *Wichita Business Journal*, April 18, 2003, p. 1.

406. "Council approves AirTran contract with subsidies", *Wichita Business Journal*, May 14, 2004, p. 28.

407. Lori O'Toole Buselt, "AirTran offers nonstop service from Wichita, Kan., to Orlando, Fla," *Wichita Eagle*, August 6, 2004.

408. Molly McMillin, "AirTran Airways Bills Wichita, Kan., for More Than $600,000," *Wichita Eagle*, November 1, 2003.

409. Mike Pare, "Chattanooga, Tenn., Airport Hopes to Land AirTran Service," *Chattanooga Times/Free Press*, September 28, 2002.

410. Mary Jane Credeur, "AirTran shifts its focus," *Atlanta Business Chronicle*, April 15, 2005, p. 1A.

411. M. Paul Jackson, "AirTran Airways to discontinue service at Greensboro, N.C., airport," *Winston-Salem Journal*, July 23, 2004.

412. Kyle Stock, "The Post and Courier, Charleston, S.C., tourism column," *Post and Courier*, August 16, 2004.

413. Kyle Stock, "Low-Fare Carrier Independence Air to Touch Down in Charleston, S.C," *Post and Courier*, May 19, 2004.

414. Mary Jane Credeur, "AirTran chips away at Delta," *Atlanta Business Chronicle*, May 14, 2004, p. A1.

415. David Bond, "Sounding Off," *Aviation Week & Space Technology*, August 2, 2004, p. 27.

416. Evan Perez and Nicole Harris, "Clipped Wings: Despite Early Signs of Victory, Discount Airlines Get Squeezed; AirTran Faces Dual Threat From a Revitalized Delta And New Set of Insurgents; The Trouble With Independence," *Wall Street Journal*, January 17, 2005.

417. Todd Pack, "Southwest foils Orlando, Fla.-based AirTran's plans for Chicago airport's gates," *Orlando Sentinel*, December 17, 2004.

418. "Southwest Airlines Celebrates 20 Years in Chicago!", http://phx.corporate-ir.net/phoenix.zhtml?c=92562&p=irol-newsArticle&ID=686671&highlight= accessed on May 12, 2006.

419. Trebor Banstetter, "Discount Air Carriers Design Business-Specific Lines to Capture New Market," *Fort Worth Star-Telegram*, May 17, 2004.

420. "AirTran Holdings Inc.: Profit Slid 95%, but Fuel Hedges Prevented a Loss During Period", *Wall Street Journal*, January 26, 2005, p. 1.

421. Jerome Greer Chandler, "Atlanta's Phoenix AirTran emerged from ValuJet as a profitable and expanding airline with its sights keenly focused on safety and reliability," *Overhaul & Maintenance*, May 2003, p. 37.

422. Jason Lynch and Mark Dagostino, "Man in Motion," *People*, Aug 26, 2002, p. 89.

423. Eryn Brown, "A Smokeless Herb," *Fortune*, May 28, 2001, Vol. 143, p. 79.

424. Ibid.

425. Barbara S. Peterson, *Blue Streak: Inside JetBlue, the Upstart That Rocked an Industry*, New York: Penguin Group, 2004, p. 13.

426. Ibid., p. 24.

427. Ibid., pp. 15–16.

428. James Wynbrandt, *Flying High: How JetBlue Founder and CEO David Neeleman Beats the Competition-Even in the World's Most Turbulent Industry*, New Jersey: John Wiley & Sons, Inc., 2004, p. 43.

429. Ibid., p. 60.

430. Ibid., pp. 60–61.

431. Barbara S. Peterson, *Blue Streak*, p. 40.

432. Ibid., p. 43.

433. Ibid., p. 38.

434. Ibid.

435. Frances Fiorino, "JetBlue Pursues Growth While Staying 'Small'," *Aviation Week and Space Technology*, June 10, 2002, Vol. 156, p. 41.

436. Amy Rottier, "The Skies are JetBlue," *Workforce*, September 2001, Vol. 80, p. 22.
437. Melanie Wells, "Lord of the Skies," *Forbes*, October 14, 2002, Vol. 170, p. 130.
438. Barry Estabrook, "In the Air, on the Cheap," *The New York Times*, April 4, 2004, p. 5.9.
439. James Wynbrandt, *Flying High*, pp. 146–48.
440. Ibid., p. 101.
441. Ibid., p. 89.
442. Ibid., p. 91.
443. Ibid., p. 97.
444. Ibid., p. 75.
445. Susan Carey, "The Importance of Not Being Earnest— JetBlue Spooks Commercials of Rivals, But Airline Says Spots aren't Mean-Spirited," *Wall Street Journal*, June 5, 2003, p. B.10.
446. Barbara S. Peterson, *Blue Streak*, p. 89.
447. Laurence Zuckerman, "Ambitious Low-Fare Carrier Names Itself JetBlue Airways," *New York Times*, July 15, 1999, p. C9.
448. Sally B. Donnelly, "Blue skies," *Time*, July 30, 2001, Vol. 158, p. 24.
449. Barbara S. Peterson, *Blue Streak*, p. 121.
450. James Wynbrandt, *Flying High*, p. 161.
451. Ibid., p. 205.
452. Ibid., pp. 115–16.
453. Robert Carey, "Nothing but blue skies," *Successful Meetings*, July 2002, Vol. 51, p. 74.
454. Bob Mims, "Head of JetBlue Airways Stresses Commitment to Worker, Customer Satisfaction," *Knight Ridder Tribune Business News*, February 22, 2003, p. 1.
455. James F. Peltz, "Upstart JetBlue Flies High Despite Travel Slump; Airlines: The Carrier isn't Cutting Operations or its Work Force to Survive, and Aircraft Delivery is on Track," *Los Angeles Times*, October 12, 2001, p. C1.
456. James Wynbrandt, *Flying High*, p. 204.
457. Perry Flint, "It's a blue world after all," *Air Transport World*, June 2003, Vol. 40, p. 36.
458. James Bernstein, "Analysts say JetBlue, Southwest face eventual fight for market," *Knight Ridder Tribune Business News*, July 19, 2004, p. 1.
459. Barbara S. Peterson, *Blue Streak*, p. 171.
460. "JetBlue Leaves Atlanta As Delta Battles AirTran", *Airline Financial News*, November 3, 2003, Vol. 21, p. 1.

461. Susan Carey, "JetBlue Orders 100 Embraer Planes," *Wall Street Journal*, June 11, 2003, p. A2.

462. David Neeleman and Dave Barger, "Letter to Stockholders (2003)," April 26, 2004, accessed March 30, 2005, http://www.curran-connors.com/jb2003/letter.html.

463. Susan Carey, "JetBlue Flies Into High Pressure; Rapid Growth, New Competition Squeeze Profit Margin, Revenue," *Wall Street Journal*, January 30, 2004, p. B3.

464. Micheline Maynard, "JetBlue Will Begin Flying Out of La Guardia," *New York Times*, June 24, 2004, p. C6.

465. James Wynbrandt, *Flying High*, p. 237.

466. James Bernstein, "JetBlue to add terminal to New York City's Kennedy Airport," *Knight Ridder Tribune Business News*, August 6, 2004, p. 1.

467. Tommy Fernandez, "Timing's right as JetBlue revs up in NY," *Crain's New York Business*, July 5, 2004, Vol. 20, p. 1.

468. Susan Carey, "JetBlue Flies Into High Pressure; Rapid Growth, New Competition Squeeze Profit Margin, Revenue," *Wall Street Journal*, January 30, 2004, p. B3.

469. "JetBlue Lands at Top of Quality List," *Wall Street Journal*, April 6, 2004, p. D3.

470. Tommy Fernandez, "Timing's right as jetBlue revs up in NY," *Crain's New York Business*, July 5, 2004, Vol. 20, p. 1.

471. Felix Sanchez, "JetBlue Airways profits dip 71 percent in third quarter," *Knight Ridder Tribune Business News*, October 29, 2004, p. 1.

472. "JetBlue Announces Fourth Quarter and Full Year 2004 Earnings," JetBlue Press Release, January 27, 2005, accessed March 30, 2005, <http://www.jetblue.com/learnmore/pressprint.asp?newsID=295>.

473. Matthew Brelis, "High-Flying Start-Up Finds Niche in Not-So-Friendly Skies," *Knight Ridder Tribune Business News*, January 19, 2003, p. 1.

474. James Wynbrandt, *Flying High*, p. 162.

475. Micheline Maynard, "Low-Fare Airlines Decide Frills Maybe Aren't So Bad After All," *The New York Times*, January 7, 2004, p. C1.

476. Kristi Sue Labetti, "Motivating a blue streak," *Potentials*, September 2002, Vol. 35, p. 75.

477. Wendy Zellner, "Is JetBlue's Flight Plan Flawed?," *Business Week*, February 16, 2004, p. 74.

478. James Wynbrandt, *Flying High*, p. 231.

479. Ibid., p. 241.
480. Frances Fiorino, "JetBlue Pursues Growth While Staying 'Small'," *Aviation Week and Space Technology*, June 10, 2002, Vol. 156, p. 41.
481. James Wynbrandt, *Flying High*, p. 204.
482. Chuck Salter, "And Now the Hard Part," *Fast Company*, May 2004, p. 66.
483. Siobhán Creaton, *Ryanair—How A Small Irish Airline Conquered Europe*. London: Aurum Press Ltd., 2004. p. 5.
484. Ibid., p. 2.
485. Ibid., pp. 10–14.
486. Ibid., pp. 19–20.
487. www.ryanair.com, "About Ryanair", accessed on December 14, 2004.
488. Siobhán Creation, *Ryanair*, p. 20.
489. Ibid., pp. 22, 27.
490. Ibid., pp. 23, 25–26.
491. Ibid., p. 24.
492. Siobhán Creaton, *Ryanair*, pp. 32–34.
493. Ibid., p. 4.
494. Ibid., pp. 35–38.
495. Ibid., p. 62.
496. Ibid., p. 43.
497. Arthur Reed, "Southwest Style in Europe." *Air Transport World*. Cleveland: August 1995. Vol. 32, No. 8; pp. 63–64.
498. Siobhán Creaton, *Ryanair*, pp. 44.
499. Ibid., p. 45–47.
500. http://www.ryanair.com/investor/download/quarter 2_05.pdf "Appendix 1 -Ryanair Number 1 for Earnings" accessed on May 11, 2004.
501. Siobhán Creaton, *Ryanair*, pp. 54–55.
502. Ibid., p. 137.
503. Ibid., pp. 61–62.
504. Simon Calder, *No Frills—The Truth Behind the Low-Cost Revolution in the Skies*. London: Virgin Books Ltd., 2002. p. 62.
505. Ibid., p. 24.
506. Arthur Reed, "Southwest Style in Europe."
507. Ibid.
508. Keith Johnson and Daniel Michaels, "Big Worry for No-Frills Ryanair: Has It Gone as Low as It Can Go?", *Wall Street Journal*, July 1, 2004, p. A1.

509. http://www.ryanair.com/investor/download/quarter 2_05.pdf "Inflight Entertainment System", accessed on March 10, 2004.
510. Graham Bowley, "How Low Can You Go?", *Financial Times*, London, June 20, 2003.
511. Kevin Done, "Pilot's Unions Link Up to Test Ryanair," *Financial Times*, London, October 19, 2004.
512. Graham Bowley, "How Low Can You Go?", *Financial Times*, London, June 20, 2003.
513. Siobhán Creaton, *Ryanair*, p. 90.
514. Ibid., p. 93.
515. Ibid., p. 98.
516. Siobhán Creaton, *Ryanair*, p. 110.
517. William Underhill, "Next: No-Frills Pizza?; The Founder of easyJet has Plans for Cruises, Buses, Phones..."; [Atlantic Edition], *Newsweek*, New York, May 10, 2004, p. 44.
518. Miller Freeman, "Air Rianta Deal would Boost Ryanair Traffic.", *Travel Trade Gazette*, Tonbridge, October 21, 1998, p. 6.
519. Siobhán Creaton, *Ryanair*, pp. 165–71.
520. Jane Spencer, "The Discount Jet-Set: Europe's Budget Airlines; As Their Ranks Swell, Carriers Drop Prices— and Amenities; London to Berlin for $25.", *Wall Street Journal*. New York, April 27, 2004. p. D1.
521. Daniel Rogers, "Can Ryanair Keep Flying High?", *Marketing*, London, June 5, 2003, p. 22.
522. Ibid.
523. Ibid.
524. *Commuter Regional Airline News International*. Potomac, May 26, 1997. Vol. 10, No. 11, p. 1.
525. http://www.ryanair.com/about/abouthome.html, accessed on December 16, 2004.
526. Graham Bowley, "How Low Can You Go?", *Financial Times*, London, June 20, 2003.
527. Jane Spencer, "The Discount Jet-Set", *Wall Street Journal*.
528. Simon Calder, *No Frills*, p. 92.
529. www.ryanair.com 12/15/2004. Customer Service FAQ, Punctuality Figures, "Ryanair has beaten easyJet on punctuality every week this year," accessed on December 15, 2004.
530. Jane Spencer, "The Discount Jet-Set," *Wall Street Journal*.
531. Graham Bowley, "How Low Can You Go?", *Financial Times*.

532. Ibid.
533. Ryanair 2004 Annual Report. www.rayanair.com Investor relations.
534. http://www.ryanair.com/abouthome.html, accessed on December 17, 2004.
535. http://www.ryanair.com/investor/download/quarter2_05. pdf, accessed on March 6, 2005.
536. "New Owners To Turn Air Asia into No-Frill 737 Airline," *Aviation Week*, September 14, 2001, p. 6.
537. Cris Prystay, "Tune Air Founder Goes Against the Odds To Establish a Low-Cost Asian Airline," *Wall Street Journal*, Eastern edition, New York, December 10, 2001, p. 1.
538. Ibid., p. 2.
539. Eirmalasare Bani, "Air Asia, MAS Likely to Complement Each Other," *Business Times*, January 24, 2002, p. 1.
540. "Malaysia Approves Expansion of Second-Tier Carriers," *Aviation Daily*, Washington, January 25, 2002, p. 5.
541. Seelen Sakran, "Soaring High on Low Fare," *Malaysian Business*, Kuala Lumpur, July 16, 2003, p. 29.
542. Ibid.
543. Michael Shari, "A Discount Carrier Spreads Its Wings," *Business Week*, September 1, 2003, p. 27.
544. Dalila Abu Bakar, "Tune Air claims unfair competition over MAS move to cut domestic fares," *Business Times*. Kuala Lumpur, August 7, 2002, p. 1
545. Ibid.
546. S. Jayasankaran and Cris Prystay, "Fare Fight: Upstart Shakes Up The Clubby World Of Asian Flying; Air Asia's Low-Cost Service Caters to New Fliers; Fending Off State Carriers; Saving on Food, Brake Pads," *Wall Street Journal*, July 20, 2004, p. A1.
547. "Malaysia Government Eyes MAS, Air Asia Fare War," *Aviation Daily*, August 9, 2002, p. 6.
548. Jake Lloyd-Smith, "Malaysia Blazes Trail with No-Frills Airline Venture," *Knight Ridder Tribune Business News*, Washington, June 16, 2003, p. 1.
549. "Air Asia forms agreement with GE Capital Aviation Services for 11 Boeing Aircraft," *Airline Industry Information*, Coventry, June 18, 2003, p. 1.
550. "Malaysia Blazes Trail with No-Frills Airline Venture," *Airline Industry Information*, Coventry, June 18, 2003, p. 1.
551. Michael Shari, "A Discount Carrier Spreads Its Wings," *Business Week*, September 1, 2003, p. 27.

552. Anonymous, "Air Asia moves into Indonesia, *Airline Business*, London, December 2004, p. 26.

553. William Dennis, "Low-Cost Challenger; Thailand's skies are becoming crowed as carriers vie for tourists and business fliers," *Aviation Week & Space Technology*, December 1, 2003, p. 52.

554. William Dennis, "Thai Air Asia Leasing 737s For Flights to Vietnam, Cambodia," *Aviation Daily*, August 11, 2005, p. 5.

555. William Dennis, "Thai Airways To Share Routes With Thai Air Asia," *Aviation Daily*, Washington, February 16, 2005, p. 8.

556. William Dennis, "Air Asia Posts Profit For Fiscal First Half," *Aviation Daily*, February 24, 2005, p. 5.

557. Boonsong Kositchotethana, "Budget pioneer enters consolidation phase: Air Asia to focus on core countries," *Knight Ridder Tribune Business News*, August 1, 2005, p. 1.

558. William Dennis, "Air Asia Adds 20 More A320s To Its Existing MOU For 40," *Aviation Week*, March, 28, 2005, p. 5.

559. Anonymous, "Award Winners Optimistic, Realistic," *Air Transport World*, Cleveland, April 2005, pp. 76–78.

560. Alex Ortolani, "Asia's Budget Airlines Head for Shakeout; For No-Frill Carriers, High Fuel Prices, Stiffer Competition Boost Pressure to Keep Costs Low," *Wall Street Journal*, April 4, 2005, p. B2.

561. John Lancaster, "India is Fertile Soil for Budget Airlines; Companies See Vast Market in Middle Class," *The Washington Post*, February 22, 2005, p. E1.

562. Neelam Mathews, "South Asia's First with e-tickets and Turboprops, Air Deccan is Aiming at India's Business Travel Market," *Aviation Week & Space Technology*, August 19, 2003, p. 41.

563. Anonymous, "Private airlines in India on a high, seek more freedom," *Knight Ridder Tribune Business News*, Washington, December 30, 2004, p. 1.

564. Ibid., p. 41.

565. Max Kingsley-Jones, and Justin Wastnage, "Turboprops are back," *Flight International London*, June 28–July 4, 2005, p. 35.

566. Lancaster, N. 5620.

567. Ibid.

568. K. Giriprakash and V.K. Varadarajan, "Air Deccan bets on volume game," *Businessline*, Chennai, February 14, 2005, p. 1.

569. Manjeet Kripalani in New Delhi and Stanley Holmes in Seattle, with Carol Matlack in Paris, "Dogfight Over India," *Business Week*, May 2, 2005, p. 20.

570. "Air Deccan Inks $17.5 m Deal with ATR," *Knight Ridder Tribune Business News*, February 12, 2005, p. 1.

571. Ibid., p. 1.

572. Kriplani, No. 5700.

573. Cuckoo Paul, "The Captain Who Gave the Common Man Wings," *Knight Ridder Tribune Business News*, July 30, 2005, p. 1.

574. See Chapter 4 on "Predatory Pricing" in the United States.

575. Aarati Krishnan, "Low-cost Airlines: They May Need More Than a Wing and a Prayer," *Businessline*, Chennai, June 26, 2005, p. 1.

576. Anonymous, "Air Deccan appoints Ryanair official as COO," *Businessline*, Chennai, June 24, 2005, p. 1.

577. Frank Swoboda, "Doubts About Airlines' Course; Wall St. Unimpressed with Carriers Despite Recent Profits," *The Washington Post*, July 26, 1998, p. H2.

578. "Major Airlines Climb to Heightened Earnings in Latest Quarter," *Airlines Financial News*, January 26, 1998, Vol. 13, p. 1.

579. Frank Swoboda, "Doubts About Airlines' Course."

580. Ibid.

581. Ibid.

582. Peter Keating, "The Best Airlines to Fly Today," *Money*, November 1997, Vol. 26, pp. 118–23.

583. "Major Airlines Climb to Heightened Earnings in Latest Quarter," *Airlines Financial News*, January 26, 1998, Vol. 13, p. 1.

584. Sonoko Setaishi, "Dividing Up the Skies—Major U.S. Airlines May Slip Into the Red," *Wall Street Journal*, January 9, 2001, p. A6.

585. Frank Swoboda, "Doubts About Airlines' Course."

586. "Southwest is Rated Top Airline for a Third Year; Transportation: But an Annual Quality Survey Shows that Passenger Dissatisfaction with Carriers is at an All-Time High," *Los Angeles Times*, April 21, 1998, p. 1.

587. Peter Keating, "The Best Airlines to Fly Today."

588. Frank Swoboda, "Airline Service Dips In 3 of 4 Categories," *The Washington Post*, April 11, 2000, p. E.01.

589. James Ott, "Market Focus," *Aviation Week & Space Technology*, June 21, 1999, Vol. 150, p. 15.

590. Virginia Postrel, "Even in Good Times, Airlines Depend on a Hairline Balancing of Supply and Demand," *The New York Times*, October 11, 2001, p. C2.

591. Steve Lott, "Airlines Slammed by Weak Revenues, Post First Net Loss in Years," *Aviation Daily*, June 13, 2001, Vol. 344, p. 9.

592. Alex Berenson, "A Plunge in Profits is Raising Risk for Stock Market and Economy," *The New York Times*, July 29, 2001, p. 1.1.

593. "Airlines Industry Likely to Suffer $1.4 Billion Hit in 2001", *Airlines Financial News*, July 30, 2001, Vol. 19, p. 1.

594. Ibid.

595. Scott McCarney, "Frightened Workers and Investors Buffet Airlines," *Wall Street Journal*, September 18, 2001, p. A3.

596. Ibid.

597. Amy Joyce, "Atlantic Coast Finds Profit In Slump; Regional Airline Picks up More Fliers, Routes from Bigger Carriers," *The Washington Post*, October 10, 2001, p. E1.

598. Ibid.

599. Ibid.

600. Keith Alexander, "United Airlines Lost $1.15 Billion; Quarter is Worst in Carrier's History; Delta Reports a Loss of $259 Million," *The Washington Post*, November 2, 2001, p. E3.

601. Henry Canaday, "Layoffs Strike Maintenance (Relatively) Glancing Blow; Maintenance Departments Didn't Get Hit as Hard as Some Airline Groups," *Overhaul and Maintenance*, Jan/Feb 2002, Vol. VIII, p. 49.

602. Dave Woodfill, "Southwest Airlines Won't Rest on Success," *Knight Ridder Tribune Business News*, June 20, 2002, p. 1.

603. Ibid.

604. Matthew Belis, "Airline Industry Struggles to Rebound," *Knight Ridder Tribune Business News*, August 12, 2002, p. 1.

605. Ibid.

606. Jane Engle, "News, Tips & Bargains; Travel Insider; Low-cost Airlines Prompt Majors to Play Their Game;

American, United, Delta Take Page from Competitors to Vie for Dwindling Customers," *Los Angeles* Times, July 27, 2003, p. L3.

607. Edward Wong, "Pass Ideas to Center Aisle. American Needs 'Em," *The New York Times*, July 21, 2002, p. 31.

608. *The Need for Domestic U.S. Airfare Structure Reform*, Association of Corporate Travel Executives, Arlington, VA: 2002.

609. Ibid.

610. Ibid.

611. Trebor Banstetter, "Continental Airlines Suffers Fifth Straight Losing Quarter," *Knight Ridder Tribune Business News*, July 17, 2002, p. 1.

612. "Low-Fare Carriers to Triumph in 'Near or Distant Future'", *Airlines Financial News*, March 24, 2003, Vol. 21, p. 1.

613. Ibid.

614. Trebor Banstetter, "Business Travel Report Says Focus on Cheap Fares Won't Help Major Airlines," *Knight Ridder Tribune Business News*, October 1, 2004, p. 1.

615. Amy Tsao, "Seven Solutions to the Airlines' Woes," *Business Week*, August 24, 2004.

616. Julius Maldutis, "Legacy Airlines: Wolly Mammoths or Their Own Saviors?", *Aviation Week & Space Technology*, March 22, 2004, Vol. 160, p. 66.

617. Ibid.

618. Trebor Banstetter, "Continental Airlines Suffers Fifth Straight Losing Quarter."

619. "The Right Price," *Aircraft Economics*, September 1, 2003, p. 1.

620. Matthew Belis, "Airline Industry Struggles to Rebound."

621. "Mixed Signals", *Airlines Business*, March 2003, Vol. 19, p. 7.

622. Jerry Seper, "Delta Joins Northwest, Continental Airlines in Alliance," *Knight Ridder Tribune Business News*, January 18, 2003, p. 1.

623. Keith Alexander, "United Official to Look Out for Customers," *The Washington Post*, May 13, 2003, p. E1.

624. Eric Torbenson, "Major U.S. Airlines Evaluate Next Moves in Competition to Stay Afloat," *Knight Ridder Tribune Business News*, August 18, 2002, p. 1.

625. James Ott, "'De-Peaking' American Hubs Provides Network Benefits 'Rolling Hub' Saves Airlines $100 Million a Year, Cuts Block Time and Creates a New Flow That

Appeals to Hub Vendors," *Aviation Week & Space Technology*, February 17, 2003, Vol. 158, p. 53.

626. Evan Perez, "Delta Unveils Its Turnaround Plan; Strategy Includes Cutting 7,000 Jobs, Abandoning Dallas-Fort Worth Hub," *Wall Street Journal*, September 9, 2004, p. A3.

627. Mary Jane Credeur, "Operation Clockwork Radical, Risky," *Atlanta Business Chronicle*, January 21–27, 2005, pp. A1, A31.

628. Ibid.

629. Russell Grantham, "Delta's Big Wager," *The Atlanta Journal-Constitution*, January 31, 2005.

630. Susan Warren, "Continental Profit Outlook Brightens," *Wall Street Journal*, June 3, 2005, p. B2.

631. Steve Josselson, "Phoenix Rises," *Air Finance Journal*, December 2003, p. 1.

632. Ibid.

633. Mike Beirne, "Are These the Little Airlines That Could," *Brandweek*, March 29, 2004, p. 31.

634. Jeff Clabaugh and Tony Goins, "Independence All Ceases Operations," http://www.bizjournals.com/columbus/stories/2006/01/02/daily1.html, Business on April 5, 2007.

635. Steven Lott, "Indy Air Must Keep Costs Low, Stimulate Traffic, Report Says," *Aviation Daily*, May 14, 2004, p. 4.

636. "Independence Air Losses Less Than Expected, But Bankruptcy Fear Is Real," *Airline Business Report*, March 14, 2005, p. 1.

637. Micheline Maynard, "US Airways and America West Plan to Merge," *The New York Times*, May 20, 2005, pp. C1, C8.

638. Dan Reed and Barbara De Lollies, "Merger Talks Revive Notion of Consolidation," USA Today, April 21, 2004, pp. B1, B2.

639. Micheline Maynard, "2 US Airlines Weigh the Perks of Togetherness," *The New York Times*, April 21, 2005, p. C1.

640. James Rowley and John Hughes, "US Airways' Wolf Calls Merger Vital," *The Washington Post*, March 22, 2001, p. E6.

641. David Wessel, "Airlines May Have to Fly Without Lifeline," *Wall Street Journal*, June 2, 2005, p. A2.

642. Jagdish N. Sheth and Rajendra Sisodia, *The Rule of Three: Surviving and Thriving in Competitive Markets*, New York: Free Press, 2002.

About the Authors

Jadish N. Sheth is Charles H. Kellstadt Professor of Marketing at the Emory University. He is also the Founder and Director of the Centre for Relationship Marketing of the same university. He has written several books and articles for international journals. He is an advisor to the Economic Development Board, Singapore; the NTIA, Department of Commerce, USA; Department of Transportation, USA; and the Georgia Public Service Commission and a board member of Centre for Telecommunications Management, USC; Wipro Limited ; PacWest Telecomm, Inc; Shasun Chemicals & Drugs (India); and Cryo-Cell International.

Fred C. Allvine is Professor Emeritus, Georgia Institute of Technology. He has authored and co-authored several books including a marketing textbook and two books on competition in the oil industry. He has also been a consultant to the Department of Justice and state regulatory bodies.

Can Uslay is Assistant Professor of Marketing, Argyros School of Business and Economics, Chapman University. He has written several articles in international journals and presented papers in international conferences across Europe and North America. He is also an ad hoc reviewer for the *American Marketing Association Conferences* and several academic journals. Uslay's research interests include the airline industry, marketing strategy, and marketing theory construction.

Ashutosh Dixit is Assistant Professor of Marketing, Cleveland State University. He has co-authored several articles with leading academicians in journal of international repute. He has also won several awards for his research.

Susan Mitchell has written nine bestselling books which document and narrate the vital and dynamic role of women in our society. Her books have been published in Australia, the United States, the United Kingdom, Germany and Holland.

Her passion for writing is matched by her passion for communicating with the widest possible audience. Apart from being a full-time writer, she is a freelance journalist, public speaker and broadcaster. She has presented radio programs on both the ABC and commercial radio as well as her own television program, 'Susan Mitchell: In Conversation'. Previously, she was a senior lecturer in Communications at the University of South Australia.

Susan lives in Sydney and travels to New York regularly.